TAXIFORNIA

JAMES V. LACY

TAXIFORNIA

Liberals' Laboratory to Bankrupt America

POST HILL PRESS

CONTENTS

ABOUT THE AUTHOR

JAMES V. LACY IS a third generation native Californian. Born in Oakland, he is a graduate of Bellarmine College Preparatory in San Jose, received his undergraduate degree at the University of Southern California in Los Angeles and his Juris Doctorate from Pepperdine University School of Law at Malibu. Lacy is admitted to practice law in California and the District of Columbia, and serves as a member of the Board of Visitors of Pepperdine University School of Law. He was a delegate from California to the 1976 Republican National Convention, pledged to Ronald Reagan for President. In 1978, he served as an aide to Howard Jarvis, the author of Proposition 13. Lacy worked for Reagan's election again in 1980 and after Reagan's victory, joined the Administration in Washington, D.C., where he served all eight years, including as a senior executive at the Commerce Department and as General Counsel to the U.S. Consumer Product Safety Commission. Lacy and his wife Janice, a former Deputy Chief Counsel of the Republican National Committee, are partners in their law firm and a political communications company. The Lacys live in Dana Point, California, where Jim has served as Chairman of the Planning Commission and was elected to the City Council. Jim Lacy is a member of the Board of Directors of the American Conservative Union, the publisher of the California Political Review, www.capoliticalreview.com, an online magazine on California politics and news, and is a blogger on the influential California politics website www.flashreport.org.

THE AUTHOR AND HOWARD JARVIS, 1978

To Howard Jarvis
1903–1986

FOREWORD

By: Rep. Darrell Issa (49th Congressional District of California),
Chairman of the House Committee on Oversight and Government Reform

CALIFORNIA.

No matter where you live, what you do, how much you earn, everyone has a picture in their mind of what the "Golden State" means to them.

To some, it's the home of companies at the forefront of innovation like Apple or Google. To others, it's where storied franchises such as the Los Angeles Lakers or the San Francisco 49ers play every week. For visitors, it's Disneyland, Hollywood, the Golden Gate, beaches, deserts, mountains, and wine.

California is a place where so many have come from somewhere else hoping to find a better quality of life. The Golden State   rich with opportunity.

My wife and I were no different.

We had a business that started at a kitchen table in Cleveland, Ohio that we wanted to grow and make into something bigger and long-lasting.

California was a state that had everything: farmers and factories, teachers and scientists, entrepreneurs and immigrants. Potential was limitless. Success was celebrated. Hard-work was expected. Government had limitations.

In 1967, speaking in Long Beach, then-Governor Ronald Reagan outlined the guiding principles that would take California down the "right road." He talked about it as the "road ahead to a better, more responsible, more meaningful life for all our citizens, a life in which they are allowed to develop and pursue their aims and ambitions to the fullest, without the constant interference and domination of big spending, big brother government."

That is the kind of vision that brought businesses, large and small, to California because it embraced possibility and understood that the lynchpin of progress was to foster prosperity.

Today's California is virtually unrecognizable. A state that welcomed job creators now penalizes them. A state that attracted businesses is now losing them.

A state that enabled millions of working families to prosper is now the one that just takes more and more away from them.

The inescapable reality is that California has lost some of its luster. It still has a world-class economy, but that is a legacy of the past century. Many of today's best and brightest are looking elsewhere – discouraged by a high cost of living and a tax and regulatory climate that is hostile to entrepreneurship and the free market.

California has twice as many jobless workers as it had five years ago. The state's income tax rate is the highest in the nation. The corporate income tax rate is America's fifth highest. Californians pay an additional 53.5 cents per gallon in gas taxes. All-the-while, state government spending grew 35% per capita in just the past ten years.

So what changed? The State's capital, Sacramento, is now a one Party town. Progressive Democrats have dominated both houses of the state legislature for more than a decade. Unchecked, they have legislated, taxed, and regulated with zeal. For this bunch, government is a means to an end. It exists to limit the excesses of the free market, to redistribute wealth, to advance a far-left social agenda.

When you look at the overall fiscal picture of our nation, Jim Lacy's "Taxifornia" strikes numerous chords. Nationally, we are in the midst of a struggle surrounding the proper province of government in our lives.

"Taxifornia" illustrates what can happen when a government is guided by a "take more" philosophy. Jobs are poached. Tomorrow's innovators innovate somewhere else. Small businesses shut down. Big businesses look to other places to expand and build.

With what is happening in Washington today, "Taxifornia" foreshadows what the consequences for our nation will be if we continue down this broken path of more taxes, more regulations and more government.

Other nations will steal our jobs. Our competitors in the global market will take our best and brightest. Innovation in America will suffocate as other world powers build new economies with the talented innovators that we have chased away.

For policymakers, "Taxifornia" is a blueprint offered by someone who witnessed California's evolution from over-taxation to taxpayer revolt—and its slide back.

Jim Lacy was there at the beginning of one of the most important movements in California's history—the successful passage of Proposition 13. That movement evolved into the Howard Jarvis Taxpayer's Association, which to this day, is the state's most influential voice for limited government.

Lacy's "Taxifornia" is a cautionary tale of what can and will happen to America if Washington follows the lead of what Sacramento has done in the past decade.

By the end of last year, California had lost 73,000 businesses.

Other states like Texas and New York are running campaigns in California hitting the message that California is bad for business and companies large and small should leave now before it gets worse.

If Washington continues to grow government instead of growing business, the jobs leaving California for other states will instead be leaving the United States for Brazil or China.

Barack Obama and Nancy Pelosi have a common vision with Sacramento's ruling class. Government in Washington has greatly expanded its reach under Obama's rule, limiting our healthcare choices, raising the cost of energy, taxing more money out of our paychecks.

There is still time. We can restore California to prosperity and trim back national government. But it is up to us to do it, to demand it.

Jim has spent his entire life devoted to the simple idea that the only change that can come is one that is derived from the will of the people—sometimes it's in the act of an electoral revolt.

Recent history reminds us that it's possible.

In 2003, with distrust of government at an all-time high and facing an avalanche of new taxes and fees, Californians took unprecedented and historic action by recalling Governor Gray Davis. With one, unified and deafening voice, Californians sent a message to Sacramento that they wanted change and reform.

Jim's counsel was essential to the success of the recall campaign. We saw firsthand, the raw emotion that propelled it forward. Up-and-down the state, I heard from Republicans, Democrats, Libertarians, Independents who all felt the same way, that government had abandoned them and was completely out-of-touch with the needs of working people.

Yet, here we are a decade later and there are fewer jobs, less opportunities, higher taxes and no end in sight. Californians are paying more for gas, more for groceries, more for electricity, more for education but have less in their paychecks.

How did Sacramento politicians respond? The Democrat-controlled State Legislature introduced 110 new bills that raise taxes.

These taxes touch on the everyday things. Ask yourself, can you afford to pay new taxes on tires, cars, sodas, and mattresses?

That's Sacramento's answer. It sounds a lot like what Washington is telling the American people today.

And as businesses abandon California, job opportunities continue to decline and the people are left to fend for themselves, big government will tell you that they are the solution, not the problem.

Truthfully, until the people stand-up and demand better for themselves and for their families, government will continue to get away with it because right now, no one is holding them accountable.

California once embodied the American Dream. It was once a place where small businesses grew into large ones. Where ordinary people achieved extraordinary things. Where the circle of success was in reach for all who worked for it and where people expected the best for themselves and their future.

Unless something changes, that future is in doubt.

Think about the world-renowned institutions in California: Berkeley, Stanford, USC, UCLA, and UCSD to name a few. Imagine sending your kid to one of those institutions believing in the idea that doing so will ensure a better future for your child. Now imagine your son or daughter graduating with a law degree and knowing that half of the people who graduated with your kid won't be able to find a job.

That's the reality of today's California. That could be the reality of tomorrow's United States—which is why Lacy is so insistent that now is the time to stand-up and fight back.

You see they've stopped listening to you in Sacramento because you aren't talking loud enough. They've stopped caring about the consequences of their actions, so you have to be the ones to hold them accountable.

What would you do to ensure your child's future? What would you say to someone who after a long day's work, decided that half of what you earned now belonged to them?

What Governor Reagan said is just as applicable today as it was in 1967, "We intend to put an end to that kind of thinking – an end to the philosophy that government has a right to match taxes to whatever it wants to spend instead of spending only what needs to be spent."

Each and every person can be the instrument that begins to change California, and the country, for the better. Californians can be the substance of their own prosperity but first, they must be the instruments of change that hold Sacramento politicians accountable.

Lacy's "Taxifornia" is our call to action.

INTRODUCTION

CALIFORNIA IS NO LONGER the Golden State, and liberalism is to blame. Tax-and-spend liberals who are in control have created a state that taxes and regulates more than any other state in the country, and have engineered a rotting economy with among the highest unemployment of any state in the nation. No wonder that businesses and residents are fleeing the state. It is a state that educates the worst but pays the best to its teachers; a place that is widely considered by most CEOs to be one of the worst locations in the nation to run a business, where local governments are going bankrupt, and where an out-of-control public employee pay and pension system threatens to gobble up and divert almost all available taxpayer resources to a point where cities and counties simply cannot afford to pay for police, fire, or road maintenance anymore. California has an outdated environmental policy and an energy policy that makes the state almost totally dependent on one source of power: imported natural gas. It is a place where the public employee union worker who controls traffic in the Bay Area Rapid Transit District maintenance yard in poverty-stricken and near bankrupt Oakland is paid more annually than the Chief Justice of the United States Supreme Court in Washington, D.C.

Once upon a time, the state of California, the biggest and most important state in America, was much different. It was a land of opportunity with a wonderful climate. There a person could get a great job or, with a good idea, open a business and succeed—rich or poor, young or old, educated or not, any race or creed. Success could be opening yet another new hamburger joint or a shoe-shine stand, baking a new type of chocolate chip cookie, making a new type of science fiction movie, or inventing the personal computer in one's family garage. One could buy a slick automobile, even a convertible, for a $100 down payment (almost regardless of credit history), come to own their own home, raise children to be educated in the best public colleges and universities in the country, or just drop-out and live life in the finest weather God's earth could offer. At one time the whole country was "California Dreamin'."

But times have surely changed. California is very different today from when I was a young boy living in the San Francisco Bay Area in the late 1950s, when Edmund G. "Pat" Brown was Governor. And I am surely not the only observer to note the profound change for the worse. As San Jose State University political science Professor Larry Gerston has written:

> "Fifty years ago, California was a national trendsetter with its infrastructure. Outstanding public education, modern highway systems, and reasonably priced housing adorned the state to the envy of the rest of the nation. The state smelled "new," looked clean, and operated smoothly….Today, California is almost totally disconnected from its past."[1]

The change that has occurred over these decades surely is complex and is many-faceted, but two aspects are particularly distinct: demographics and politics. As to the former, California has surely become much more culturally diverse; but as to the later, California's former competitive balance in state power has, in the last generation, simply disintegrated. With few exceptions, state power is almost completely dominated by political liberals, and their powerful, deep-pocketed

---

1 Larry N. Gerston, *Not So Golden After All, The Rise and Fall of California* (Boca Raton, CRC Press, 2012), 14.

Left-wing special interest union allies. Their hold on power is so strong, and so one-sided, there is no longer any "swing of the pendulum" in state politics. It is this utter stranglehold on state policy by liberals that has ruined California today.

Migration in and out of the state, both legal and illegal, as well as the recession, have surely pressured government institutions and infrastructure. Yet in recent years, California has seen more people exiting the state than immigrating to it. Some observers think immigration is California's single biggest problem. I disagree.

Rather, *liberalism is the problem*. Long-term liberal dominance of California's levers of power has brought a pervasive philosophy to government up-and-down the state that results in far too much spending and too much taxation. Over-taxing and over-spending is now catching up with state and local governments, saddling them with truly incredible financial problems and a mountain of debt that may hamper government services for decades to come. The tax-and-spend liberal philosophy has caused low achieving public schools; local government bankruptcies; some cases of grossly overpaid public employees; huge, under-funded public employee pension liabilities; a hyper anti-business, job-killing regulatory climate; and unacceptably high persistent unemployment, especially in minority communities. Things have never been worse for California and its citizens. In March of 2013 The Field Poll reported that 72% of California voters described California's economy as being in bad times; while 61% described unemployment as very serious in the state and just 36% expected job opportunities to improve in the coming year.[2] As one of America's leading taxpayer advocates, Grover Norquist told the *San Francisco Chronicle* editorial board about California's high-tax, job killing policies not too long ago: "this is a state that used to have people move to it. In the last decade 1,200,000 net people have

---

2 http://www.field.com/fieldpollonline/subscribers/Rls2444.pdf. A USC/Los Angeles Times poll a few months later reported that a lower majority, of 50%, said the state remains on the wrong track. http://www.latimes.com/news/local/political/la-me-pc-california-economy-jerry-brown-20130604,0,7019041.story

walked out the door. And this is not taken as a wake-up call?"[3]

Liberalism has failed to offer rational new policies to fix California's problems— even when some of those solutions are obvious. With its hundreds of public institutions running amok in deficit spending, Californians are suffering as a result. The promise of a bright future for California's citizens has never been threatened more than now. Many of those who once thought California would forever be their home are having second thoughts, as citizens and industry flee the state for better opportunities and less government oppression. As one observer has written:

"At a time of political polarization, the choice between living in a red or blue state is virtually a matter of choosing citizenship in separate nations. If you're in search of low taxes, light regulations, the ability to own a gun with minimal hassle, and an absence of nanny-state meddling, go red, young man. If you're charmed by progressive taxation, a strong union influence, pervasive environmentalism, and public sector obesity, blue's for you. Unsurprisingly, the results of this experiment are lopsided. Look at the states leading the nation in net domestic outmigration and you'll see liberalisms starting lineup: Illinois, New York, Michigan, and, of course, California. Among those reaping the most new inhabitants are Texas, Florida, North Carolina, Georgia, and Arizona."[4]

And for Californians themselves, perhaps unappreciated in the mix of all these problems is exactly how the liberals have wrecked havoc on the state, and what we are all losing as a result. The liberal elites who control California will not admit their culpability in California's awful condition, and a compliant media helps in the cover-up. Instead, they obfuscate, and blame its problems on, among

---

3 Audio interview with Norquist by John Diaz, http://blog.sfgate.com/opinionshop/2013/04/08/norquist-on-california-example-of-what-not-to-do/.

4 Troy Senik, *Orange County Register*, http://www.ocregister.com/opinion/state-501594-states-blue.html

other things, "the special interests." Liberals and their media allies have so far been successful in advancing a fantasy about California's problems, alternately blaming them on a real property tax-cut initiative passed in 1978 known as Proposition 13, or "political dysfunction" caused by citizens occasionally engaging in direct democracy by voting on a handful of initiative laws or being able, rarely, to recall elected officials.[5] The liberals in control would have the people believe that the special interests ruining California are greedy, polluting energy, tobacco and telecommunications corporations, aided by a minority of crazed right-wing Republicans who have temporarily left their caves for the legislature.

These claims of the liberals are just poor excuses for the long list of bad decisions California's liberal policymakers have made in bringing the state to the brink of economic destruction. A 35-year old tax-cut is not to blame for California's current problems.

Public employee unions are without question the biggest source of special interest money in the state, literally dwarfing the lobbying efforts of the state's business community; yet you wouldn't know it from most media reports. California's current problems stem from the successes and near complete control of the political process by these powerful unions, and the decisions of liberal officeholders they put in place—not a handful of laws passed by initiative. Unfortunately, today, moderate and conservative solutions to address the state's problems simply don't have a chance to be implemented because the state has lost political balance. California's dwindling business community and loyal opposition party in Sacramento are essentially powerless in the political environment. Even Democratic political leaders who offer more moderate solutions are silenced and eviscerated. California today is a "one-party" state dominated by the liberal faction of the California Democratic Party and their union and environmental

---

5 California Supreme Court Justice Ronald M. George, in a 2009 speech, termed "frequent amendments" to the state constitution as somehow rendering state government "dysfunctional", with no further explanation of what that meant. http://www.latimes.com/news/opinion/la-oe-mathews19-2009oct19,0,6083414.story.

lobby cronies. It is their policies that have been adopted, again and again, in the last generation, and their policies have failed. They are the over-taxers and over-spenders. They are the cause of the high taxes, high unemployment, record number of bankruptcies, lousy business climate and economic suffering of today.

The failure of California's media and so-called "neutral" political observers to correctly identify the real "special interests" in the state is spellbinding. That's one of the goals of this book: to focus on and identify the "special interests" harming California. Such clarity in "naming names" on California's most troublesome special interests is necessary because most other authorities, undoubtedly liberals themselves, continually dodge that question. And the liberal media lets them get away with it. For example, political science Professor Gerston has written an entire college-level textbook devoted to rooting out and exposing the state's ills and proposing solutions, while attempting to chronicle the "Rise and Fall" of California. Yet the three words, "California Teachers Association," do not appear anywhere in Gerston's textbook, *not even once*. The teachers union is unquestionably the largest and most powerful special interest in the state. Since 2000 it has spent almost $300,000,000 to influence policy outcomes and elections in the state, much more than any other special interest, including big oil, big tobacco, or big business *combined*. It is perplexing that Gerston would miss that point in his textbook. Besides teaching at San Jose State, Gerston is an oft-quoted and seemingly respected political analyst on Bay Area radio and television stations and is sought after for commentary in the press. He has received deserved accolades for his work. But in reality, Gerston is hardly a neutral observer. Gerston's failure to acknowledge the California Teachers Associations as a special interest might not be so benign. The California Teachers Association has more than 1,300 chartered affiliates throughout the state and one of them is the California Faculty Association, which does collective bargaining with the State University system representing professors like Gerston.[6] I have no doubt professor Gerston is an honorable man, but as an example of what the media considers a fair and neutral observer, he is a failure. Given the credibility as a commentator he has otherwise achieved, his failure is not an excusable one; rather, it is symptomatic of what a compliant media lets liberals get away with. Gerston's kid-glove treatment of the teachers union in his text about California's problems reveals the ingrained partisanship of the liberal elites that run California, who are not being called to account for the economic devastation they have levied on the state, and why this book is necessary.

What happens in California is important not only to its residents but also to the rest of the nation. As one observer has written:

> "California supplies not only vast amounts of capital to the Democratic Party and its infrastructure, but supplies also the spiritual inspiration for the policies those Democrats seek to impose on the rest of America. The state represents a possible future for the entire nation, and the preferred future of the American left: environmentally stringent, demographically heterogeneous, Pacific-oriented, inequality-obsessed (and inequality prone), and devoid of conservatives in positions of influence."[7]

Taxifornia seeks to identify and examine the true cause of California's decline, which is liberal dominance, and how the over-weighted influence of Left-wing special interests is destroying the state's economic future and threatening personal freedoms. Having identified the problem correctly, this book also offers some observations about

---

6 http://www.calwatchdog.com/2013/05/10/
two-wings-of-cta-have-low-opinion-of-much-bigger-wing/

7 http://freebeacon.com/the-california-captivity-of-the-democratic-party/

what can be done to restore political balance in the state, as well as some rational ideas for how California can fix its economic problems. But the economic and political situation in California today is at such an extreme, whether California can ever return to the broad prosperity of the past and once again lead the nation, is a very open question.

TAXIFORNIA

CALIFORNIANS TODAY ARE VICTIMS of the heaviest taxation of any citizens in the country, and those high taxes are now steadily destroying the state's economy.[8] State residents not only join all Americans in paying higher rates on their federal income taxes, but they must also pay the highest marginal state income in the country, 13.3%, as a result of the passage of Governor Jerry Brown's "Proposition 30" tax-rate hike in November 2012.[9] California's state income tax is 21% higher than the second highest state income tax in the nation (Hawaii) and 34% higher than the third highest state income tax (Oregon).[10]

In addition to these high federal and state income taxes, Californians must also pay the highest sales taxes in the country, ranging in localities from 7.5% to up to 10%, the legal limit.[11] California's

---

8 According to the Legislature's own Legislative Analyst's Office, as of 2010, even before California's most recent tax increases, the tax burden in the state was conceded to be higher than all neighboring states, 10th highest of the 50 states, above the national average, and of the most populous states only New York's tax burden as of 2010 was considered higher. CalFacts, LAO, 2013.

9 http://taxfoundation.org/sites/taxfoundation.org/files/docs/ff2013.pdf

10 Id. Calculations published by Richard Rider, www.RiderRants.BlogSpot.com.

11 http://taxfoundation.org/article/state-and-local-sales-tax-rates-2011-2013

corporate income tax rate at 8.84% is one of the highest of any state west of the Mississippi River, other than Alaska, and ranks 5th highest in the nation.[12]

The California State Board of Equalization recently approved a 9% increase on the state excise tax on gasoline—raising it to 39.5 cents a gallon,[13] which is the highest state excise tax on gasoline at the pump in the nation.[14] Added to the cost of fuel is another 14 cents per gallon for other state taxes and fees, making California's total take at the pump at 53.2 cents per gallon also the highest in the nation.[15]

Though Californians continue to enjoy protections on big jumps in their real estate property taxes as a result of the historic "Proposition 13" tax-cut, property taxes in the state on both commercial and residential properties rank well above the national average.[16]

All of these taxes are in addition to the significant taxes and fees California and its localities require for attending a community college or university, or starting up, licensing and maintaining a corporation, at the highest annual minimum tax rate in the nation.[17] Localities in California often impose significant additional fees on hotel occupancy.[18] Additional state taxes include the 3rd highest

---

12 http://taxfoundation.org/article/2013-state-business-tax-climate-index

13 http://articles.latimes.com/2013/apr/17/opinion/la-oe-billingsley-california-taxes-20130417

14 CNBC "Fast Money Halftime Report," July 1, 2013.

15 http://www.api.org/oil-and-natural-gas-overview/industry-economics/fuel-taxes

16 http://taxfoundation.org/article/property-taxes-owner-occupied-housing-state-2004-2009

17 California's minimum mandatory corporate tax is $800, regardless of profit. Oregon has the next highest such annual tax at $150. http://tinyurl.com/CA-800-tax.

18 Most California cities raise revenue not only through property taxes and sales taxes, but also in part through a so-called "TOT" or "transient occupancy tax." In Anaheim, where Disneyland is located, the "TOT" is 15% of a room charge, among the highest in the state. A three-day visit to the Disneyland Grand Californian Hotel for a family of three in the summer of 2013 costs $1,500 plus tax. Tax calculated at the TOT tax rate of 15% and would add an additional $225 to the room charge. State sales taxes are added for food and beverage services, and there is a "voluntary" state tourism tax collected of $1 per room per day.

workers compensation insurance rates in the nation, at 3.4%, paid by employers and deducted from workers paychecks.

Invariably, the motivating force behind these taxes are spending programs of California's liberal politicians and the special interests behind them, and these elites now have total control of California state government. Left-wing special interest groups dominate political spending in the state, win most of the elections, and burden the tax system again and again with their perpetual appetite for more and more special interest public spending. Indeed, California is among the top ten states for public spending growth in the nation, with a 35% spending increase in the last decade.[19] The strain on California's tax system is so bad, that people and businesses have every incentive to flee the state, and are leaving, to the detriment of the long-term tax basis. No wonder then that Republican Congressman Devin Nunes of Visalia advocates tax reform in our country, and especially in California, and concludes, "(o)ur excessive tax and regulatory burden is killing businesses and driving them to other states."[20]

Historian Arthur Schlesinger is credited with the development of the so-called "cyclical theory" that describes fluctuations in American politics as a continuing shift that occurs when politics get out of balance.[21] According to the theory, when one extreme of the political debate gets too much control, the public rises up and corrects the balance by a shift in political outlook and mood toward the other side of the debate. The cycle and balance is seen as necessary to the health of political institutions. At the extremes, political issues arise that can "detonate," or cause the shift in the other direction to begin to occur.[22]

Taxes and government regulation are far too oppressive in California today, and the special interest groups that support them have

19 http://www.capradio.org/articles/2013/07/23/
california-among-top-ten-in-nation-for-government-spending-growth/

20 http://www.ocregister.com/opinion/tax-504889-business-reform.html

21 Arthur M. Schlesinger Jr., *The Cycles of American History* (New York, Mariner Books, 1999).

22 Id., p. 35.

too much control. Applying Schlesinger's theory to California, it seems the state should be at the verge of a political mood shift.

For example, there have been other times in California's history when taxes topped those in other states, and anger about them came to a boiling point among voters, and even gained national attention—most notably the passage of the historic Proposition 13 real property tax cut in 1978, when 4.2 million Californians, nearly 66% of the electorate, voted to cut their property taxes by 57%. Howard Jarvis, a co-author of the measure, made the cover of *Time* magazine and was a runner-up for its' coveted "Person of the Year." On election night Jarvis told *Time's* reporter, "[g]overnment simply must be limited. Excessive government leads to either bankruptcy or dictatorship."[23] Proposition 13 can be seen as "detonating" a tax revolt against the big spending liberals of that era. The adoption of the measure not only had national ramifications with the election of California's Governor Ronald Reagan as President in 1980, but also served to propel Republican candidates into 16 years of continuous control of the Governorship of the state from 1982-1998.

But 35 years have passed since California voters famously decided to cut their taxes, and in the meantime the taxation pendulum in the intervening decades has decidedly shifted in the opposite direction. Some observers might even say that Jarvis' prediction of excessive government leading to bankruptcy and one-party political dictatorship in California has been fulfilled.

High taxes hurt all Californians, but they are especially problematic for businesses and wealthier individuals who are the so-called "job creators." The well-off surely have an obligation to pay their taxes. But tax rates on high-income taxpayers have become so dangerously high in California, that even a fairly neutral political observer, such as columnist Dan Walters, has written California's "increasing reliability on high-income taxpayers is perilous."[24]

---

23 *Time* magazine, June 19, 1978, p. 13.

24 http://www.sacbee.com/2013/05/17/5427418/dan-walters-a-perilous-tax-trend. html#mi_rss=Dan%20Walters?utm_source=feedly

And business flight has become endemic. Companies like San Fernando Valley-based Superior Industries, a manufacturer of aluminum wheels, recently decided to expand and open its fourth new, $135 million manufacturing facility—in Chihuahua, Mexico.[25] A few years earlier, Superior decided to close its Van Nuys wheel factory, which had been operating for 30 years, at a loss of 290 area jobs.[26] At one time, Superior employed 1,200 people, but costs of operating its manufacturing plant in California became too excessive over time, and as the economy tanked during the recession, Superior simply couldn't keep its doors open in the state. Cereplast, Inc., a bioplastics manufacturer whose resins are used to make disposable food containers, has announced it plans to move its headquarters from El Segundo to Seymour, Indiana, "in order to turn profitable."[27] Defense industry giant Raytheon, whose Space and Airborne Systems unit is a $6 billion business with headquarters also based in El Segundo, has announced it is moving the division to McKinney, Texas, losing California at least 170 high-paying jobs at an average salary of $250,000.[28] The fact that Superior is now investing off-shore rather than reopening its California facility, that Cereplast must leave the state to become profitable, and that Raytheon, after many years in California, has been lured away to the better tax environment in Texas, are just more clear examples of how liberal policies are damaging California's economy by making the state too expensive for business.

The inherent disincentives in California's current onerous tax system are vividly illustrated in research by Matt Blumenfield of Americans for Tax Reform that touches on Sacramento Mayor Kevin Johnson's determined attempts to keep the Kings NBA professional

25 http://sfvbj.com/news/2013/apr/16/superior-adds-fourth-wheel-plant-chihuahua/

26 http://www.dailynews.com/ci_11448583

27 http://labusinessjournal.com/news/2013/may/07/cereplast-move-hq-indiana/

28 http://www.bizjournals.com/dallas/news/2013/05/02/raytheon-moving-california-hq-to.html

basketball team in his troubled city and prevent them from moving.[29] Johnson, himself a three-time NBA All-Star, now retired from the game, has proposed, even over voter rejection at the polls, that cash-strapped Sacramento contribute $258 million in taxpayer funds it doesn't have to build a new arena just to keep the Kings in the city. But for the players themselves, there is room for ambivalence to stay or even want to play in California, because of the state's high marginal tax rates, and also because of yet another tax referred to as the "jock" tax, first assessed by California in 1991.

Thus, according to Blumenfield, a Sacramento Kings player currently must pay a top marginal tax rate of 56.7% of his income, comprising: a 39.6% Federal income tax (increased in the "fiscal cliff" debate at the end of 2012); a 13.3% state income tax (increased by Governor Brown's Proposition 30 enactment in November, 2012); and a 3.8% Medicare tax. The 56.7% marginal rate of course does not include any additional real property taxes, vehicle fees and taxes, local taxes, and sales taxes paid on goods. And because of the jock tax, when an out-of-state team visits Sacramento to play a game, (Blumenfield uses the example of Kings NBA player DeMarcus Cousins, the Kings top scorer, for purposes of calculating the tax) a player at Cousins pay level would have to pay California a special tax of $29,247.98 per game. That is in addition to all other taxes paid by the player.

Worse still for California, if the Kings were actually to move out-of-state, the players would get to keep a whole lot more of their hard earned money. Cousins' top marginal tax rate would be reduced to 43.4% if the kings moved to Seattle, for example, since Washington state does not have an state income tax or a "jock" tax. According to Blumenfield's analysis, Cousins would be able to keep over $500,000 more of his average $3,950,033 annual salary[30]

---

29 http://www.flashreport.org/blog/2013/04/16/
sacramento-mayor-to-use-taxpayer-funds-in-rushed-arena-proposal/

30 http://www.spotrac.com/nba/sacramento-kings/demarcus-cousins/

if the Kings relocated out-of-state to Seattle. The tax policy seems to indicate that California is literally taxing its professional sports teams out of the state.

And the current state tax policy is no better at encouraging investment in California. While some Silicon Valley technology companies are thriving, and in some cases building new headquarters facilities in California for high-paid white-collar home office employees[31], actual investment in California manufacturing facilities is apparently not so attractive. Tim Cook, the CEO of Cupertino-based Apple, a giant of Silicon Valley, has announced that its new domestic assembly plant will be in Texas, not California, and the plant will use components and equipment made in other states, namely Florida, Illinois, Kentucky and Michigan.[32] An editorial in the *San Diego Union-Tribune* suggests the reason Apple passed on more business investment in California is the high cost of energy as a result of environmental regulations, putting California "on track to have the highest energy costs of any state."[33] A few miles down Highway 101 from Apple's headquarters, Google Inc. has made the decision that its subsidiary, Google Fiber, will avoid installing new internet networks in California, in favor of Missouri, Kansas, Texas, and Utah, because of California's lousy business reputation. "[W]e go where it's easy to build, if you make it hard for me to build and there are other places where it's easy to build, I will probably go to those other places," said Milo Medin, vice president of Google Access Services, to an audience at the Fiber to the Home Council America conference in Kansas City this year.[34] Despite 18% profit growth, and with a horde of $50.6 billion in cash, San Jose-based technology giant

---

31 http://www.mercurynews.com/business/ci_23386132/apple-new-campus-2-cupertino-mothership-jobs-spending?source=rss&utm_source=feedly

32 http://www.utsandiego.com/news/2013/may/26/apple-builds-in-texas-not-california/

33 Id.

34 http://www.bizjournals.com/kansascity/blog/2013/05/google-fiber-california-network.html?page=all

Cisco will cut 4,000 jobs (5% of its workforce) beginning in 2014.[35] The job losses are intended to reduce costs,[36] and follow an earlier workforce reduction announced in July 2011 of an additional 6,500 employees.[37] Company officials did not specifically take California's business environment to task in their announcement of the job cuts, but most of the cuts will presumably affect California-based employees. Cisco Chairman John Chambers blames the most current round of reductions on a "disappointing economic recovery."[38] Cisco's performance is "widely regarded as a bellwether for the technology industry."[39]

Even the occasional bright spot comes with a glitch. Though it moved its two big aircraft modernization programs for the C-130 Hercules military transport aircraft and the B-1 bomber from Long Beach to Oklahoma City in 2010 in a cost-cutting effort,[40] Boeing has announced it will shift 300 engineering jobs from Washington state to its longtime facility at Long Beach, after years of downsizing, where the "company's commercial work in Southern California has dwindled over the years."[41] Boeing's announcement of the engineering jobs shift predated reports of problems airlines are now experiencing with the 787 Dreamliner, and it is unknown whether those issues will affect Boeing's plans. The 300 new engineering jobs also were promised before Boeing subsequently announced another 1,000 job layoffs in Long Beach by 2015 after completion of its

---

35 http://money.cnn.com/2013/08/14/technology/enterprise/cisco-earnings/index.html

36 http://www.reuters.com/article/2013/08/14/us-cisco-results-idUSBRE97D16W20130814

37 http://money.cnn.com/2011/07/18/technology/cisco_layoffs/

38 Id.

39 http://www.sfgate.com/business/technology/article/Cisco-s-1Q-revenue-falls-below-estimates-4980979.php

40 http://www.dailynews.com/news/ci_23365210/lockheed-moving-f-22-maintenance-work-from-palmdale?source=rss&utm_source=feedly

41 http://articles.latimes.com/2013/jun/01/business/la-fi-boeing-long-beach-jobs-20130601

C-17 cargo plane deliveries to the Air Force and few new orders from foreign governments.[42]

Campbell's Soup Company closed its big, 125-acre plant in Sacramento in July 2013 with a loss of 700 workers. The plant had been in operation since 1947 and was the oldest facility for the company in the United States. Production has been shifted to plants in North Carolina, Ohio, and Texas.[43] The closure was said to be in part about "trimming costs."[44] "This one hurts," said the director of Business Forecasting at the University of the Pacific, "[t]hese are middle class jobs."[45] A Campbell Soup spokesman said "[t]he business reason to close Sacramento is pretty clear because it has the highest production cost per case of any plant in our network."[46] At about the same time as the announcement of the Campbell's plant closure, high technology firm Comcast announced it was shifting 1,000 jobs out of state "because of the high cost of doing business" in California.[47] Comcast said its calling centers in Natomas, Morgan Hill, and Livermore would be closed and the jobs moved to Colorado, Oregon, and Washington state. The company said it "arrived at the decision after thoughtfully and methodically studying the market and our potential options. We determined that the high cost of doing business in California makes it difficult to run cost-effective call centers" in the state.[48]

---

42 http://www.laobserved.com/biz/2013.09/boeing_to_end_c-17_p.php?utm_

43 http://www.bizjournals.com/sacramento/news/2013/01/10/campbells-first-wave-of-job-cuts.html

44 http://sanfrancisco.cbslocal.com/2012/09/27/sacramento-campbell-soup-plant-closing-700-jobs-cut/

45 http://www.bizjournals.com/sacramento/news/2012/09/27/campbell-soup-pulling-out-of-sacramento.html?page=all

46 http://www.bizjournals.com/sacramento/news/2012/09/27/campbell-soup-pulling-out-of-sacramento.html?page=all

47 http://sacramento.cbslocal.com/2012/09/25/comcast-to-close-3-california-call-centers-shift-1000-jobs-out-of-state/

48 http://sacramento.cbslocal.com/2012/09/25/comcast-to-close-3-california-call-centers-shift-1000-jobs-out-of-state/

Hardly a day goes by without a news report of more job reductions. Lawrence Livermore Laboratories in the San Francisco Bay Area recently invited 600 employees to quit.[49] Dignity Health is laying off 400 workers, 300 of them in bankrupt Stockton, as a result of an acquisition by an out-of-state firm.[50] Mattel is moving 100 employees from its Fisher-Price unit in El Segundo to New York.[51] Nexicore, a computer-hardware leasing company, has filed a notice with the state disclosing it is laying off 108 workers at its Simi Valley headquarters.[52] The company says the layoffs are caused by "the recession and slowing recovery" in the economy,[53] but there were no similar announcements of lay-offs at its facilities in Florida, Illinois, or Canada.

Wells Fargo has announced it is reducing its national workforce by 2,323 jobs, and hard-hit California will lose the largest share, 500 of them, from its mortgage division.[54] Shortly after the press reports of the job losses Wells Fargo's public relations department went to work and the bank announced it was hiring 5,000 new employees in its brokerage division, but it was unclear how many of the positions would be full-time and how many would be in California,[55] and the jobs will not be new jobs, rather, they will primarily fill positions otherwise lost through attrition.[56] On the heels

---

49 http://www.bizjournals.com/sanfrancisco/news/2013/05/08/livermore-lab-asks-600-people-to.html

50 http://www.sacbee.com/2013/05/14/5419700/dignity-health-will-lay-off-150.html

51 http://www.scpr.org/news/2013/05/23/37389/mattel-is-moving-some-fisher-price-jobs-from-ny-to/?utm_source=feedly&utm_medium=feed&utm_campaign=Feed%3A+893KpccSouthernCaliforniaNews+%28KPCC%3A+News%29

52 http://sfvbj.com/news/2013/may/30/nexicore-services-lay-108-simi-valley/

53 Id.

54 http://www.bizjournals.com/sacramento/news/2013/08/21/wells-fargo-cutting-employees-country.html?ana=e_du_pub&s=article_du&ed=2013-08-21&page=all

55 http://capoliticalnews.com/2013/08/27/great-news-wells-fargo-firing-2300-people-then-hiring-5000/

56 http://www.bizjournals.com/sanfrancisco/blog/2013/08/bank-of-america-wells-fargo-layoffs.html?ana=e_du_pub&s=article_du&ed=2013-08-30

of the Wells Fargo job reduction announcement, Bank of America, like Wells Fargo headquartered in San Francisco, disclosed a similar job reduction of 1,000 positions.[57] Symantec in Mountain View is laying off an estimated 1,700 employees, following 900 layoffs at neighboring NetApp in Sunnyvale, and 520 at the San Francisco-based Zynga social gaming company.[58] GAF, the largest manufacturer of roofing materials in North America, is closing its Fresno plant, which was built in 1963, and 60 employees are being laid off.[59] California Cart, a manufacturer of food trucks and trailers based in Lake Elsinore, is dropping the word "California" from its name and moving its manufacturing plant to Dallas out of frustration with an aggressive regulatory environment and tax policy. Having tangled with the California Air Resources Board over installation of diesel-fueled generators on trucks and trailers, Cart's Elma Eaton said "[y]ou have to beat them up to win...I'm tired of fighting... [t]hey're just looking for another layer of taxation or fee to impose on us."[60] Volcano, a manufacturer of medical devices in San Diego, reported it would lay off 39 people in the first week of September 2013, following a loss of an additional 290 employees during 2011 and another 105 let go during 2010.[61]

After a few months of growth, the San Francisco Bay Area was "jolted" by a reported actual loss of 2,300 jobs in July 2013, according to state labor officials.[62] Year-to-year job growth statis-

---

57 Id.

58 http://www.mercurynews.com/rss/ci_23452499?source=rss

59 http://www.fresnobee.com/2013/06/25/3360320/north-american-roofing-giant-gaf.html

60 "California Cart Builder moving manufacturing to Texas," *North County Times*, September 27, 2012.

61 http://www.bizjournals.com/sacramento/news/2013/07/16/volcano-corp-plans-39-layoffs-by-fall.html?ana=e_sac_rdup&s=newsletter&ed=2013-07-16&u=slyE44urV4bo6o4GHwHIqylywCD&t=1373990890

62 http://www.insidebayarea.com/business/ci_23877085/bay-area-jolted-by-loss-2-300-jobs

tics show the San Francisco Bay Area is rapidly losing new jobs.[63] "Government fiscal policies have also had a dampening effect on the region's job growth" said an economist for Beacon Economics. Even the U.S. Air Force is moving maintenance work on its F-22 Raptor jets from Palmdale to Hill Air Force Base in Utah, a move that could eventually impact as many as 3,000 Palmdale employees, and that will immediately add 200 long-term jobs at the Utah facility.[64]

California is not just losing jobs, it is losing small businesses, and the causes for both may be inter-related. "Why Are California's Businesses Disappearing?" is the question asked in a recent article in *Businessweek*.[65] According to Bloomberg News' review of Bureau of Labor statistics, there is simply no doubt that small businesses, the engine of new employment in any healthy economy, are literally vaporizing. Bloomberg's research has found that at the end of 2012, there were 1.3 million businesses based in California, 5.2% fewer than in the previous year. A total of 73,000 businesses were gone at the end of the year, dwarfing the loss of 5,200 businesses in Massachusetts, the next highest total nationwide.[66]

And not just businesses are being lured out of California as a result of higher taxes as exemplified in Proposition 30, but high-income citizens as well. Hit by the combined 51.9% federal-state income tax on earnings over $1 million a year, the well-known wealthy who have gone on the record about leaving the state include champion golfer Phil Mickelson, who reportedly said he would leave the state over its tax policy, and thereby join "a line of athletes and entertainment figures, among them Tiger Woods, who left for states like Florida, which has no personal income tax."[67] Of the so-called "millionaire

---

63 Id.

64 http://www.dailynews.com/news/ci_23365210/lockheed-moving-f-22-maintenance-work-from-palmdale?source=rss&utm_source=feedly

65 http://www.businessweek.com/articles/2013-07-03/why-are-californias-businesses-disappearing#r=rss

66 Id.

67 http://www.nytimes.com/2013/02/07/us/millionaires-consider-leaving-california-over-taxes.html?_r=0

migration," Ed Botowsky of Chapwood Investments, who is a financial manager for high-income Californians, said "[y]ou'd be a fool to not leave California."[68] California's high taxes have even inspired a new, standard real estate agency pitch for home-buying in nearby Nevada that includes "California's Proposition 30 has made communities like Incline Village, Glenbrook, Zephyr Cove, Nevada on Lake Tahoe's North Shore and particularly the area in Reno attractive options for buyers looking for tax relief..."[69] Nevada is one of seven states that do not have a state income tax.

California's liberal policymakers seem mute on the subject of the flight of capital and businesses out of state. When asked about companies and individuals leaving the state because of California's poor economy, Howard Jarvis Taxpayers Association President Jon Coupal offered his opinion on Jerry Brown's response: "Joe Vranich, who is with the business thing called the Relocation Coach, in 2011 he documented 247 companies (that moved or expanded out of the state) . . . I think the census data are pretty strong. Somebody just did a study tracking high-wealth individuals moving out of state and Jerry Brown derided that study saying it was only people getting divorced or something—sort of a flippant remark. His job is to be a cheerleader for the state, I get that, so I'm not going to hold that against him but I think he ignored some of the trends."[70]

News of job losses has sadly become common in the Golden State. In 2010 the Sacramento region even led the nation in job losses according to the Bureau of Labor statistics.[71]

Persistent unemployment in California simply cannot be effectively tackled when tax and spending policies invite businesses to leave. In March 2013 there were 18.6 million Californians in the

68 http://www.breitbart.com/Big-Government/2013/02/01/
California-Tax-Hike-Sparks-Millionaire-Migration

69 http://buytahoehomes.com/blog/tag/proposition-30/

70 http://www.utsandiego.com/news/2013/jun/01/
fixing-california-taxpayer-advocate-jon-coupal/

71 http://sacramento.cbslocal.com/2011/03/21/
sacramento-led-nation-in-job-losses-last-year/

workforce, with 1.75 million of them unemployed, establishing an official unemployment rate of 9.4%, one of the nation's highest.[72] But because of changes in how the Obama Administration calculates "workforce participation," and the number of people who have given up looking for jobs, one observer has noted that California's actual jobless rate might be closer to 13%.[73] As the country has shown faltering signs of emerging from the recession, unemployment growth nationwide has started to reverse track. By May 2013 even California's official unemployment rate improved to 8.6%, perhaps causing some liberal Democrats to cheer about a California renaissance. But that unemployment rate was still the sixth worst rate among the 50 states.[74] And now, the latest statistics are even more grim: as reported in September 2013, California's unemployment rate has reversed itself and is back up to 8.9%.[75] "The labor market appears to be going sideways" in California, said the chief economist for the Los Angeles County Economic Development Corporation.[76]

Though the still high unemployment rate nationwide might show limited signs of easing a bit, that is not happening in California. Observers are not convinced the overall employment picture will consistently improve, for example, as actual payroll job growth decelerated a full percentage point between March and May to just 1.6 in San Diego County,[77] with similar patterns throughout the state. In interpreting the statistics, the conclusion of the chief economist at Point Loma Nazarene University was "[w]e have lost momentum in the last couple months."[78]

72 http://www.sacbee.com/2013/05/05/5395670/dan-walters-californias-workforce. html#mi_rss=Dan%20Walters?utm_source=feedly

73 Id.

74 "County's Jobless Rate Fell to 6.7% in May," *San Diego Union-Tribune*, June 22, 2013.

75 http://www.latimes.com/business/la-fi-california-jobs-20130921,0,5426857.story

76 Id.

77 "County's Jobless Rate Fell to 6.7% in May," *San Diego Union Tribune, June 22, 2013.*

78 Id.

The California jobless rates are higher than the national unemployment rates, and even into the summer of 2013 as new jobless claims start to drop nationwide according to U.S. Labor Department statistics, California is still reporting the largest jump in people claiming unemployment insurance of all other states.[79] Joblessness is so bad in California, even professionals are feeling the pinch, for example, a new study reveals that about one-sixth of recent law school graduates in the state do not have a job.[80] Fewer jobs of course means a smaller tax base, and if job-creating businesses are contracting at the same time unemployment is increasing in California, the economic dangers to the state become all the more obvious and intensified, and cry out for rational solutions.

Conservative policy favoring lower taxes and less government spending is premised on a philosophy that when government taxes and spends too much, it diminishes personal liberties, and the more it does so, the more it impacts and reduces everyone's personal freedom, including one's ability to get a good job. The Nobel Prize-winning economist Milton Friedman, who campaigned for Proposition 13 and inspired Ronald Reagan and British Prime Minister Margaret Thatcher in adopting job-creating economic policies that raised two great nations out of economic crisis, famously observed that liberal-inspired tax systems increasingly penalize work, while subsidizing non-work through welfare.[81]

But one doesn't need to get caught up in too deep of a philosophical debate on the false wisdom of high taxes to see that even New York state is rejecting them, and in a big way in a national media campaign to lure job creating businesses to the Empire State. The "New New York" media campaign, airing on financial networks

79 http://m.bizjournals.com/losangeles/news/2013/05/23/california-jobless-claims-shoot-up.html?ana=e_du_pap&s=article_du&ed=2013-05-23&u=slyE44urV4bo6o4G HwHIqylywCD&t=1369497019&r=full

80 http://www.sacbee.com/2013/05/22/5438494/dan-wallters-california-state.html#mi_rss=Dan%20Walters?utm_source=feedly

81 http://www.brainyquote.com/quotes/quotes/m/miltonfrie 161888.html

such as CNBC, promises the "lowest middle-class tax rate in half a century," "tax-free zones," lower taxes and incentives for businesses, and a better business regulatory environment both for small and big business.[82]

Governors and representatives from areas around the country have flocked to California to lure businesses and jobs out of state with promises of lower taxes and a more rational regulatory climate. In 2012 the Greater Phoenix Economic Council flew 100 California CEOs to Arizona for complementary stays and tours of the metropolitan area.[83] Both Texas Governor Rick Perry and Iowa Governor Terry Branstad have visited the state for the express purpose of luring away businesses and jobs for their states, as have Virginia Governor Bob McDonnell and Utah Governor Herbert.[84] According to *Forbes Magazine*, Utah is very business friendly and has been the "Best State for Business and Careers" in the nation for the last three years, while Virginia is currently ranked the second best in the nation.[85] States are ranked by overall costs to business to operate in the state, labor supply, a positive regulatory attitude towards business, and a good economic climate. California is ranked 41st of the 50 states,[86] making it among the least business-friendly states in the nation. The American Legislative Exchange Council has ranked California as the 47th state for economic outlook, and *CEO* magazine has rated California as the worst state to do business for eight years in a row.[87]

California's reputation among business leaders nationwide is at an all time low. According to a survey of Chief Executive Officers by Chief Executive.net asking CEOs to grade states on taxes and

82 http://www.thenewny.com/Stories/BusinessSuccesses.aspx

83 http://cronkitenewsonline.com/2012/11/
business-leaders-aim-to-capitalize-on-california-tax-hike/

84 http://www.calwatchdog.com/2013/04/30/governors/

85 http://www.forbes.com/best-states-for-business/

86 Id.

87 http://www.hjta.org/california-commentary/shakedowns

regulation, quality of workforce, and living environment, Texas ranked first for the ninth straight year, and California continued to rank "dead last."[88] "(A) good state is one that understands the private sector pays for the public sector and makes it easy for the private sector to conduct business and grow" said David N. Willis, CEO of a Baltimore-based wholesale distribution company.[89] "California, New York, and Illinois have high costs of living, high taxes and regulation," observed Mark Larsen, CEO of a mid-size financial services firm.[90] Austin, Texas, is particularly becoming a fast growing technology center, and a place where programmers and technology engineers can enjoy a housing cost index 300% lower than in San Francisco.[91]

There is little question that California is failing to keep existing business investment in the state and to attract new business investment from other states. While California businesses report receiving regular calls from recruiters from other states, and never receiving similar calls from California officials,[92] the Governor's own office has failed to create a media or advertising campaign to attract outside investment in the state. The likely reason for that is that given liberal policies that have created such an awful business climate in the state, there isn't much such an advertising program could say that would be convincing. California's current lackluster interest in promoting business investment was expressed by Kish Rajan, the director of the Governor's Office of Business Development, when he told the *Sacramento Business Journal*, "(a)round here, we all take our lead from Gov. Jerry Brown. He's in charge and he sets the tone and defines the culture we all work in. He's really not about sizzle."

---

88 http://chiefexecutive.net/
states-more-aggressive-in-competing-with-one-another-2013

89 Id.

90 Id.

91 Id.

92 http://www.bizjournals.com/sacramento/print-edition/2013/05/10/is-california-losing-race-business.html

That is not to say that Jerry Brown has taken absolutely no steps regarding business investment. He did lead a group of 90 Californians to the opening of a new trade office in Shanghai intended to help California exporters.[93] China is a buyer of California nuts and wine, and as much sensitive technology as they can get. Production of pistachios in the state is set to double to a billion pounds a year by 2020 on a gamble that sales will grow in China.[94] But such efforts might be a little late in the game. The Rhodium Group, an economic research firm, concludes the total value of Chinese investment deals that California has secured during 2000-2011 "was less than other states hauled in," and that California has had less success with state-owned enterprises, "where the money is."[95]

Yet at the same time that New York was wooing people and businesses with promises of lower taxes, and just after making California's marginal income tax the highest in the country, liberal Democrats returned to Sacramento in 2013 not with job-creating reforms, but rather with a mountain of even more measures to extract further taxes from the businesses left in the state. In early 2013 after enactment of record-setting tax increases, Democrats in the legislature had 110 new bills introduced that would raise state taxes in general, including a new car tax.[96] Despite Jerry Brown's campaign promise to hold off on new taxes if Proposition 30 passed, Democrats in the legislature are now able to over-ride his veto with two-thirds of the members in each chamber; and what these reflexive liberals want is more tax revenue, period.[97]

---

93 http://www.economist.com/news/
united-states/21576111-old-relationship-presents-fresh-opportunities-chasing-dragon

94 http://www.sacbee.com/2013/05/26/5446939/its-raining-pistachios-growers.
html#mi_rss=Business?utm_source=feedly

95 http://www.economist.com/news/
united-states/21576111-old-relationship-presents-fresh-opportunities-chasing-dragon

96 http://capoliticalnews.com/2013/03/22/
return-of-the-car-tax-and-why-legislators-should-say-no/

97 http://www.capradio.org/187382?utm_source=feedly&utm_medium=feed&utm_
campaign=Feed%3A+CapitalPublicRadioLatestNewsRSS+%28Capital+Public+Radio%
3A+Latest+News+RSS%29

Among the 110 new tax increase proposals that the legislature is approving in "one committee vote after another,"[98] several have made their way to the governor's desk. The biggest tax increase is AB 8, which would raise $2.3 billion a year in new revenues by increasing taxes on tires, automobiles, and boats, in part to establish a network of "hydrogen" filling stations across the state, paid for by the government, for H2O-emitting automobiles that do not yet exist on the consumer market. The bill sailed out of the legislature with several Republican votes and is expected to be signed into law by Governor Brown.[99] Other bills include new fees on prepaid mobile phone cards, [100] and Senate Bill 254, which would impose a new $25 fee on mattresses.[101]

Other legislation that will be considered into 2014 includes Senate Bill 622 which would raise the tax on sweetened beverages by one-cent an ounce, adding nearly $1 of tax for a six-pack of 16 ounce sodas.[102] [103] Senate Bill 782 would impose a $10 entry fee tax at bars and restaurants offering adult entertainment.[104] Senate Bill 700 would require a payment of 5 cents for every paper or plastic

---

98 http://www.ocregister.com/articles/taxes-508807-state-tax.html

99 "Jerry Brown will sign bills extending fees, incentives to reduce emissions," Sacramento Bee, September 16, 2013. http://blogs.sacbee.com/capitolalert-latest/2013/09/jerry-brown-will-sign-bills-extending-fees-incentives-to-reduce-emissions.html

100 http://www.boe.ca.gov/legdiv/pdf/0300ab041613cw.pdf

101 http://articles.latimes.com/2013/mar/28/business/la-fi-mattress-tax-20130329

102 http://www.latimes.com/news/opinion/commentary/la-oe-billingsley-california-taxes-20130417,0,787442.story

103 http://leginfo.ca.gov/pub/13-14/bill/sen/sb_0601-0650/sb_622_bill_20130530_status.html

104 http://leginfo.ca.gov/pub/13-14/bill/sen/sb_0751-0800/sb_782_bill_20130530_status.html

shopping bag used at a grocery store.[105] Senate Bill 768[106] would add $2 a pack to the already hefty cigarette tax,[107] despite warnings from the California Retailers Federation that passing a 230% tax increase on a pack would cost jobs in the state while increasing the traffic in black market sales of cigarettes from neighboring states with greatly lower tobacco taxes.[108] Nevada, for example, already imposes an 80 cents per pack excise tax on cigarettes; while AB 768 would set the California excise tax at $2.87,[109] making just one carton of cigarettes purchased in nearby Las Vegas close to $21 cheaper than across the border in California. For smokers, AB 768 is about as expensive as a weekly bus ticket to Vegas.

Energy resources are undoubtedly the most mismanaged industry by government in California. Rather than embracing academic research that reveals millions of tax-base expanding jobs could be created by opening California's immense reserves for further high-tech exploration and extraction, liberals instead foreclose such efforts and seek to tax energy all the more at job-killing levels. Senate Bill 241 would impose an additional 9.9% new tax on oil extraction.[110] Northern California liberal Democrats in the legislature, such as its author State Senator Noreen Evans, crow that such a tax could generate $3 billion a year in new tax revenues for the state.[111]

---

105 http://leginfo.ca.gov/pub/13-14/bill/sen/sb_0651-0700/sb_700_bill_20130530_status.html

106 http://leginfo.ca.gov/pub/13-14/bill/sen/sb_0751-0800/sb_768_bill_20130530_status.html

107 https://leginfo.legislature.ca.gov/faces/billNavClient.xhtml?bill_id=201320140SB768&search_keywords=

108 http://www.foxandhoundsdaily.com/2013/05/the-economic-and-criminal-consequences-of-raising-the-tobacco-tax/?utm_source=rss&utm_medium=rss&utm_campaign=the-economic-and-criminal-consequences-of-raising-the-tobacco-tax

109 http://www.ncsl.org/issues-research/health/2011-state-cigarette-excise-taxes.aspx

110 http://leginfo.ca.gov/pub/13-14/bill/sen/sb_0201-0250/sb_241_bill_20130530_status.html

111 http://www.sfchronicle.com/politics/joegarofoli/article/Oil-tax-could-get-boost-from-billionaire-4432908.php?t=cade6155985133445b

But the liberals ignore the research on how detrimental such a tax increase would be on California's economy. George Runner, a Republican elected official on the state's Board of Equalization, which deals with tax resolution issues, is highly critical of AB 241 and further taxes on oil, citing the fact that the state and its localities already impose a severance tax and other taxes on oil including property taxes, sales taxes, and corporate taxes.[112] Runner cites a 2008 analysis to debunk liberal arguments that oil companies in California aren't taxed enough.[113] The study, by Jose Luis Alberro and William Hamm, found that if the severance tax encompassed by AB 241 were enacted, California would have established a tax system for oil well above the national average, that oil production would be reduced as a result, prices would rise at the gas pump contributing to inflation, reliance on foreign oil would be increased, and the tax could eliminate as many as 10,000 jobs as a result.[114]

In 1978 despite the opposition of big business, labor, and liberal Democrats, who were all claiming dire consequences if Proposition 13 passed, voters overwhelmingly approved the Proposition 13 tax-cut because real property taxes in the state had indeed become among the highest in the nation. Voters were concerned that homeowners, and especially senior citizens would be "taxed out of their homes," as Jarvis would say, as a result of rapidly inflating tax bills during the real estate boom of the era.[115] The desperate mood of some taxpayers was captured by Joel Fox, a former President of the Howard Jarvis Taxpayers Association, as he recounts in his book the story Howard Jarvis often told of the time Jarvis accompanied a middle-aged woman to the Los Angeles County Hall of Administration in the mid-1960s to plead her case: her real property taxes,

---

112 http://www.vcstar.com/news/2013/apr/14/
george-runner-a-severance-tax-will-cost-jobs/?partner=RSS

113 Id.

114 Id.

115 http://www.latimes.com/news/local/la-me-dell-property-20130505,0,6993978.
story?track=rss&utm_source=feedly

which had escalated dramatically as a result of California's real estate inflation, were simply outrageous and needed to be reduced because she could not afford to pay them. According to the story, county officials told her that her taxes had been calculated correctly and there was nothing they could do for her, and she must pay the tax bill. Frustrated and in shock, the woman had a heart attack in the building and died.[116]

Proposition 13 offered a stable and rational alternative to skyrocketing valuations of homes: it pegged the annual taxable value of homes at 1% of the original purchase price of a home, put a cap of 2% a year on increases in the assessed value for tax purposes, and allowed for reassessment to full market value when the property was next sold.[117]

And Proposition 13 has helped, not hurt California. Its benefits to the state at the time of passage, despite the dire warning of opponents to the contrary, were predictable, gaining the support of Nobel-prize winning economist Milton Friedman, who actually appeared in a television commercial for Prop. 13, saying "don't let the politicians fool you."[118] Another top economist, Arthur Laffer of the University of Southern California, who would go on to gain fame as influencing the economic expansion policies of the later Reagan Administration as the creator of the "Laffer Curve," also was an ardent supporter of Proposition 13. Laffer predicted that if Proposition 13 passed, "with property taxes lower, businesses will expand their activities within the state. This expansion will create new jobs, more investment, and higher real wages. Sales, incomes, and other forms of activity will expand. Sales taxes, income taxes, etc., all will rise."[119]

And economic expansion envisioned by Laffer is exactly what happened. According to Laffer, in the ten years after passage of Proposition 13, incomes in California grew 50% faster than the

---

116 Joel Fox, *The Legend of Proposition 13*, (City: Xlibris, 2003), 19.

117 Id.

118 Joel Fox, *The Legend of Proposition 13*, (City: Xlibris, 2003), 86.

119 Joel Fox, *The Legend of Proposition 13*, (City: Xlibris, 2003), 61.

nation as a whole, and jobs were created at twice the pace of the rest of the country.[120] Laffer has observed that after Proposition 13 passed, in 1978 property tax revenues fell $5 billion, but this drop in revenue "was largely offset by higher revenues in every other major tax category,"[121] and the increase in personal incomes allowed the tax base to expand enough, with more people paying taxes, to offset the reduction in property tax rates and allow for tax revenue growth for years to come. It took just six years, to 1985, for property tax revenues themselves to return to pre-Proposition 13 levels, as the economy expanded.[122] Indeed, by 1987, Republican Governor George Dukemejian not only was able to sign a balanced budget for the state, but because of a surplus of state revenues, also called for a 15% rebate of income taxes already paid by Californians,[123] a unique rebate that was approved by the legislature in a time of economic growth.

Stephen Moore has written that Proposition 13 didn't result in an "undertaxed" California. Citing Tax Foundation statistics, Moore concluded that Proposition 13 "merely moved California from one of the highest tax states in the nation to a slightly above-average tax state."[124]

Today, Arthur Laffer concludes that California's taxes are once again too high, and makes the case that California's tax policies continue to bear an inverse relationship to job creation and personal incomes in the state in relation to the rest of the country. When taxes are high in California in relation to the rest of the country, as they are now, jobs are lost. When taxes are lower than the rest of the country, job creation flourishes better than the rest of the nation.[125]

---

120 Arthur Laffer with Wayne Winegarden, *Eureka! How to Fix California*, San Francisco, Pacific Research Institute, 2012), 107.

121 Id., 111.

122 Id., 112.

123 http://articles.latimes.com/1987-07-07/news/mn-1592_1_income-tax-rebate

124 http://www.cato.org/publications/commentary/proposition-13-then-now-forever

125 Arthur Laffer with Wayne Winegarden, *Eureka! How to Fix California*, (City: Pacific Research Institute, 2012), 111, Exhibit 45.

Liberals today do not share the view that lower taxes are helpful to the economy. Rather, they support high levels of taxation, and they are eager for Jerry Brown and his Proposition 30 tax hike to succeed. The *New York Times*, for example, has editorialized "Brown Cheered in Second Act, at least So Far," and has said that when Brown was elected Governor, California "seemed caught in an intractable reversal of fortune" and implies Brown and his tax hikes are changing things for the better.[126] That conclusion is simply liberal hubris. A more credible assessment is provided by long-time *Sacramento Bee* columnist Dan Walters, whose outlook is not stuck in any political camp. Walter's response to the predicable gushing of the *New York Times* on the slightest improvement of economic news coming from California attributable to Brown and the tax hike was candid and to the contrary: "California's economic recovery may be slowing, the latest employment figures indicate, and the state still has nearly 1.7 million jobless workers, nearly twice as many as it had five years ago."[127]

California's taxes are too high and they are hurting, not helping the state's economy. The current tax policy seems very much out of balance, and according to Arthur Schlesinger's theory of cycle of balance, California should be ripe for a big change in its politics based on the devastating economic results its out-of-whack taxes created. So the question becomes, what is the mood of California citizens themselves on the taxes? Polls show that California voters are not inclined to accept any more taxation. A USC/*Los Angeles Times* poll of California voters months after the passage of Proposition 30 found that most opposed making it easier to pass new taxes for school funding, and Dan Schnur, director of the poll said voters were "not in the mood to either pay higher taxes now or to make it easier to raise taxes in the

---

126 http://www.nytimes.com/2013/08/17/us/brown-cheered-in-second-act-at-least-so-far.html?pagewanted=all&_r=0

127 http://www.sacbee.com/2013/08/25/5678747/dan-walters-jerry-browns-agenda.html#mi_rss=Dan%20Walters

near future." [128] Similar results were found in another statewide poll released in March 2013 that showed a majority of Californians oppose making it easier to raise local parcel taxes.[129] But the best tests of voter sentiment are elections. There are perhaps some signs of the beginning of a shifting balance on tax reform, even among California's minority communities, depending on the tax. On the same ballot as the Proposition 30 tax hike in the last election, nearly 67% of voters in the Bay Area city of Richmond defeated at the polls an additional new tax on soft drinks.[130] Richmond has a large Black/African American community making up more than 26% of the residents.[131] In El Monte in Los Angeles County, where Latinos comprise 69% of the residents,[132] 77% of voters similarly rejected a measure on the same ballot to raise taxes on sodas.[133] More recently, in the Democrat-dominated city of Los Angeles' 2013 off-year elections, a measure that would have raised sales taxes was handily defeated with close to 55% of the voters opposing the tax hike.[134]

It remains to be seen whether citizen dissatisfaction with California's taxes is reaching the fevered pitch that lead to Proposition 13's historic passage in 1978 and is headed for a major cyclical mood shift, or perhaps a mass exodus; nevertheless, regardless of the opinion writers of the *New York Times*, California's terribly high tax burden remains an obstacle to economic growth and job creation and people are suffering because of it.

---

128 http://dornsife.usc.edu/usc-dornsife-la-times-poll-taxes-education-march-2013/

129 http://www.hjta.org/press-releases/
pr-new-poll-shows-majority-california-voters-oppose-lowering-parcel-tax-voting-thresh

130 http://latimesblogs.latimes.com/lanow/2012/11/soda-taxes-lose-big-in-california.html

131 http://www.bayareacensus.ca.gov/cities/Richmond.htm

132 http://quickfacts.census.gov/qfd/states/06/0622230.html

133 http://latimesblogs.latimes.com/lanow/2012/11/soda-taxes-lose-big-in-california.html

134 http://ballotpedia.org/wiki/index.php/
City_of_Los_Angeles_Sales_Tax_Increase,_Proposition_A_%28March_2013%29

THE NEW CALIFORNIA

CALIFORNIA IS A BEHEMOTH. It is the largest state in the nation, with over 38 million residents,[135] of whom 18,008,380 are registered voters and live in 9,867,964 households.[136] One in eight Americans call California their home. California has the ninth largest economy in the world, larger than even Russia.[137] Gross domestic product in 2011 was almost $2 trillion. Federal spending in California is $330 billion, in the form of payments to individuals, state and local governments, businesses and nonprofits (payments for Medicare and Social Security), spending on goods and services, grants, and other procurements.[138]

There is no question that California has also been a leader: as Joe Mathews has written, the state "attracts more venture capital than the rest of the country combined," and tops the charts in agriculture sales, high-wage services, fast-growing companies, and patents and inventions, among other categories.[139]

---

135 http://quickfacts.census.gov/qfd/states/06000.html

136 http://www.politicaldata.com/Pages/ReportCount.aspx

137 CalFacts, LAO, 2013.

138 Id.

139 http://www.dailynews.com/opinions/ci_23348218/
joe-mathews-are-californians-flaky-no-we-work

But California is changing. Despite its vast mineral resources, it is no longer a leader in energy production.[140] The movie and television industry are seeing production move out-of-state, perhaps epitomized by the announcement that after four decades, the "Tonight Show" was moving back to New York City.[141] The problem is so intense that newly elected Los Angeles Mayor Eric Garcetti has declared a "state of emergency" as movie and television production studios leave Hollywood.[142] A bad economy, lack of tax incentives, and bad business regulatory environment are taking their toll. "Too difficult, too expensive" to do business in Los Angeles anymore, said one experienced location manager to a reporter from *Variety*.[143]

Businesses are indeed fleeing the state, and unemployment and poverty rates are among the highest in the nation. Sadly, California's poverty rate has over time become the highest of any state in the nation. According to the most recent statistics of the U.S. Census Bureau, the poverty rate was 23.5% in 2011.[144] The method by which the Obama Administration calculates poverty has recently changed, resulting in a sharp jump in California's statistics, and there has been some criticism of the new method of data evaluation, which is seen as inflating the true number of those actually in poverty.[145] Nevertheless, what is considered a "a steep climb" in the rate is, according to the *Sacramento Bee*, "driven largely by the state's high cost of living."[146] That "cost of living" of course includes not only higher costs of rent and food, but

---

140 http://www.utsandiego.com/news/2012/Nov/14/
california-should-lead-oil-shale-revolution/

141 http://www.presstelegram.com/opinion/20130326/
tonight-show-news-puts-hollywood-woes-in-spotlight-opinion

142 http://variety.com/2013/biz/news/l-a-mayor-declares-state-of-emergency-as-movie-tv-production-flees-hollywood-1200589182/

143 Id.

144 http://www.census.gov/prod/2012pubs/p60-244.pdf

145 http://www.huffingtonpost.com/2012/11/14/california-poverty_n_2132920.html

146 http://blogs.sacbee.com/capitolalertlatest/2012/11/californias-poverty-rate-highest-in-us-by-new-federal-measure.html

also the highest taxes in the nation, and specifically the highest sales taxes in the nation, which have a disproportionately negative effort on the poorest families and contribute to their poverty. The state has 6.1 million people living in poverty, and more children than any other state in the nation in poverty,[147] and the statistics support a connection between poverty and family structure. Families headed by a single parent are much more likely to be living in poverty than in a traditional family structure. [148] Education is also connected to poverty, and in California, counties with the lowest high-school dropout rates like Placer, Marin and El Dorado, are also the counties that have the lower poverty rates.[149]

Unemployment has become a persistent problem in California. From July 2007 through February 2010, the state lost a staggering 1.4 million jobs.[150] Less than half of those lost jobs have been recovered since.[151] The percentage of those unemployed for more than six months has steadily risen over the past five years.[152] There are close to 2 million unemployed workers in California today. Since the recession began, California's unemployment rate has consistently exceeded the national unemployment rate by 2 to 3 percentage points.[153] But there is a huge bright spot in the changing California. The Golden State leads the nation in almost all technology sectors. Technology employment accounted for nearly 1 million jobs and a payroll of $120 billion in 2012.[154] No other state comes even close to California's leadership in technology employment.

---

147 http://www.ocregister.com/articles/poverty-510086-california-counties.html

148 Id.

149 Id.

150 CalFacts, LAO, 2013.

151 Id.

152 Id.

153 Id.

154 http://www.bizjournals.com/sacramento/news/2013/05/15/california-leads-tech-sector-payroll.html

The demographics of California are also undergoing remarkable change. For the first time in more than one hundred years, Hispanics will be the largest ethnic group in California starting in 2013, according to a California state report contained in the Governor's 2013-14 budget proposal.[155] According to the report, Hispanic and white non-Hispanic populations will reach parity in mid-2013 at 39% respectively, and then Hispanics will steadily grow into dominance, as the Hispanic population is much younger, with only 19% older than age 50, compared to only 43 percent of whites older than age 50.[156]

Californian's Asian population has tripled over the last 30 years and it is now 13.6% of the population, meaning that Hispanics and Asians combined constitute a majority of California's population.[157]

The 2010 U.S. Census found that despite growth of California's African-American population of about 2.7 million, the fifth largest of any state, it is shrinking as a share of the total population in the state and is about 50% as large proportionally as the black population in the rest of the nation.[158] The reduction in the percentage of African-Americans in California's population is threatening black office holders, as African-American voter registration dominance in at least one historically black Congressional district in Los Angeles County shifted to dominance by Latino voters as a result of the reapportionment of Congressional districts after the Census.[159] The 9th City Council district in Los Angeles, which represents downtown areas as well as parts of the Watts district in south-central Los Angeles and which has traditionally elected a member of the

---

155 *Huffington Post*, January 18, 2013, http://www.huffingtonpost.com/2013/01/18/ california-hispanic-population-largest-ethnic-group_n_2508103.html

156 Id.

157 http://www.flashreport.org/blog/2013/05/11/ whats-holding-california-republicans-back/

158 http://blogs.sacbee.com/capitolalertlatest/2011/09/californias-black-population-shrinkjng-proportionately.html

159 Id.

black community to represent it on the city council, is now 80% Latino.[160]

In Oakland—where the Black Panther Party was founded and which has produced great black Hall of Fame athletes such as Joe Morgan, Ricky Henderson, and Bill Russell, politician Ron Dellums, and entertainers such as the Pointer Sisters—the black population has declined by at least 25% over the last decade.[161] Today there are as many Latinos in Oakland as there are blacks.[162] Across the Bay in San Francisco, only one black serves on the 11-member Board of Supervisors, where the black population has plummeted by more than half since 1970 and stands at less than 6.1 percent of the population today.[163]

Blacks are clearly losing political clout because of demographic changes, not just in Los Angeles and the Bay Area,[164] but throughout the state.[165] This loss of clout is occurring not only as a result of the rise of California's Latino population, but also as a result of the migration of parts of the black community outside of high concentrations in urban areas, into the suburbs.[166]

California's elderly population is growing and will continue to grow rapidly in the next ten years, as a result of the aging of "baby boomers" and continuing drops in death rates. The growth

---

160 http://articles.latimes.com/2013/feb/22/local/la-me-9th-district-election-20130223

161 http://www.sfgate.com/bayarea/article/25-drop-in-African-American-population-In-Oakland-2471925.php

162 Id.

163 http://www.sfgate.com/politics/article/S-F-blacks-political-clout-imperiled-2353403.php

164 http://connection.ebscohost.com/c/articles/9705196304/blacks-losing-political-clout-hispanics-los-angeles

165 http://newamericamedia.org/2011/06/black-migration-changes-the-political-landscape-in-many-states.php

166 Id.

is especially accelerated for seniors age 65-74.[167] The largest overall group by age remains those 25 through 44. School- and college-age groups are projected to be slightly smaller through 2020 due to declining birth rates.

California is indeed changing. But one thing that has not changed in the last decade, as the state's demographic centers of gravity have shifted, is the continuing political dominance of liberal elites in Sacramento. Their control has only grown in strength, regardless of the other changes California is experiencing.

---

167 http://www.flashreport.org/blog/2013/05/11/
whats-holding-california-republicans-back/

CALIFORNIA'S LIBERAL SPECIAL INTERESTS

PUBLIC EMPLOYEE UNIONS ARE by far the biggest spending special interest groups in California, dumping hundreds of millions of dollars into lobbying and election campaigns that perpetuate liberal control and that result in outcomes that mostly favor union members at the expense of ordinary Californians. Their financial intervention in the political system dwarfs the spending of the big energy, banking, and telecommunications industries, the California Chamber of Commerce, realtors, doctors, insurance companies, you name it. The public employee unions spend more on politics in California than any other interest group. They spend hundreds of millions on politics in the state and with their cronies, the liberal Democratic officeholders in Sacramento, they run the state, rendering a once robust business community afraid to challenge their liberal monopoly of power. In so doing, these liberals are able to perpetuate the tax-and-spend policies that prop-up irrationally high public employee salaries and pensions, and saddle the state economy with high taxes, high unemployment, and a dwindling business community. They have thrown the state wildly out of political balance.

Of course, political spending by unions, not just in California but across the nation, has become endemic. According to the *Wall*

Street Journal, union disclosures to the Labor Department on their total political spending on Federal, state, and local candidates, political activity like polling and research, and lobbying, total a whopping $4.4 billion from 2005 to 2011.[168] These donations invariably assist Democratic candidates and liberal policies. According to the *Journal,* 92% of union political spending on candidates in 2008 went to Democrats.[169] The top union political spender nationwide is the Service Employees International Union (SEIU), and in California it is topped by the California Teachers Association (CTA).

Public employee union money has particularly dominated political spending in California, and can be identified as the real reason for Californian's one-sided politics today. In 2010 California's Fair Political Practices Commission issued a paper entitled "Big Money Talks" which studied and reported on nine years of disclosed political spending by special interests in California state government from the beginning of 2000 to the end of 2009. The report identified the top 15 special interests in the state and tallied that they collectively spent a whopping $1 billion to influence elections and legislation in the time period. Of the total, the California Teachers Association ranked as the single biggest spending special interest in the state, at almost $212,000,000, eclipsing the combined spending of Chevron Corporation, AT&T, Philip Morris USA, and the Western States Petroleum Association. CTA's spending was twice as much as the next big spender, the SEIU in California, at $107,467,272, leaving behind the paltry spending of the California Chamber of Commerce at just $39 million over the nine year period.

Special interest spending in California is surely not on the decline either, and CTA not only remains on top as the single biggest spending interest in the state, but its spending also is growing. From 2000 through the last public disclosure period ending mid-2013,

---

168 http://online.wsj.com/article/SB10001424052702304782404577488584031850026.html

169 Id.

CTA has spent an incredible $290,000,000 on influencing California elections and legislation.[170] That is almost $2 million spent on state politics every month for the last 12 ½ years. CTA's political spending in this period exceeds by a factor of six times the spending of the California Chamber of Commerce, and even swamps the SEIU at $136,000,000. Between CTA and their public employee union allies in the California Correctional Peace Officers Association and the SEIU, unions representing public employees have spent half a billion dollars to influence politics in California in just a little more than ten years. Their influence helps ensure that the $300 billion a year the state spends from all sources flows the way they want it to flow.[171]

The SEIU is California's largest public employee union and one of the top special interest spenders in the state. Its leader, Yvonne Walker, recently expressed SEIU's sense of political entitlement to a labor rally for higher public employee wages on the State Capital steps: "We're letting them know this is our house!"[172] During the 2012 campaign to oppose Proposition 32, a measure that would have ended the practice of allowing mandatory union dues for politics, the 700,000 member strong union spent about $15 per employee on the anti-Prop. 32 campaign, over $10 million.[173] The California Association of Professional Scientists gave the equivalent of $40 per member, and with a small base of just 2,500 members, their contribution was still $100,000 to the political campaign. The 13,000 member Professional Engineers in California Government gave about $46 per member, or close to $600,000.[174] Nevertheless, SEIU's money dwarfed most of the other unions in the 2012 campaign.

---

170 Calculations based on public disclosure reports compiled by the author.

171 http://www.sacbee.com/2013/07/21/5583075/dan-walters-big-money-in-california.html

172 http://www.mygovcost.org/2013/06/19/
this-is-our-house-government-unions-own-the-capitol/

173 http://blogs.sacbee.com/the_state_worker/union-spending/

174 Id.

Total Money Spent by Top 18 California Special Interest Groups: Campaign Spending and Lobbying Spending (January 1, 2000 - June 30, 2013)

Special Interest Group	Total $ Spent
California Teachers Association	$290,614,400.28
California State Council of Service Employees	$136,791,567.37
Pharmaceutical Research and Manufacturers Association	$108,343,940.23
Chevron Corporation	$90,892,858.07
Philip Morris USA	$90,673,213.37
Morongo Band of Mission Indians	$86,449,390.74
Pacific Gas and Electric Company	$74,795,674.37
Pechanga Band of Luiseno Indians	$74,365,330.50
AT&T Inc.	$73,141,221.03
California Association of Realtors	$61,238,803.60
California Hospital Association	$54,479,368.81
Western States Petroleum Association	$51,509,508.22
California Chamber of Commerce	$51,291,230.65
Southern California Edison	$51,227,727.29
Agua Caliente Band of Cahuilla Indians	$51,083,542.17
California Correctional Peace Officers Association	$49,465,448.10
California School Employees Association	$49,347,917.60
Aera Energy LLC	$36,451,062.10

Among those workers the SEIU represents includes healthcare workers at facilities such as Kaiser Permanente Hospitals, where 45,000 workers are members of the union.[175] The union has been criticized by the National Labor Relations Board for engaging in unfair tactics in organizing workers,[176] and is sometimes at odds

---

175 http://www.sacbee.com/2013/05/02/5391189/giant-seiu-claims-victory-in-fight.html#mi_rss=Business?utm_source=feedly

176 Id.

with another influential union in the state, the California Nurses Association. Ten public employee unions including the SEIU, the California Labor Federation and the California Professional Fire-fighters Association are so incensed that the conservative Koch Brothers might become owners of the newspaper-publishing Tribune Company, the parent company of the *Los Angeles Times*, that they have rallied liberal Democratic legislative leaders to join them in threatening the current largest shareholder of Tribune, Oaktree Capital Management, with retaliatory withdrawal of pension fund investments should Oaktree make the sale.[177] Such thuggery seems not too far afield from racketeering, and stands out as an example of how far California's major unions will go to silence a different view. So much for promoting competition of ideas in California.

A beneficiary of all this public employee union special interest spending is the California Democratic Party. At the end of 2012, after crushing Republican candidates for office up and down the state, the California Democratic Party disclosed spending in excess of $26 million with "cash on hand" of over $10 million at year's close.[178] In contrast, the California Republican Party reported just under $10 million in total expenditures during the same period, ending the year with a cash balance of $155,541.52.[179] And this tremendous money advantage of the Democratic Party is just the tip of the iceberg of the liberal establishment's supremacy in campaign finance.

There is another reason for the tremendous money advantage for Democrats in political campaigns, even beyond its support from

---

177 http://www.latimes.com/local/lanow/la-me-pc-unions-lawmakers-line-up against koch brothers 20130508,0,2671523,story?track roo&utm_source=feedly&utm_medium=feed&utm_campaign=Feed%3A+lanowblog+%28L.A.+Now%29

178 http://cal-access.sos.ca.gov/Campaign/Committees/Detail.aspx?id=1018392&session=2011&view=general

179 http://cal-access.sos.ca.gov/Campaign/Committees/Detail.aspx?id=1030435&session=2011

public employee unions, and it is because they are the ones in control of the levers of power. Business and other special interests that have a concern about government are simply wasting their money on helping otherwise like-minded Republican candidates for office, because of the total dominance Democrats have in the legislature. For example, when Adidas, a firm that had never been a big campaign donor in the state, successfully sought legislation in 2007 to legalize the sale of kangaroo leather in its running shoes, just two days after it was signed into law they not so surprisingly donated $2,360 to the Democratic State Senator (currently under FBI investigation for bribe-taking involving different legislation), who authored the legalization bill, while also donating another $13,600 to the California Democratic Party a few months later. [180] "Such is the way of Sacramento, enabled by politicians who control the town," observed one prominent journalist.[181] Jon Coupal, the head of the Howard Jarvis Taxpayers Association, writes of a "pay-to-play culture in the state capitol" that allows "members of the majority party" to press "politically vulnerable industries for campaign contributions."[182]

And those union allies are hardly nonpartisan about their politics or their goals. Left-wing union activism, echoed with approval by their media allies, especially in San Francisco, has hit an almost absurd level. Formerly non-union hotel chains like Hyatt are "blacklisted" by the California Federation of Labor,[183] guests are disturbed and subjected to strikes[184] and the company's neighbors

---

180 http://www.sacbee.com/2013/06/09/5480550/money-lures-politicians-and-fbi.html#mi_rss=Opinion

181 http://www.sacbee.com/2013/06/09/5480550/money-lures-politicians-and-fbi.html#mi_rss=Opinion

182 http://www.hjta.org/california-commentary/shakedowns

183 http://www.hotelworkersrising.org/HotelGuide/boycott_list.php

184 http://www.tripadvisor.com/ShowUserReviews-g60713-d81103-r118469695-Hyatt_Regency_San_Francisco-San_Francisco_California.html

are also disturbed until they bow to the pressure.[185] The nurses at the University of California's hospitals, including U.C. San Francisco, went on strike over, among other things, their objections to "unprecedented executive excess."[186] U.C officials reportedly say the real reason for the strike is that the union that represents the nurses, the Federation of State, County and Municipal Employees, doesn't want to change employees' generous pensions. "The union has refused to agree to UC's pension reform started in 2010 to address underfunding of the plan," said a U.C. spokesperson.[187] U.C. patient care workers are reportedly balking over increasing their own pension contributions from 5% to 6.5%, after nearly two decades of "holiday" when neither employees nor U.C. were making any contributions to their pension plans.[188] Such short-sighted management of retirement obligations by both labor and management is symptomatic of the larger pension funding crisis throughout California, let alone the public employee unions' desire to place all the risk for their members retirement compensation on the taxpayer.

Even the Symphony in liberal San Francisco finds a reason to go on strike, causing cancellation of what was termed a "prominent East Coast tour."[189] Something seemingly as docile as the annual meeting of San Francisco-based Wells Fargo Bank is forced out of their own headquarters city, where the meeting has been held each year for 15 years, and placed instead in Salt Lake City, for fear of "Occupy" protesters, cheered on with support from the California

---

185 http://www.bizjournals.com/sanfrancisco/blog/2013/07/hyatt-union-group-end-three-year.html?page=all

186 http://www.bizjournals.com/sacramento/news/2013/04/19/workers-vow-strike-at-uc-hospitals.html?ana=e_sac_rdup&s=newsletter&ed=2013-04-19&u=slyE44urV4bo6o4GHwHIqylywCD

187 Id.

188 http://calpensions.com/2013/08/12/public-pensions-become-issue-in-labor-strikes/

189 http://www.sfgate.com/music/article/SF-Symphony-players-ratify-con-tract-4432391.php

Teacher's Association[190], disrupting the meeting.[191] Concession workers at AT&T Park staged a game-long strike during a San Francisco Giants game, reportedly about wages and health benefits, chanting a few feet away from the statue of Willie Mays at the park's entrance, "...don't buy the food. We are on strike!"[192]

The California Teachers Association is considered one of the most powerful forces in Sacramento.[193] The published mission statement of the CTA is straightforward enough. It states CTA, first and foremost, "exists to protect and promote the well-being of its members."[194] CTA sees itself as the "preeminent voice for public education in California," and exists to "maintain and expand its membership so as to remain effective in defending and advancing members' interests." However, the actual role CTA plays in the political process is more insidious.

The year 2013 marked the 150th anniversary of the creation of the California Teachers Association. Founded in 1863 as the California Educational Society by state schools superintendent John Swett,[195] it has grown from less than 100 members to its current powerhouse status of more than 325,000 members. CTA describes its contribution to California's history as follows:

> "CTA's long history is full of the sounds of school strikes and teachers chanting on picket lines, the shouts of victory on countless election nights, and the quiet conversation of educators waiting to speak out in crucial legislative hearings over the decades in Sacramento."[196]

---

190 http://www.cta.org/Issues-and-Action/School-Funding/Tax-Fairness/Occupy-Wall-Street.aspx. CTA supports the Occupy protesters by providing financial support for posters, placards, flyers and other organizing support.

191 http://capoliticalnews.com/2013/03/28/san-fran-left-thinks-city-govt-and-business-sold-out-unions-to-capitalism-horrors/

192 http://www.sfgate.com/politics/joegarofoli/article/AT-amp-T-Park-concession-workers-1-day-strike-4548739.php?utm_source=feedly

193 http://articles.latimes.com/2012/aug/18/local/la-me-cta-20120819

194 http://www.cta.org/About-CTA/Who-We-Are/Mission-Statement.aspx

195 http://www.cta.org/en/About-CTA/Who-We-Are/CTA-150th-Anniversary.aspx

196 Id.

CTA indeed has a long history, which includes consistently opposing efforts to lower taxes and restrain government spending. CTA successfully opposed Governor Ronald Reagan's efforts to convince the legislature to place controls on local government spending of their share of the skyrocketing property tax revenues that were being collected as a result of steep real estate inflation during that era.[197] And it was CTA in 1973, Reagan's last year in office as Governor, that helped block at the polls Reagan's own failed statewide initiative, Proposition 1, a spending limitation measure that eventually served as a precursor to the historic Proposition 13 real property tax-cut in 1978. Proposition 1 was a proposed state constitutional amendment to restrict government spending through strict tax-rate limitations and other limits on the legislature to raise taxes. It was vigorously supported as a ballot measure by the conservative Republican Governor during a time when California state government was "awash in revenue after years of fiscal crisis,"[198] (author Lou Cannon's words) after seven years of Reagan's tenure. Reagan had indeed been successful in controlling government spending during his years as Governor, and he didn't want government after him to recklessly spend all the excess unbudgeted tax revenue his years in office and a good economy were generating. But CTA disagreed, and even with ample campaign funding and Reagan's salesmanship for the proposition, CTA played a leading role in beating the measure on election day.[199]

CTA is allied with the California Federation of Teachers,[200] a smaller teachers' union that represents an additional 120,000 employees in 135 local unions chartered by the national American Federation of Teachers.[201] CTA's national affiliation is with the larger National Education Association.[202]

---

197 Lou Cannon, *Governor Reagan: His Rise to Power*, (New York, Public Affairs, 2003), 334.

198 Id., p. 370.

199 Id., p. 375.

200 http://latimesblogs.latimes.com/california-politics/2012/03/california-tax-teachers-poll.html

201 http://www.cft.org/about-cft/who-we-are.html

202 http://www.cta.org/About-CTA/Who-We-Are/CTA-Fact-Sheet.aspx

CTA really became the powerhouse it is today just after Reagan left office in 1974. The start of CTA's real ascent to power in California began when a younger Governor Jerry Brown, Reagan's successor in office, signed into law in 1975 a bill known as the "Rodda Act." The Rodda Act was the first collective bargaining law enacted in California for public school employees.[203] The new law allowed labor associations throughout California, such as the California Federation of Teachers, to organize bargaining units at local schools on wages, hours, health and pension benefits, evaluation procedures, employee safety, and discipline procedures. The Act provided for exclusive representation of a single employee organization to act as the representative of the teachers in the bargaining unit, whether the teachers joined the union or not.[204] This "agency shop" treatment handed the teachers' union a monopoly of labor power in education in the state. During the following years, CTA and its affiliates rapidly grew, gaining additional dues-paying members through their monopoly hold on teachers contracts. And as they grew, they gained more and more influence and made an increasingly successful impact on California elections and policy outcomes, including defeating a private school voucher initiative in 1993, two education related initiatives in 1998 backed by Republican Governor Pete Wilson, and another voucher initiative in 2000.[205]

By the time a politically naïve and wide-eyed reformer named Arnold Schwarzenegger started thinking seriously about running for Governor, CTA had established itself as the real power in the State Capitol. Schwarzenegger's first public act of statesmanship on his road to election as Governor was his sponsorship of a statewide initiative, the "After School Education and Safety Act," on the 2002 ballot, and Schwarzenegger's choice of subject matter was intentional—he actively sought the approval of CTA for his initiative before putting

---

203 http://www.ggea.org/documents/Rodda_Act-A_Historical_Look.pdf

204 Id.

205 Joe Matthews, *The People's Machine*, (New York: Public Affairs, 2006), 90.

it into circulation for qualification,[206] and at his first meeting with the CTA's top lobbyist he reportedly whispered, "(i)s there any way we can work together?"

Today CTA is more than a central fixture of the Sacramento liberal power structure. According to former Democratic State Senate leader Don Perata, CTA views itself as "the co-equal fourth branch of government."[207] Regarding CTA, "Democrats kowtowed publicly and grumbled privately about the union's arrogance. Even Republicans did their best not to provoke CTA's anger."[208] According to published reports then, it might come as no surprise that a much older Governor Jerry Brown worked out the last details of his state budget in 2012 with just three people in the room: the Assembly Speaker, the State Senate leader, and the lobbyist for CTA.[209]

CTA's political war chest tips the scales again and again in local and statewide elections for candidates and measures that tow their line, and that line is not reform minded when it comes to education policy. CTA's spending outpaces all other special interests in the state, including Chevron Oil Company, AT&T, and even the next largest spender, the SEIU. CTA's spending included close to $5 million to help Brown become Governor again in 2010.[210]

Surely CTA is not the only special interest group engaged in California politics, but it is by far the largest and most influential. Other unions and industry groups of course lobby the legislature and contribute to candidates, and their activities are generally subject to public disclosure. Sometimes well-meaning "watch-dog" groups will attempt to compile spending statistics to gage for the public who the biggest spenders are. But often such research misses the true mark of influence and control, because it focuses on just

---

206 Joe Matthews, *The People's Machine*, (New York: Public Affairs, 2006), 91.

207 Id.

208 Id., p. 90.

209 http://articles.latimes.com/2012/aug/18/local/la-me-cta-20120819

210 Id.

one aspect of political involvement, such as direct contributions to candidates, rather than also including direct "independent expenditures" to support or oppose candidates, as well as expenditures on statewide and local ballot measures and lobbying. When groups fail to consider the total political spending a special interest group engages in, an inaccurate picture is painted of that interest's activities in comparison to other interests, whose total involvement may really be minor in relation. One well-meaning group, the Center for Investigative Reporting (CIR), recently compiled total campaign spending reports and correctly concluded that Democrats in the State Assembly in the 2012 election were able to raise more than $43 million in direct campaign contributions from interests ranging from the healthcare industry such as the California Medical Association and California Dental Association($4.8 million); building and trade unions($2.8 million); Indian tribes ($1.8 million); "public employee unions" such as firefighters ($1.5 million); the California Teachers Association ($1.1 million); and telecommunications firms such as AT&T ($1.4 million).[211] The statistics CIR reports on direct political contributions to Assembly Democrats (which dwarf contributions to Republican rivals) may be correct, but the reporting of the information is misleading in two ways. First, CIR separates the CTA involvement from the "public employee union" category which works to minimize the apparent total involvement of public employee unions, which far exceeded $1.5 million. Second, and more importantly, CIR's report does not paint an accurate picture of true special interest influence in these elections or in the state because other critical spending, such as independent expenditures, support or opposition to ballot measures, and lobbying, are not included in the tallies. When all the expenditures are taken into account, CTA's total spending crushes that of any other union or industry group in the state.

---

211 http://cironline.org/reports/
interest-groups-play-major-role-democrats-campaign-funds-analysis-finds-4503

CTA funds its huge political treasury through compulsory fees that every teacher in the state system is required to pay, whether the teacher is a member of the union or not, or whether the teacher believes in CTA's anti-reform minded education philosophy or not. Such mandatory fees for political activity can be as high as $1,000 a year per teacher.[212] Efforts to outlaw the practice of requiring mandatory fees for political activity of California's public employee unions, known as "paycheck protection" measures, have failed in the legislature and at the ballot box.[213] A small group of California teachers associated with the Christian Educators Association who object to CTA's political positions is currently suing CTA under a claim that California's so-called "agency shop" law violates their constitutional rights by forcing them to pay dues for political activity they actually object to.[214] That Federal lawsuit is pending.

CTA rabidly opposes changes to teacher tenure rules, seniority protections, teacher evaluations linked to pay, merit pay, teacher accountability reforms, and private-school vouchers, all reforms that could dramatically improve the quality of education for California's school children.

Other, more local public employee unions seek power and control in California's major cities, including Los Angeles, where the electrical workers union gave an incredible $2.1 million to an independent effort to elect Wendy Greuel as Mayor.[215] The union electricians work for the

---

212 http://washingtonexaminer.com/
california-teachers-sue-nea-over-forced-1000-union-dues/article/2528510

213 Proposition 32 on the November, 2012 ballot, which would have prohibited compulsory dues from union members for political purposes, was defeated. The California Teachers Association was one of the principle funders of the successful opposition campaign.

214 http://washingtonexaminer.com/
california-teachers-sue-nea-over-forced-1000-union-dues/article/2528510

215 http://www.latimes.com/local/lanow/la-me-ln-dwp-union-wendy-greuel-20130511,0,310517.story?track=rss&utm_source=feedly&utm_medium=feed&utm_campaign=Feed%3A+lanowblog+%28L.A.+Now%29

City's Department of Water and Power and earn an average $100,000 a year in salary, which is 50% more than the average salary of other city employee's and 25% more than electricians make at comparable private and public sector jobs, according to a study by the *Los Angeles Times*.[216] There are claims that the same International Brotherhood of Electrical Workers $10 billion pension fund is seriously underfunded and actuarially unsound, which might help to explain the vigorous intervention by union electricians in the Mayor's race.[217] In the meantime Los Angeles residents who pay for the water and power delivered by the city, (many of whom live at or below the poverty line) will be looking at paying higher rates to meet the costs of high wages and benefits imposed on them by the Department of Water and Power and the electricians' union.[218] The electricians' union is not the only public employee union that intervened in the Mayor's race for Greuel, who also was backed with another $1.43 million from the Los Angeles Police Protective League.[219] "Spending by city employee unions in the mayoral contest has been hotly debated because City Hall faces continued budget troubles caused in part by rising costs of employee salaries and benefits," wrote one *Los Angeles Times* report on the millions being poured into Greuel's campaign by public employees.[220] Greuel ended up losing the election to Eric Garcetti as news of the "pot of money" public employee unions put into her race ended up trashing her reputation as a fiscal hawk with moderate and Republican voters in the San Fernando Valley from which she hailed.[221]

---

216 Id.

217 http://www.citywatchla.com/lead-stories-hidden/4996-bully-bo-d-arcy

218 Id.

219 http://articles.latimes.com/2013/may/08/local/
la-me-ln-police-union-greuel-20130508

220 Id.

221 http://www.latimes.com/local/lanow/la-me-ln-for-city-unions-split-
result-20130522,0,5530353.story?track=rss&utm_source=feedly&utm_
medium=feed&utm_campaign=Feed%3A+lanowblog+%28L.A.
+Now%29

California's public employee unions do not win every single election in which they intervene. However, there is no question that they have managed to win all the important elections in state government, and their continued dominance is both remarkable and dangerous to California's economic future.

THE DESCENT OF THE GOP AND STAMPING OUT OPPOSING VIEWPOINTS

ON ELECTION NIGHT, NOVEMBER 6, 2012, Governor Jerry Brown and his liberal Democratic allies turned California, already one of the nation's "bluest" states, into one in which the liberals "have all but complete political control."[222] Jerry Brown himself is not the cause of California's current remarkable imbalance in political power, but Brown and especially the liberal special interests behind him are surely the ones in control today.

Jerry Brown has had more than his share of election nights in California. Sharing his father's birthplace in San Francisco, he is the son of liberal Democratic politician Edmund G. "Pat" Brown. Pat Brown had unsuccessfully run for State Assembly as a Republican, and again for District Attorney before he was finally elected as a Democrat as San Francisco District Attorney in 1943. He was a successful prosecutor, and was twice elected as state Attorney General, and then won two terms as Governor of California (1959-1967). Pat Brown has the distinction of winning his second term as Governor by beating Richard Nixon in 1962, only to be

---

222 http://www.reuters.com/article/2012/11/08/
us-usa-campaign-california-idUSBRE8A70BV20121108

defeated four years later by Ronald Reagan by more than one million votes. Son Jerry moved south and after a brief stint in a Jesuit seminary in the state, entered politics himself and won a seat on the governing board of the then brand new Los Angeles Community College District. He went on to become California's Secretary of State (1971-1975), served two terms as Governor (1975-1983), ran unsuccessfully for President, became Chairman of the California Democratic Party (1989-1991), moved back north and was elected Mayor of Oakland for two terms (1999-2007), served as state Attorney General (2007-2011), and was elected to his third term as a Governor in 2010. Jerry Brown has indeed had a stake in plenty of election nights in California. But no other election night has been more successful for California's Democratic Party than November 6, 2012, when liberals gained total and absolute political control of state power.

Liberals had been dominant, entrenched and building power in California for more than the last decade. The 2012 elections handed them complete and total control. In California there are eight state constitutional officers, specifically, the Governor, Lt. Governor, Attorney General, Controller, Treasurer, Secretary of State, Insurance Commissioner and Superintendent of Public Instruction, and two United States Senators elected statewide. Today, the incumbent in every single one of those ten statewide positions is a registered Democrat.

On election night 2012, Democrats took control of 68.75% of the seats in the California State Assembly, with 55 seats, as opposed to just 25 seats going to the Republicans. In the State Senate, the dominance of the Democrats was even greater, with 29 seats or 72.5% control of the Senate, and just 11 seats, a paltry 27.5%, going to Republican members. California's Congressional delegation did not fare much better, with the state's 53 Congressional representatives being split between 38 Democrats, almost 72%, and just 15 Republicans. Two-thirds control of both houses of the state legislature means that Democratic officeholders have a free hand to enact legislation without any Republican input.[223] Indeed, *Salon* reported the last election night results as "The GOP's Horrible California Nightmare."[224] And polling a few months after the election found that most California voters think that the Democrat's two-thirds control of the legislature is a good thing.[225]

To think that during the late 20th Century, California sent two Republican favorite sons, Richard M. Nixon and Ronald Reagan to the White House as Presidents, that a Republican Governor, Earl Warren served as Chief Justice of the U.S. Supreme Court, and that today a Republican has practically no chance at winning any state-wide elective office. This is bitter testimony to Republicans of their rock-bottom status and lack of influence in state politics. The total control of all statewide elective offices and both houses of the state legislature today by liberal Democrats evidences something more: a state very much out of political balance.

A major factor in the California GOP's decline has to do with its failure to attract support from Latinos. California has always had a large presence of Hispanic residents who dominated the state from the time of the Conquistadors and Spanish and Mexican colonists. However, there is a political aspect to the Hispanic re-emergence today that has boded very poorly for Republicans in the state and that has helped empower the liberal elites that run California. This problem has been traced to what some observers see as the mistaken enthusiasm of the California Republican Party for a statewide ballot proposition that passed in 1994 known as "Proposition 187."

Prop. 187 established a state-run citizenship screening program to prohibit illegal immigrants from accessing publicly supported

---

223 Two-thirds control of both houses of the state Legislature also means that Democrats can override a veto of their legislation by Governor Jerry Brown.

224 http://www.salon.com/2012/11/07/the_gops_horrible_california_nightmare/

225 http://www.field.com/fieldpollonline/subscribers/Rls2438.pdf. 55% of all voters agreed that the Democrats two-thirds control of both legislative houses was a good thing, with 39% saying it was a bad thing. 76% of Democrats were positive, and 86% of Republicans were negative on the development.

healthcare, education, and social services paid for by the state.[226] The law was aimed at reducing services and costs for an estimated 1.3 million illegal immigrants residing in the state, which included approximately 300,000 children. Incumbent Republican Governor Pete Wilson, whose re-election campaign had been sagging in the polls, enthusiastically embraced the measure, which was on the ballot at the same time as his own re-election. Political observers agree that Wilson's support for the measure helped him win re-election.[227] But the GOP support for that proposition, which was later declared unconstitutional by a Federal court, and more-than-lingering perceptions that Republicans in the legislature oppose immigration reforms, have greatly hurt the Republican party and alienated it from Latino voters, many of whom poll as a naturally conservative voting bloc in the state.

For example, in 1984, Republican President Ronald Reagan received 47% of the California Latino vote for his re-election, but by 2008, Republican Presidential candidate Mitt Romney's share of the Latino vote had sharply fallen to 21%.

Clearly, the Republican Party's sustained poor showing with Hispanic voters has been a big element in its own failures, aiding the dominant status of the Democratic Party today. But otherwise, politics and policy in California have until the recent generation had a history of cycle and balance. For example, the last time Democrats had a "supermajority" in the State Senate was in 1965,[228] but within a year, conservative Republican Ronald Reagan was elected Governor in a landslide. Other GOP Governors such as George Dukemejian, Pete Wilson, and more recently even Arnold Schwarzenegger offered some political balance to general Democratic majorities in the state legislature. At one time California

---

226 http://www.congressionalresearch.com/97-543/document.php

227 Cathleen Decker and Daniel Weintraub, "Wilson Savors Win; Democrats Assess Damage," *Los Angeles Times*. November 10, 1994.

228 http://www.mercurynews.com/breaking-news/ci_21946080/democrats-seek-supermajority-state-senate

politics and policy seemed dominated by liberal black San Francisco criminal attorney Willie Brown, who served 30 years in State Assembly and 15 years in the powerful position of Speaker. Yet in 1994 Republicans captured a majority in the State Assembly for one election cycle and even then, after some effort, were able to retire Brown from both his Speakership, as well as the state legislature, aided by a new six-year "term limit" initiative enacted by voters in 1990 that was animated in part by voter disapproval of Brown's long tenure in office. Within two years, however, the resourceful Willie Brown was Mayor of San Francisco.

The difference between the past and the present is that today, aided by truly enormous public employee union political spending, competition between the parties has completely eroded. Added is that California Republican Party registration at 29% statewide is at its lowest point in its 159-year history as a party.[229] In the last decade, California has lost 100,000 registered Republicans, even though the state's voter roles have grown by 2.9 million.[230] The overall GOP registration has declined 7 percentage points in the last ten years, to a percentage that cannot match the Democrats almost 44% party registration statewide. Judged by huge public employee union political spending and a big disparity in political party affiliation, the pendulum of "cycle and balance" in California's politics has swung so hard and far to the political Left, that it may have become completely stuck there. This greatly unbalanced political situation threatens the state's political and economic health now, and into the future.

Despite their total control, liberal Democrats nevertheless remain unmercifully partisan to their feeble opposition and any differing ideas about policy. Republicans, who were already suffering from an "image" problem going into the current decade, are now branded as

229 http://www.mercurynews.com/california-budget/ci_22693009/
california-republican-party-convention-gop-attempts-recover-from

230 http://www.bizjournals.com/sacramento/news/2013/08/30/report-voters-calif-
republicans-decline.html?ana=RSS&s=article_search

"old, white, racist, and losers" by University of Southern California political science Professor Darry Sragow."[231] Among Sragow's comments in the USC classroom:

> "We discovered, and this is generally true, the least flexible voter in America, the person who's less likely to change their mind about anything, is an old white guy. Old white guys are stubborn sons of bitches."

> "The Republican Party is increasingly the last refuge of old angry white people who don't like what is going on in this country."

> "The Republican Party in California…is the last vestige of angry old white people."[232]

Sragow's unacademic rant in the USC classroom is not exactly the truth about the California GOP. In fact, registered Republican candidates, men and women, young and old, are quite successful in being elected to the thousands of "non-partisan" offices throughout California, such as city council, school board, or Mayor, on ballots where identification of party affiliation is not permitted. A recent study by GrassrootsLab published in the *Los Angeles Times* revealed that close to half of the state's 2,500 local non-partisan offices are held by registered Republicans.[233] But when the elections are for so-called "partisan" races in which the ballot identifies the political party of the candidate, such as for Congress and the State Legislature,

---

231 http://www.campusreform.org/blog/?ID=4702. Sragow was caught in a video making the statement in a classroom. In the video he also seems to endorse a classroom statement by his Teacher's Assistant that Black Panthers should be placed at polling stations to further diminish the Republican vote through intimidation. Sragow also happens to be a professional political consultant for Democratic party candidates and causes, which was his full-time profession before being allowed onto the USC political science faculty.

232 http://www.nationalreview.com/articles/345659/sragow-s-leftist-rants-dennis-prager

233 "GOP thrives at local level," *Los Angeles Times*, September 4, 2013.

Republicans fall far short and lose many more elections than they win. The contrast in "non-partisan" successes where the Republican brand is not revealed to voters, and the persistent "partisan" election losses, calls further attention to the contentions of those who think there is something wrong with the "Republican brand" in California in general. Former San Diego-area Republican Assemblyman Nathan Fletcher, a capable legislator with a military background, left the Republican Party during a bitter primary election fight with other Republicans for Mayor of Republican-voter rich San Diego. Much of the acrimony in the campaign focused on which of the candidates was the "more Republican," and Fletcher, a moderate, lost that battle and the primary election. But the Republican who beat Fletcher in the primary, who was tarnished himself in the process, was defeated in the run-off election by a former Congressman, Democrat Bob Filner (who later resigned as a result of a scandal). Fletcher himself re-registered as a member of the Democratic Party after the election and had this to say about leaving his former political party:

"It was because I thought their policies provided the best access to the American Dream. I no longer believe that is true. In my opinion, the GOP today is more focused on protecting those who have already achieved the American Dream than allowing others access to it."[234]

Some other prominent Republicans who have failed in their aspirations for higher office have, rather than leaving the Republican Party, instead simply left the state. A widely unreported story in California is the fact that of the three major Republican candidates for United States Senate in 2010, two quickly emigrated to other states after their election defeats. Former California Assemblyman Chuck DeVore, a strong conservative who finished third in the

234 http://www.voiceofsandiego.org/news/article_84f097c0-b502-11e2-860c-001a4bcf887a.html

GOP primary election in June of 2010 for U.S. Senate, is now a fellow at the Texas Public Policy Foundation and resident in Austin, Texas. Former Lucent and Hewlett-Packard executive Carly Fiorina, who actually won the primary election but was beaten by incumbent liberal Democrat Barbara Boxer in the November 2010 general election, has been seen more recently as a frequent guest ably representing the Republican position on nationally televised talk shows, but according to a local news report has been "out of the spotlight" in California for the last three years. While DeVore has done so, Fiorina has not been on the agenda at any statewide Republican party-building functions in California since she ran for Senate. She now resides in Virginia,[235] where the Governor there appointed her to the Board of Visitors of James Madison University, a state college.[236]

It does not assist the credibility or help build the future of the California Republican Party, when volunteers and the public are whipped-up to support and invest in a statewide candidate, only to see the same candidate make an exit from the state after an unsuccessful race.

Statewide nominees of the Republican Party have increasingly been untested wealthy newcomers to the political scene, such as Arnold Schwarzenegger, Meg Whitman, and Fiorina, who self-fund their campaigns, and usually have no real connection to the party's rank-and-file volunteers or demonstrated personal investment in the party's success beyond their own elections. None of these candidates had a history of political involvement or genuine support for a political cause before they ran for office, unlike Ronald Reagan, who famously campaigned for Barry Goldwater for President in 1964 and had been President of the Screen Actors Guild. Successful GOP Governors Pete Wilson and George Dukemejian were party activists who ran for and held lower elective offices and came to

---

235 http://conservative.org/news/
acu-announces-carly-fiorina-as-new-chairman-of-foundation/

236 http://www.jmu.edu/visitors/about/members.shtml

their top positions through the ranks, where they had many years to learn the craft of politics, study and engage in public policy, and had an incentive to help in the building of a lasting party organization. This was not the case, especially with Whitman and Fiorina, both of whom were dogged during their campaigns about failures to vote, and even failures to register to vote, let alone be engaged in GOP party-building before their decision to run for office.

In Whitman's case, a newspaper investigation found she had not even registered to vote before 2002 and had only registered as affiliated with the Republican Party in 2007,[237] less than three years before her disastrous run for Governor against Jerry Brown, which she lost badly in the midst of a clumsy, self-inflicted political scandal involving her housekeeper's legal status. As a successful Silicon Valley business executive, Whitman's decision to expose herself to politics and engage in the rough-and-tumble process in an effort to help reform California was highly commendable. As discussed in a subsequent chapter, California could benefit from more political engagement by Silicon Valley entrepreneurs, but with a focus on not just fielding a candidate, but rather public policy problem solving to counterbalance liberal control.

Fiorina joined Whitman in apologizing for her own voting record during her unsuccessful run for U.S. Senate in 2010. She said she voted in six of 14 elections in California since 2000, but lived in New Jersey for the previous 10 years where she admitted to never voting.[238] Fiorina and Whitman were surely fresh faces to the political scene in California, who could also afford to pay for their own advertising, but their inexperience and even earlier disinterest in politics probably harmed rather than helped their campaigns.

Even top leaders of the California Republican Party readily acknowledge their party is in very deep trouble. Jim Brulte, the state

237 http://www.huffingtonpost.com/2009/09/29/meg-whitman-on-her-voting_n_303681.html

238 http://www.cbsnews.com/2100-250_162-5549879.html

chairman of the GOP and a respected veteran of the California Leg-islature, has identified the source of the GOP's sorry condition as a "failure to recognize changing demographics" and has said that Republicans have been too reluctant to venture into communities outside of their traditional power base. "If we want to be successful we have to get outside of our comfort zone," Brulte said. "Too many Republican party leaders or Republican elected officials spend all their time talking to the choir."[239] Jon Fleischman, a former Execu-tive Director of the California Republican Party and publisher of the influential FlashReport.org comments, "The challenge for Republicans in California is immense. On the short term, there must be a laser-like focus on recapturing enough legislative seats in the Senate and the Assembly to block the Democratic supermajori-ties. Long term, however, the path back for the California GOP involves increasing market share with minority voters—and creating relevance with younger voters. Winning the White House would help, because we have no Republican luminaries in this state to take a winning message to those groups. In the meantime, going into those communities and having a presence is the first step. You can't win someone over if you aren't talking to them."[240]

The collapse of the California Republican Party reflects not only the fact that its "brand" is deeply tarnished and needs much work, but also the broader reality that a genuine competition for ideas in the State Capitol really no longer exists. This collapse has stifled the advancement of the more moderate and conservative policy solu-tions needed in the state that Republicans, independents and many Democrats themselves advocate, but that liberal Democrats, particu-larly the powerful public employee unions, reflexively reject. Liberal Democrat leaders like USC Professor Sragow simply disregard dif-fering views, virtually run the state, have been running it, are intent

239 http://blogs.sacbee.com/capitolalertlatest/2013/06/john-burton-jim-brulte-spar-over-crime-campaigns-and-fate-of-gop.html

240 Interview with the author, September 23, 2013.

on stamping out anything that doesn't fit their liberal ideology, and in the end, are running it all very poorly.

Regardless of minority voter dissatisfaction with the Republican party, the current one-party control of California has occurred more clearly as a result of the pervasive influence and political success of liberal special interests. And the liberal Democrats in control don't just have Republicans in their sights. Democrats are even urged to attack other reform-minded Democrats by the liberal California Teachers Association, if the issue has anything to do with reforming California's abysmal education system.

As former Democratic State Senator Gloria Romero has observed, "(f)or years, Democrats simply acquiesced to the demands of the CTA and the National Education Association."[241] Romero is not just any politician. She holds a Ph.D degree in psychology from the University of California, Riverside, and is the former majority leader of the Democrats in the California State Senate, being the first woman ever to hold that position.[242] She has taught as a professor at state universities and has served as President of the Board of Trustees of the Los Angeles Community College District.[243] Romero is an advocate of reforms to improve test results of poor and minority children in underperforming schools, an effort that Romero contends is "increasingly bipartisan."[244]

Romero is correct that such efforts are receiving increasing bipartisan support, and a growing number of Democrats, Republicans and Independents are setting aside party differences and coming together to attempt to solve the problems of underperforming schools. A common goal of such reform is to link teacher performance to student outcomes, and streamlining rules for hiring good teachers and firing bad ones.

---

241 http://www.ocregister.com/articles/delegates-505240-education-reform.html

242 http://en.wikipedia.org/wiki/Gloria_Romero_%28California_politician%29

243 Id.

244 Id.

Such efforts have found support in both the Bush and Obama Administrations, and even in the city of Los Angeles, where New York Mayor Michael Bloomberg, an independent and former Republican, donated $1,350,000, along with a $500,000 contribution from Los Angeles business leader Eli Broad, and $25,000 from Republican Frank Baxter, to support a reform-minded effort lead by Democratic Mayor Antonio Villaraigosa, to elect new candidates to the Los Angeles Unified School District ("LAUSD") Board of Education who support Superintendent John Deasy's modest plank of reforms that include use of student test scores in teacher evaluations.[245] LAUSD is a troubled school district desperately in need of reform, and Deasy has also taken strong steps to address a variety of teacher-related problems including not only poor test scores, but also corporal punishment, verbal and physical abuse, and apparent widespread sexual misconduct of teachers reported in classrooms. After a sex-abuse scandal at Miramonte Elementary School, Deasy initiated a "zero-tolerance" policy in February of 2012, and since then has sidelined 100 teachers for misconduct, and accepted the resignations of 200 more that were about to be terminated.[246] An astounding 300 additional teachers accused of inappropriate behavior have been taken out of the classroom while their cases are investigated.[247] But actual dismissal of the offending teachers will be very tricky because according to California's arcane teacher dismissal regulations, heavily influenced by the CTA, a dismissal must be approved by a three person administrative panel that includes not only an administrative law judge, but also a representative appointed by the school board and a third member appointed by the accused teacher or union representative. One keen observer has noted that the process usually

---

245 http://www.latimes.com/news/local/la-me-school-money-20130421,0,1982149.story?track=rss

246 http://www.dailynews.com/news/ci_23220307/lausd-cracks-down-teacher-misconduct-100-fired-200?source=rss&utm_source=feedly

247 Id.

results in a "union-friendly" panel process that has seen fewer than 10 dismissals for cause a year out of a universe of more than 300,000 teachers, and hundreds of cases annually[248]

So, according to Romero, CTA President Dean Vogel took to the stage at a recent California Democratic Party convention "to warn delegates that no reform passes the legislature unless it goes through his union,"[249] and insisted that delegates adopt a resolution to that effect, which they did without even a roll call vote,[250] an explicit shot at Romero and other advocates of education reform in the Democratic Party. The teachers' unions can't stand that a former Democratic elected official like Gloria Romero might speak out with authority and have a different view about education than they do.

But Romero is not their only target to silence or vilify. The same resolution CTA had passed at the California Democratic Party convention ripped into an education reform organization named "StudentsFirst."[251] Sacramento-based education reformer Michelle Rhee, the former Chancellor of the District of Columbia school system and head of the StudentsFirst organization, has been referred to as "disgraced" on the United Teachers of Los Angeles (a CTA affiliate) website, simply because she supports modest reform legislation introduced by a Democratic State Senator that requires teachers be evaluated for their proficiency.[252] To add insult to injury, CTA president Dean Vogel told the same group of Democrats at their state convention that StudentsFirst should be shunned as "backed by moneyed interests, Republican operatives, and out-of-state Wall

---

248 http://www.capoliticalreview.com/top-stories/teachers-union-outraged-at-l-a-school-chiefs-move-to-remove-sadists-pedophiles-from-classroom/

249 Id.

250 Id.

251 http://blog.cta.org/2013/04/15/
public-education-a-high-priority-at-ca-democratic-convention/

252 http://www.utla.net/print/4084

Street billionaires dedicated to school privatization and trampling on teacher and worker rights."[253]

Rhee, an Asian-American, is the wife of Democrat Kevin Johnson, an African-American and the Mayor of Sacramento. She started her career as an inner-city school teacher in lower-performing schools. She became Chancellor of the D.C. school system in 2007 and served for three years until 2010. Rhee was known there for an aggressive, reform-minded agenda that emphasized student performance on tests, reducing administrative costs, and encouraging performance-based merit pay for teachers. Rhee negotiated a new contract with the D.C. teachers union that allowed for the dismissal of more than 200 poorly performing teachers.[254] Over her term, the D.C. Comprehensive Assessment System reading rates increased 14%, and math rates increased 17%.[255]

After leaving her position in D.C., Rhee formed StudentsFirst. The organization is an education advocacy group that has been involved in more than 15 states to reform education to include teacher performance evaluations.[256] It has received significant support from the philanthropic community nationwide, including the Walton Foundation.[257] In early 2013 StudentsFirst generated debate by issuing a report ranking states on teacher tenure, pensions, governance of school districts and use of student test scores in teacher evaluations. California was among 6 states receiving a grade of "F." But Democrat political operative Richard Zeigler, the chief deputy superintendent of California schools, put a spin on things by calling

---

253 http://blogs.sacbee.com/capitolalertlatest/2013/05/studentsfirst-under-scrutiny-from-the-left.html

254 http://en.wikipedia.org/wiki/Michelle_Rhee

255 Id.

256 http://www.washingtonpost.com/blogs/answer-sheet/wp/2013/05/01/walton-foundation-giving-8-million-to-rhees-studentsfirst-plus-2012-donations/?wprss=rss_national&utm_source=feedly

257 Id.

the rating "a badge of honor,"[258] dismissing Rhee's efforts by saying "[t]his is an organization that frankly makes its living by asserting that schools are failing.....I would have been surprised if we had got anything else."[259]

In California, Rhee and her organization are trying to offer leadership and strength to both Democrats and Republicans in the legislature who may feel bullied by CTA's ardent opposition to education reform, especially on the issue of teacher evaluations, as even some Republicans on the State Senate Education Committee have been compelled to oppose the reform measure,[260] most likely because they fear political reprisals in their re-election campaigns from CTA and its liberal allies.

Labor's bullying in the Democratic party on behalf of public employee unions includes McCarthy-era tactics such as "black-listing" of Democrat professional political operatives who work not for opposition Republican candidates, but for the wrong Democrats. Steve Glazer, a talented advisor to Governor Jerry Brown, was placed on a "do not hire" list by the California Labor Federation because Glazer helped a handful of Democratic candidates supported by the California Chamber of Commerce.[261] A total of six Democratic consultants were placed on the same "do not hire" list on "a motion submitted by the California Professional Firefighters, the American Federation of State, County, and Municipal Employees, and the State Building and Construction Trades Council" to encourage all unions, labor councils, "allies and candidates seeking our support" to not hire them.[262]

---

258 http://www.nytimes.com/2013/01/07/education/studentsfirst-issues-low-ratings-on-school-policies.html?_r=0

259 Id.

260 http://blogs.sacbee.com/capitolalertlatest/2013/05/am-alert-students-first-rallies-troops-for-california-teacher-evaluation-bi.html#mi_rss=Capitol%20and%20California; http://blogs.sacbee.com/capitolalertlatest/2013/05/california-teacher-evaluation-bill.html

261 http://blogs.sacbee.com/capitolalertlatest/2013/07/former-jerry-brown-aide-among-consultants-blacklisted-by-labor.html

262 http://www.rollcall.com/news/california_labor_group_bans_controversial_consultants_shop_talk-226559-1.html

The work of liberal Democrats to stamp out differing views sadly includes concerted efforts in the last decades to undermine Californian's constitutional right to initiative, referendum, and recall. Though liberal Democrats are in total control of statewide offices and with super-majorities in both Houses of the state legislature, citizens retain the right on their own to place a law on the ballot, veto a law once passed, or remove an elected official from office, when enough voters sign a petition to do so and an election is held. These special rights are unique to California and a number of mostly western states and arise from the Progressive Movement of the early 1900s. The intention of these rights is to allow citizens to bypass their elected officials and the special interests they may represent.

These "petition" rights are seen by some liberal elites as a threat to their power, and they have responded with a series of laws to "reform" and dilute these rights by making it harder to qualify an initiative measure and limiting the number of elections where measures can appear on the ballot to just one every two years. As one keen observer has written, "[i]t is no secret that politicians and bureaucrats detest the initiative process."[263] Though normal public disclosure rules are applied to initiative campaigns, a plethora of other special rules regulating initiatives have been enacted by the liberals in control, including rules on how signatures are collected, the size of paper and type-face used to print a petition, and disallowance of on-line signature gathering. These rules have had the effect over time of making it harder and harder for the people to exercise their constitutional rights to initiative.

In an era when liberals in the legislature advocate election-day voter registration, voter information to be provided to inmates at county jails and state prisons, expansion of voting rights for felons, on-line voter registration, and acceptance of absentee ballot requests over the phone, those same liberals in control refuse to even discuss

---

263 http://www.hjta.org/california-commentary/
government-insiders-threaten-initiative-process

online qualification of initiative, referendum and recall petitions, which would greatly reduce the cost of campaigning in the state and thereby reduce the influence of special interests money. Liberal Democrats have no problems making exercise of the petition process so expensive, because then only the special interests that the petition system is designed to protect against, such as the California Teachers Association, can afford to mount a petition campaign.

The so-called political dysfunction and teetering economy in California can very clearly be laid on the doorstep of CTA's and other public employee unions' massive power and money, and the pervasive, selfish influence and control exercised by public employee unions in the state. These unions do not always win every election, especially when voters understand what is at stake, but they win most of them, and are completely in control of the state government of California right now and they deserve the blame for the state's ills today. The California Republican Party, with a continuing need to burnish its "brand" is not going to be able to alter liberal Democrats control very easily or too soon, or on its own. As its new chairman Jim Brulte told me, "we are going to have to rebuild from the bottom up, that is going to take time, and that is what I am committed to do."[264] Small but important achievements, like whittling away at the Democrats "supermajority" status in the state legislature, are in Brulte's sights for now.

Nevertheless, there will not be even modest reform or improvement in California until the unhealthy controlling influence of the CTA and its allies is counter-balanced by a broad range of Californians "waking-up" and demanding real change.

---

264 Email exchange between Jim Brulte and the author.

THE IMPLOSION OF PUBLIC EDUCATION

STUDENT ACHIEVEMENT TEST SCORES in California have been on a steady decline in the last 50 years. While test results of students nationwide are also no longer in the top tier of nations globally, California's scores in many cases rank toward the bottom half of our general national decline, when compared to other states.

The long-professed partisan opinion of the liberal establishment, which dominates education policy in the state, is that students in the California public school system perform poorly on standardized tests in comparison to other states because there is not enough tax revenue devoted to education. Their opinions are summarized in the commonly-expressed liberal view of Richard Zeiger,[265] chief deputy superintendent of public instruction at the California Department of Education, who told the *New York Times* that demographic changes and "a sustained disinvestment in public education, made all the more severe by the Great Recession," are the reasons for poor student

---

265 Richard Zeiger "is responsible for managing and coordinating all functions of the California Department of Education." http://www.nagb.org/newsroom/naep-releases/mega-states/bio-zeiger.html. For 14 years Zeiger has was a staff member in both the State Senate and Assembly for Democratic elected officials and "chief of staff to leaders of the state Senate and Assembly," id., all Democrats.

achievement results in California.[266] Zeiger's boss is state Superintendent of Public Instruction Tom Torlakson, a career Democratic politician, who was elected to his office in 2010 with $3.9 million in campaign spending by a coalition of union groups led by the California Teachers Association.[267]

The liberal Democrats and their teachers' union allies support their arguments that more and more money is needed by pointing out that state spending on education per capita is 48th of the 50th states, that student-teacher ratios, number of computers per classroom, and number of books in school libraries rank 50th in the nation.[268] But what they don't tell you is that at the same time money is not reaching the classroom, California's teachers are among the best paid teachers in the nation.[269]

The disconnect between teacher pay at the very zenith of the country, and classroom assets and performance ranked at the very bottom of the nation, seems lost on most of California's liberal power-brokers in the legislature, and especially to the general public whom should be holding them accountable for better education results for the state's students.

The liberal educational lobby has Californians convinced that all they need do is spend more and more money on education and things will improve. But a number of academic studies do not support that thesis. A study from State Budget Solutions supports that "throwing money at education" isn't working, and that states that are

---

266 Motoko Rich, "Test Scores of Hispanics Vary Widely Across 5 Most Populous States, Analysis Shows," *New York Times*, February 21, 2013.

267 http://www.latimes.com/local/la-me-0821-state-supt-20130821,0,7898584.story

268 Larry N. Gerston, *Not So Golden After All, The Rise and Fall of California* (Boca Raton, CRC Press, 2012), 15.

269 http://usatoday30.usatoday.com/news/education/2002-11-21-ca-teacher-salaries_x.htm. In a 2002, the National Educations Association ("NEA") reported that California teachers were the most highly paid teachers in the nation. More recently the NEA has reported that California teachers are the second highest paid teachers in the nation, after New York, and that beginning teacher salaries are the fifth highest in the nation. http://www.nea.org/home/38465.htm

spending the most do not have students with the highest test scores, and they do not have the highest graduation rates.[270] Even studies that liberals might cite to justify more spending on education in California do not support that student test scores or academic success will rise under the current system. For example, a recent Obama Administration U.S. Census report purports to place California as spending $9,139 per pupil annually, which sets the state at 36th in spending among the 50 states and the District of Columbia.[271] But a side-by-side review by columnist Dan Walters, comparing that report to a recent U.S. Department of Education survey on high school graduation rates "reveals no correlation between spending and educational success" according to Walters.[272]

A compelling new book by Amanda Ripley, a writer for *Time* magazine, entitled "The Smartest Kids in the World and How They Got That Way,"[273] examines worldwide student achievement test scores for critical thinking and communication skills needed to function in the modern world. The test is focused on teenagers and was developed by the Program for International Student Assessment (PISA) at the Organization for Economic Cooperation and Development. The PISA test, first launched in 2001, is taken by hundreds of thousands of students in most nations worldwide. Students in the United States have routinely finished in the second tiers of achievement since the test was first administered, despite the fact that our nation collectively spends more on education per capita worldwide than any other nation except tiny Luxembourg. Ripley conducted research on education systems in three particularly well-performing nations in the PISA test system: Finland, South Korea, and Poland.

270 http://www.statebudgetsolutions.org/publications/detail/throwing-money-at-education-isnt-working

271 http://www.sacbee.com/2013/05/26/5448726/dan-walters-does-spending-more.html#mi_rss=Dan%20Walters?utm_source=feedly

272 Id.

273 Amanda Ripley, *The Smartest Kids in the World and How They Got That Way*, (New York: Simon and Shuster, 2013).

What she learned and shares in her book is that total spending per pupil does not necessarily correlate with academic success, as poorer nations with higher poverty rates than the United States are educating students in critical thinking, science, and math much better than we are. What matters more is ensuring that students are motivated, and whether teachers themselves actually are prepared to teach and be engaged with their students.

Thus, what the data suggests matters most for states like California is not *how much* money is spent on education, but rather, *how* it is spent.

Disregarding these facts, liberals and their special interest allies, despite their failures, still demand that even more money is needed to fix education in California. They don't see much of a linkage in student achievement test performance and teacher performance and evaluation. They don't admit there might be a value in separating good teachers from bad and retraining or reassigning the bad ones as a means to improve the quality of education in our state. The liberals just focus on money, and say they continually need more of it to fix California's poor educational achievement.

The problem is, even though they have repeatedly won that argument, when they get more money, the students' test scores still continue to spiral downward. Like Einstein's classic definition of insanity, even after California's education system receives ever new tax distributions devoted to "education," without progress in test scores, and with increasing failures among minority students, the liberal powerbrokers simply repeat their cant about not having enough money to fix education; and when they get more money, student scores continue to slide. The reality is the special interest influence of the teachers' unions just won't allow test scores to rise, because almost all that money they raise "for the kids" gets gobbled up and spent not in the classroom, but on very high comparative teacher and administrator salaries and benefits, on redundant administrative overhead caused by the existence of more local school districts than necessary and on expensive lawyers within the elaborate network of school districts who aggressively defend their liberal policies. Money is not spent on true education reform, like teaching English; lowering student-teacher ratios by hiring more new, younger teachers with more average wages; motivating students by making testing count for something; and testing teacher proficiency and using "merit pay" concepts to reward teachers whose students excel, thereby incentivizing achievement. Special interest public employee unions and their Democratic political allies in Sacramento have run the state school system for decades and therefore "own" its problems, but from their perspective, the problems will always be due to "sustained disinvestment," the tacit understanding being that somebody else out there is holding back student achievement by cutting off school funding. They label reform as "anti-union." Alternate ideas to improve student achievement through (in their opinion) crack-pot ideas like home-schooling or "private-school vouchers" or "school choice" are anathema to them. The result is the liberals and the teachers' unions will not accept responsibility for their own failures and face the fact that if education is to be improved, something very different from the current system they are responsible for needs to be accomplished. And in the meantime, the taxes and other financial burdens they continually impose on Californians to support their failing education system are wrecking the economy and everyone's economic opportunity.

For example, liberals claimed dire consequences in California if Proposition 30 did not pass on the November 2012 ballot. That ballot initiative, a brain-child of Governor Jerry Brown, purported to raise $6 billion in new revenues for schools, at the threat of cutting the school year up to 15 days if it didn't pass. After it passed, University of California, Santa Cruz President George Blumenthal said voter approval of Proposition 30 "signals a shift in the willingness of voters to support education."[274]

---

274 http://www.huffingtonpost.com/2012/11/09/santa-cruz-county-school-_n_2097935.html

But Blumenthal is completely wrong about the so-called voter "shift" in support of education. Voters in California have almost always supported education appeals. They have bought into the tax-and-spend merry-go-round of the liberal education lobby again and again, coughing up funds for "education" many dozens of times in the state. In 1988, for example, California voters gave approval to Proposition 98, which established a mandatory minimum percentage of the state budget to be directed to education spending with increases tied to inflation, thus guaranteeing an annual increase in the California education budget.[275] The baseline test of Proposition 98 requires that 39% of the state budget be directed to K-12 education whether the needs of education call for that or not, making education the largest single line-item in California's state budget, which currently totals $96.3 billion.[276] Over the years, voters have repeatedly responded to the liberal education lobby and passed numerous initiative measures supporting more funds intended for the classroom, including serial-adoption of school construction and facility bond measures (Props. 1 and 6, 1972; Prop. 1, 1974; Prop. 1, 1982; Prop. 26, 1984; Props. 53 and 56, 1986; Props. 75, 78, and 79, 1988; Props. 121, 123 and 146, 1990; Props. 152, 153, and 155; Prop. 203, 1996; Prop.1A, 1998; Props. 14 and 39, 2000; Prop. 47, 2002; Prop. 55, 2004; Prop. 1D, 2006); teacher retirement and public employee pension related measures (Prop. 6, 1970; Prop. 162, 1992); a tobacco surtax for early childhood development, (Proposition 10, passed in 1998); and establishment of a state lottery intended to provide at least 34% of its revenue *as supplemental* (not replacing tax dollars) funding for public education.[277] Proposition

275 http://www.cbp.org/pdfs/2006/0604_prop98.pdf

276 "California Legislature Approves Rare State Budget with Surplus," *San Jose Mercury*, June 14, 2013.

277 http://en.wikipedia.org/wiki/California_Lottery. However, in 2010 Governor Schwarzennegger and the State Legislature made certain changes to the allocation system empowering the "lottery board" to return "not less than 50%" of total lottery revenues to the state for public use, at a level that maximizes the "total net revenues allocated to public education."

39, a corporate tax loop-hole closure measure that passed on the November 2012 ballot, dedicates an estimated $450 million annually in additional support for schools in the coming years.[278]

All these state education funding measures enacted directly by voters are also supplemented by hundreds of local ballot box enhancements for local education in recent years, including not only local parcel taxes adopted to aide schools in wealthier communities like Palo Alto and Beverly Hills, but also actions by middle-class voters. For example, in areas like the Victor Valley Union High School District in the high desert of San Bernardino County, voters approved a $500 million bond known as Measure V by almost 68% of the vote,[279] to build a new "state-of-the-art" high school in working-class Adelanto,[280] a city of 31,000 where over 58% of the residents are Hispanic.[281] Such bond measures themselves do not come without controversy, and there is an apparent cottage industry for writing them and getting them adopted by voters among some securities firms, who profit from sales of the bonds. Government agencies are not allowed to spend money to influence the outcome of elections, but not too long ago the Garden Grove Unified School District in Orange County placed a $250 million bond on the ballot that was passed by taxpayers, after the securities firm hired to organize the nonpartisan bond information for the voter approval also spent $35,000 in political contributions to actually get voters to adopt it. After the election the same firm received a "no bid" contract to sell the bonds and pocketed $1.4 million on the sale.[282]

Californians are so reflexively supportive of school funding that

278 http://sanfrancisco.cbslocal.com/2013/05/11/
ca-lawmakers-debate-how-to-spend-900m-prop-39-revenue/

279 http://ballotpedia.org/wiki/index.php/Victor_Valley_Union_High_School_District_bond_proposition,_Measure_V_%28November_2008%29

280 http://www.sbsun.com/news/ci_23075349?source=rss&utm_source=feedly

281 http://www.usa.com/adelanto-ca.htm

282 http://www.latimes.com/news/local/la-me-bond-donations-20130603,0,4866938.story?track=rss

the liberal education lobby has for years had the local Parent Teacher Associations (PTAs) convinced they need to engage in widespread private fundraising to provide additional supplemental funds for local schools to "buy erasers and chalk." For example, the PTA in Point Dune Elementary in Malibu held golf tournaments, fundraising dinners, and book fairs to raise $2,100 per child during the 2009-10 school year to help pay for music and art programs, as well as a dedicated marine science lab.[283] Malibu sits in the Santa Monica-Malibu School District, which combines the two coastal cities into one governing board. Santa Monica, always dominated by liberal politics, is a city of 90,000 compared to Malibu's 13,000. But Santa Monica has a lower median income per family, and the PTAs in Santa Monica do not take as active an interest in fundraising projects for their own schools as do Malibu residents. Predictably, the governing board of the school district, controlled by liberal members from dominant Santa Monica, have developed a plan to "equalize" what they consider to be the "disparity" in the private PTA support within the school district. Their plan is to take control of and centralize all PTA supplemental fundraising projects in the district into one private charity controlled by the school board, and then redistribute the private contributions "equitably" between schools in Malibu and Santa Monica. In other words, donors in Malibu who want to provide supplemental funds to assist their own children in schools in their own community, will also have to give additional funds to be directed to schools that their children do not attend. The plan of course will probably result in a drop-off of PTA participation by Malibu residents in the future, and children will suffer as a result. It can be labeled classic "money redistribution" and has been called "ludicrous" by one Malibu High School parent.[284]

In radical Berkeley's school district, after the Federal government

---

283 http://www.latimes.com/news/local/la-me-malibu-district-20130428,0,7078091,full.story

284 Id.

stopped funding "gardening and cooking" classes for school children because there were not enough low-income kids to justify the program, the school board found $600,000 to keep paying for the classes and another $50,000 to pay a fundraising consultant to find private-sector support.[285] In nearby San Jose, the school district even pays teachers more than they are legally obligated to pay under union contracts and rules. The Alum Rock Union School District there has for the past 10 years paid administrators and teachers $1 million more than required in what spokespeople say is an effort to attract and retain what it considers to be good teachers.[286] The practice has been criticized by the county grand jury, which thinks the school district needs better rules to justify its generosity to the teachers.[287] While the academic value of cooking classes rather than learning ABCs for grammar school children is surely a debatable point, finding funding for such courses, and paying teachers more than their contracts exemplifies generous support for local schools. Californians are indeed generous with schools, through local funding, private philanthropy, and the ballot box.

So it might not have been a complete surprise when education-supporting Californians, responding to the same old dire but familiar warnings of liberals and a heavily financed advertising campaign paid for by liberal public employee unions, were persuaded to pass the Proposition 30 tax increase. As a result, all Californians now pay the highest state sales tax in the country, raised ¼ cent under the measure, as well as the top marginal state income tax rate in the nation at 13.3%. These new taxes have predictably become job killers and are causing a flight of businesses from the state just a few months after passage. KCRA television in Sacramento reported in early 2013 that as many as 24 of some of California's top companies

285 http://www.insidebayarea.com/breaking-news/ci_23209679/
berkeley-budget-cuts-slam-school-gardening-program?source=rss&utm_source=feedly

286 http://www.mercurynews.com/education/ci_23731645/
san-jose-school-district-paid-teachers-administrators-more

287 Id.

were committed to leave the state as a direct result of the passage of Proposition 30, with more on the way.[288]

Yet as stated earlier, tax revenues for education don't always get spent the way that proponents portray. Jerry Brown promised that funding from the Proposition 30 tax hike would go directly into classroom instruction. Yet now it is unclear whether all the extra money, even if it can be raised from a now diminishing tax base, will even reach the classroom, let alone do much to improve test scores if it does. This is in part because the state has setup a distribution system that is loosely based on $200 per unit of average daily attendance of pupils per school district. For example, the Santa Barbara Unified School District expects to receive $2.7 million this year. However, a published report says that the funds are expected to be spent by the District's liberal governing board on just more salaries and benefits for teachers,[289] rather than other instructional benefits to students.

It is also fair to question whether any of the new tax revenues will actually reach the classrooms, given the fact that the California State Teachers Retirement System, a program that handles teacher-only pensions and which is a cousin to the California Public Employees' Retirement System (CalPERS), is now seeking $4.5 billion from the state, after Proposition 30 has passed, to bolster its own underfunded pension liability for state teacher pensions. The State Teachers Pension Retirement Fund is greatly underfunded, and CTA lobbyists can snap their fingers to get the California Legislature they control to cough up funds out of the Proposition 30 windfall to bail out their own pensions. David Crane, an advisor to former Governor Arnold Schwarzenegger, predicted that teachers would attempt to grab most of the new Proposition 30 tax money for their pensions rather than allow it to be spent in the classrooms, and events appear to be proving

288 http://www.kcra.com/news/Two-dozen-companies-commit-to-leaving-California/-/11797728/18533954/-/ivlxudz/-/index.html

289 http://www.noozhawk.com/article/
sbusd_spent_proposition_30_money_on_teachers_for_current_year/

his predication may have some legs.[290] With an additional $50 billion in unfunded liability for the state retiree healthcare at CalPERS and $10 billion owed to the Federal government for the state Unemployment Insurance Fund,[291] it is very clear that California's fiscal liabilities are swamping its revenues. The state is spending far too much money on its public employees, and even more than anticipated revenues from the Proposition 30 temporary tax increases will not result in a balanced budget anytime soon for California.

California's massive overall debt surely comes into focus as the teachers attempt to bite off a bigger share of Proposition 30 revenues. Tax payments in April of 2013, the first set of payments scheduled after the enactment of Proposition 30, initially appeared to be supplying the state a somewhat more than expected in new business and personal income taxes, in the neighborhood of nearly $5 billion more than projections.[292] "We've reached an important milestone in California's economic recovery. For the first time in nearly six years, we closed out a month without borrowing..." said State Controller John Chang.[293] But the cause for self-congratulation did not last. The projections of $5 billion in extra revenue were subsequently revised downward to $2.1 billion with July tax revenue projections off by $266 million.[294] The Legislative Analyst's Office warned that sales tax revenues were falling short.[295] Proposition 30 was raising strong tax revenues, but nowhere near as strong as initial reports.

Much of that new revenue will likely be eaten up by schools and

---

290 http://www.sacbee.com/2013/04/28/5377472/dan-walters-california-legislature.html#til_iss=Dan%20Walters

291 http://www.sacbee.com/2013/06/12/5489724/dan-walters-is-californias-new.html

292 http://www.latimes.com/news/local/la-me-state-budget-20130503,0,1598116.story?utm_source=feedly

293 http://capoliticalnews.com/2013/05/08/good-news-ca-cash-deficit-is-only-5-8-billion-full-deficit-is-127-billion/

294 http://www.latimes.com/local/political/la-me-pc-california-tax-revenue-20130815,0,1909848.story?track=rss

295 Id.

community colleges as Brown promised. But Brown has also said he wants to start directing some of the new tax revenue to pay the billions of dollars of accumulated debt the state has incurred, expected to be $28 billion in state budgetary borrowings in mid-year.[296] However, the new tax revenues are a drop-in-the-bucket in a state that is drowning in debt. According to the State Auditor's report, California is $127.2 billion in deficit.[297] A review by the independent Tax Foundation confirms California's accumulated deficit isn't just its $28 billion credit line, it is a whopping $127 billion, which itself does not include unfunded liabilities for the cost of health and pensions for public employees, including teachers.[298] The recognized unfunded liability for these pension plans is $265.1 billion.[299] Assemblyman Brian Jones (R—San Diego) estimates California's long-term state government obligations for unfunded pensions for state workers and retiree healthcare benefits at $230 billion, along with another $11 billion in federal loans for unemployment insurance benefits.[300] And additionally, when the total outstanding debt of California and all of its local governments, school districts, redevelopment agencies, and special districts is calculated—using State Controller and State Treasurer data—the California Public Policy Foundation concludes total indebtedness of all governments in the state is about $648 billion,[301] a staggering amount that respected Sacramento political pundit Dan Walters says "closely approximates" his own calculations.[302]

---

296 http://www.latimes.com/news/local/la-me-state-budget-20130503,0,1598116. story?utm_source=feedly

297 http://www.washingtontimes.com/news/2013/apr/1/ california-red-1272-billion-state-auditors-say/

298 http://taxfoundation.org/blog/ california-auditor-state-has-127-billion-net-asset-deficit

299 http://californiapublicpolicycenter.org/ calculating-californias-total-state-and-local-government-debt/

300 http://arc.asm.ca.gov/member/AD71/?p=article&sid=431&id=255896

301 Id.

302 http://www.sacbee.com/2013/05/12/5413779/dan-walters-california-could-owe .html

Nevertheless, according to one observer, education spending in California has doubled anyway in the last 40 years, and the state's teachers are receiving an average salary of $67,871, one of the most generous in the nation.[303] But regardless of California's generous teachers' salaries, scoring of the National Assessment of Educational Progress revealed California's fourth-graders ranked 45th in the nation in math; 49th in the nation in science; and average Scholastic Aptitude Test scores have dropped 5%.[304]

The truth about public education in California isn't that its programs are cash starved. To the contrary, there is plenty of money for public education. The real problem with public education in the state is twofold: it suffers from what Jerry Brown himself has dubbed an "overly complex, administratively costly and inequitably distributed" funding system[305]; and California teachers are paid too much and have too generous a pension system, for too little results. And the CTA won't allow that to change.

Test scores in general have become such a problem that in a few cases some teachers have even reportedly attempted to rig the results. A third grade teacher at McKinley Elementary in Burbank was placed on administrative leave when she allegedly helped students answer questions during a state standardized test,[306] apparently seeking to improve the school's Academic Performance Index.

The decline in the quality of education California offers its young people and their resulting poor test scores have terrible long-term ramifications for the state. Concerns have been raised that California's high school standards are too low and that students in the major urban areas of the state are not receiving rigorous enough exposure

303 http://www.capoliticalreview.com/top-stories/
tax-hike-not-enough-to-fix-ca-schools/

304 Id.

305 http://blogs.sacbee.com/capitol-alert-insider-edition/2013/04/editorial-brown-fights-the-good-fight-on-school-funds.html

306 http://www.latimes.com/local/lanow/la-me-ln-test-scores-under-investigation-at-burbank-school-20130421,0,484591.story

to college preparatory work in seven key subject areas to qualify for requirements for admission to either the University of California or California State University system. According to a report commissioned by the California Public Policy Foundation, the education system leaves these students "ill-prepared for tougher courses" necessary to advance to college,[307] and that the system is pointing towards a larger share of high school dropouts in the future. Author Amanda Ripley, who studied the Finnish education system, writes in her book that if "the United States had Finland's PISA scores, GDP (Gross Domestic Product) would be increasing at the rate of one to two trillion dollars a year."[308] There is a clear link between a nation's economic well being and the academic achievement of its children. California test scores don't even meet the average in our own nation, which is trailing other nations worldwide. A less educated generation of Californians appears to be in store for the state, and unemployment, under employment, social problems, and crime all come into sharper focus in that scenario.

Even some of the schools in California's college system seem incapable of meeting students' needs. City College of San Francisco, the largest public school in California with 85,000 students, recently had its academic accreditation terminated after a one-year evaluation period by the Accrediting Commission for Community and Junior Colleges.[309] The College can appeal the termination which cited "lack of financial accountability" as well as "institutional deficiencies in the area of leadership and governance" for its decision.[310] Predictably, CTA's close ally, the California Federation of Teachers, attempted to overturn the decision in court, claiming to the U.S.

---

307 http://www.centralvalleybusinesstimes.com/stories/001/?ID=23297

308 Amanda Ripley, *The Smartest Kids in the World and How They Got That Way*, (City: Simon and Schuster, 2013), 24.

309 http://www.accjc.org/wp-content/uploads/2013/07/ACCJC_Memo_To_Field_Commission_Actions_On_Institutions_07_03_2013.pdf

310 http://www.accjc.org/wp-content/uploads/2013/07/Press_Release_on_CCSF_Accreditation_July_3_2013.pdf

Department of Education that the Accrediting Commission over-stepped its authority.[311] Nevertheless, a news report concluded that money management at City College "is rife with problems,"[312] including unauthorized payroll changes and overpaid employees. Plagued by distracting labor union issues,[313] the college was unable to address 12 of 14 serious deficiencies in the delivery of education to its students, and its future operations as an accredited college are now in doubt. City College of San Francisco does not stand alone as a failing higher educational institution in California. Compton Community College lost its accreditation in 2005.[314] As many as eight other California community colleges are currently in the "warning" process and risk losing their accreditation, likely because of fiscal mismanagement and poor administration, including two in the Los Angeles Community College system.[315] In all, as many as 20 of California's community colleges are facing some sort of accredita-tion challenge, according to the system's Chancellor.[316]

The failures of California's secondary and higher education insti-tutions put job opportunities at risk. The important relationship between attainment of higher education and employment oppor-tunities has been well measured by the Lumina Foundation of Indianapolis, Indiana. Lumina, which describes itself as a "private foundation focused solely on increasing Americans' success in higher

311 http://www.sfgate.com/education/article/City-College-of-SF-to-lose-accreditation-in-2014-4645783.php

312 http://www.sfchronicle.com/education/article/S-F-City-College-s-finances-in-disarray-4637594.php

313 http://www.sfchronicle.com/bayarea/article/State-official-tells-CCSF-to-get-moving-4184833.php

314 http://www.district.compton.edu/history/docs/Commission-letter-to-R-Cepeda-06-05.pdf

315 http://www.dailynews.com/news/ci_23596942/valley-mission-colleges-get-accreditation-warnings

316 http://www.bizjournals.com/sanfrancisco/blog/2013/08/community-colleges-accreditation-harris.html

education,"[317] believes that California is slipping in education attainment. The slippage means job opportunities will be lost in the future. According to its report, "A Stronger Nation through Higher Education," 38.7 percent of working-age Americans (25-64 years of age) had two or four-year college degrees in 2011, and the number of degree-holding Americans is growing. However, the same statistics fall far short in California, which reports an attainment rate below the national average, especially in the Central Valley, with Stockton at 26.75 percent, Fresno at 27.9 percent, and Bakersfield-Delano at just 21.35 percent. "Research tells us that 65 percent of U.S. jobs will require some form of postsecondary education by 2020," said a spokesperson for Lumina.[318] With California so far behind in educational attainment, the need for focus on educational success could not be more urgent in the state.

The current sad failures for minority students in California test scores are astounding. Hispanic students in particular accounted for more than half of all eighth graders in California in 2011, the highest such proportion in the nation. However, only 14 percent of these Hispanic students were proficient on their eighth grade reading tests administered by the U.S. Department of Education.[319]

In mathematics, the same students also underperformed in comparison to similar students in other states, with just 13% able to reach the national standard for proficiency in their age group. Hispanic students in Texas, for example, while underperforming the national standard, had a 31% proficiency which was still three times better schooled in mathematics than California Hispanic students.[320] The California students also do poorly in science, and the only recent gains appear to be among fourth-grade reading and math scores of

---

317 http://www.luminafoundation.org/about_us/

318 http://www.centralvalleybusinesstimes.com/stories/001/?ID=23631

319 http://articles.latimes.com/2013/apr/21/local/
la-me-ln-test-scores-under-investigation-at-burbank-school-20130421

320 Id.

black students, whose test scores have indeed improved over the past twenty years.[321]

In 1998 California voters adopted Proposition 227, a measure that requires all instruction in the state be conducted in English. The measure provided funds for English-immersion programs for children not proficient in English at the time, to facilitate a transition to all-English. Arguments in favor of Proposition 227 on the ballot included claims that former "bilingual" education efforts had failed in that Spanish-speaking children were not being exposed to English in their first 4 to 7 years of education, and that because English is the most common language in California and our nation, that the former bilingual system could injure non-English speaking children for life, economically and socially.[322] There is much truth to the idea behind Proposition 227. California is a state where it is claimed that more than 140 languages are spoken.[323] A common language, especially in commerce, is already well-established; education efforts that segregate a child from early exposure to the English language could hardly be seen in the long term as enhancing a child's chances for success in later life.

But apparently, years after enactment, California's education system is still not doing all that it should to enable Spanish-speaking children to learn English, which may help explain why test scores of Hispanic students in other states far exceed those same kids in California. A recent lawsuit by the American Civil Liberties Union claims that the California Department of Education has ignored its obligation under Proposition 227 to ensure that non-English speaking children receive adequate and legally required assistance to learn English.[324] The lawsuit claims that up to 20,000 young students are not being adequately provided with English language training,

---

321 Id.

322 http://primary98.sos.ca.gov/VoterGuide/Propositions/227yesarg.htm

323 Id.

324 http://www.latimes.com/health/la-me-english-lawsuit-20130425,0,5017508.story

as 250 school districts have reported they are either not providing such services or doing so at inappropriate levels. The lawsuit cites the experiences of actual students who have failed as a result of lack of English instruction, and then who excelled when such instruction was provided, including in the Compton and Oxnard School Districts.[325] And who was the major opponent of Proposition 227, even signing the official ballot argument against it? The California Teachers Association.[326] It should come as little wonder that CTA's liberal minions in the State Department of Education aren't enabling the English-only ballot measure law they opposed.

Author Amanda Ripley has observed that standardized tests like the PISA test are useful tools to measure needed critical thinking and communication skills of students in key subjects such as math, science, and reading. She also has reported that in societies where tests really matter, students do better on the PISA score—meaning that they are smarter than kids in places like California that use uniform tests that don't matter towards getting a high school diploma or for use in teacher evaluation.

California needs to start testing students in a manner that both motivates them to learn and helps their teachers to improve and do a better job. A standard test the Federal government is encouraging be administered in districts across the nation is known as Common Core. The Common Core series of tests are designed to set basic standards of what children must know to complete each grade.[327] Common Core, (like the PISA test), focuses on critical thinking and forming arguments for communication skills.[328] One idea of Common Core is to encourage children to actually learn, not just

---

325 Id.

326 http://primary98.sos.ca.gov/VoterGuide/Propositions/227yesrbt.htm

327 http://www.usatoday.com/story/news/nation/2013/08/31/more-schools-adopt-common-core-foundation/2748875/

328 http://www.kpbs.org/news/2013/sep/05/california-could-speed-transition-common-core-test/

memorize. A total of 45 states and the District of Columbia have either implemented the standards or agreed to do so by 2015.[329] California is one of the states that is just beginning to implement Common Core testing, but only in about 20% of school districts statewide,[330] including, for example, the Fresno Unified School District.[331]

Predictably the full implementation of Common Core in California is being hampered and stalled by the California Teachers Association who, along with their liberal Democratic allies in state government, is resisting incorporating standardized test scores into teacher evaluations.[332] Using test scores to evaluate teacher performance so that both students and teachers can improve is a rational reform, and Common Core is expected to be used in teacher evaluations. Yet the teachers' unions historically resist use of test scores in teacher evaluations, labeling them a "labor issue." In Los Angeles, for example, they have sued through the state labor board to sideline a new teacher performance evaluation system in the city unified school district, claiming that implementation of the management tool should have been subject to collective bargaining.[333] Meanwhile, a key deputy superintendent of classroom instruction in the school district, occupying a $250,000 annual salaried position, resigned a few days after an eight-hour school board meeting in which the school board postponed a decision, for the second time, on how to spend $113 million in state funds to implement Common Core.[334] The deputy superintendent, who had been "spearheading" the effort,

---

329 "More Schools Roll Out Tough Standards," *USA Today*, September 6, 2013, A3.

330 http://www.kpbs.org/news/2013/sep/05/
california-could-speed-transition-common-core-test/

331 http://abclocal.go.com/kfsn/story?section=news/education&id=9224531

332 http://www.mercurynews.com/central-coast/ci_24065137/
california-schools-could-lose-federal-funding-over-star?source=rss

333 http://www.dailynews.com/article/20130910/NEWS/130919973

334 http://www.dailynews.com/article/20130913/NEWS/130919740

worried that the delay would derail chances that the school district could get teachers trained in time to implement the Common Core program properly and on schedule.[335] The new school board president, Richard Vladovic, who led the charge in postponing implementation of Common Core in Los Angeles, is reportedly a "strong ally of the teachers union."[336]

In order to resist a quicker transition to Common Core testing throughout California, the teachers' unions and their liberal Democratic allies in Sacramento are proposing legislation that would shelve use of existing state accountability tests for any evaluation purposes for the next two years.[337] Federal funding of education in California is held in the balance. The Obama Administration has signaled that California's position is not acceptable, as Arne Duncan, the U.S. Secretary of Education issued a statement saying "[a] request from California to not measure the achievement of millions of students this year is not something we could approve in good conscience.... Backing away entirely from accountability and transparency is not good for students, parents, schools, and districts."[338]

Common Core is not only opposed by teachers' unions and liberal Democrats, but also some conservative organizations.[339] Conservatives object that Common Core has been developed on a national basis through the U.S. Department of Education, and see it as an intrusion on state and local control of education and curriculum.[340] But critics should rethink their opposition to such testing, which is

335 http://www.scpr.org/blogs/education/2013/09/14/14746/
updated-l-a-unified-loses-leader-of-common-core-ip/

336 http://www.dailynews.com/general-news/20130626/
lausd-board-member-richard-vladovic-accused-of-harassing-employees

337 http://www.dailynews.com/article/20130910/NEWS/130919973

338 Id.

339 http://articles.latimes.com/2013/jun/17/opinion/
la-ed-race-to-the-top-common-core-curriculum-20130617

340 http://cuacc.org/Common%20Core%20Letter%20to%20Appropriation%27s%20
Committe...pdf

an important first step to reforming education to objectively help our kids get smarter and also hold teachers accountable for both their successes and failures on the job.

Surely there are thousands of wonderful and talented teachers in California that care about their students and do more than their part to offer a quality education. California's public education problem does not rest on the shoulders of those capable educators who love their jobs and even sacrifice for them. Though their individual pay ranks high in comparison to other states, no one joins the teaching profession to become a millionaire, and that is an important point to remember. Rather, the problem with public education in the state rests with the California Teachers Association itself, which will not agree to even moderate reforms to improve the state's educational standings, and even villainizes the leading education reformers in the state, Democrat Gloria Romero and Michelle Rhee. After decades of winning funding victories, sometimes at the expense of other public services and public employee unions, and continual sub-par performance in educating our state's children, it is time for California's ever-more-taxed residents and poorly educated children to correctly call out the California Teachers Association for their role in the state's failures in education; to as stop reflexively thinking that more and more money will fix the problems; and finally demand the changes California needs to excel once again in student achievement.

CALIFORNIA'S KOOKY LIBERALISM

CALIFORNIA HAS LONG BEEN the butt of the nation's jokes about its kooky liberalism. From Berkeley and San Francisco in the north to what some call the "People's Republic of Santa Monica" in the south, attitudes about California's liberalism may conjure up images of extreme activists fighting to save a lone tree, let a prisoner out of jail, or raise taxes. Those caricatures of liberal Californians are based on real-life events that are stranger than fiction. At UC Berkeley, liberal students spent 21 months living in a giant redwood tree that stood in the way of a new athletic facility.[341] The university tried to talk the activists down by hosting a "remembrance" ceremony for the 200-year-old tree. [342] More recently, Hollywood liberals have championed a strike by California prison inmates that is being led by a white supremacist Aryan Brotherhood prison gang. As if to show just how out-of-touch these liberals truly are, even members

341 John Wildermuth, , Last stand for Berkeley stadium tree-sitters, *San Francisco Chronicle*, September 8, 2008. http://www.sfgate.com/bayarea/article/Last-stand-for-Berkeley-stadium-tree-sitters-3269915.php

342 John Wildermuth, , Last stand for Berkeley stadium tree-sitters, *San Francisco Chronicle*, September 8, 2008. http://www.sfgate.com/bayarea/article/Last-stand-for-Berkeley-stadium-tree-sitters-3269915.php

of the liberal mainstream media have criticized the "pampered elite of Hollywood" for siding with violent killers. "What blinders they wear in their rarefied world," *Sacramento Bee* columnist Dan Morain wrote in a column taking Hollywood to task for their support of the prison strike.[343]

Liberalism, in a dictionary definition of the term, may describe these actions in a more sterile and academic frame.

> "[A] political philosophy based on belief in progress, the essential goodness of the human race, and the autonomy of the individual and standing for the protection of political and civil liberties; *specifically:* such a philosophy that considers government as a crucial instrument for amelioration of social inequities (as those involving race, gender, or class)."[344]

In political science, however we know that a strict dictionary definition won't necessarily give us the fullest understanding of a term. The American 20th century philosopher Russell Kirk once complained that the problem with liberals is that they seem blindfolded to the real problems in modern life and how to address them. Kirk writes of a discussion he had with a professor of chemistry who was a political liberal, to whom Kirk described "some very real and immediate symptoms of social decay—the increase in the rate of crime, the debauchery of children's minds, the collapse of law and order in a great part of the world" to which the liberal professor responded, "But isn't all this just anxiety?"[345] To quote Kirk, so much for Aristotle's view that man is a rational creature.[346]

One internet source provides a modern, if more pedestrian, take

---

343 Dan Morain, "Dan Morain: The real story behind hunger strike," August 11, 2013, http://www.sacbee.com/2013/08/11/5638362/the-real-story-behind-hunger-strike.html

344 http://www.merriam-webster.com/dictionary/liberalism

345 Prospect for Conservatives, Russell Kirk, Regnery Gateway 1989, p. 17.

346 Id.

on liberalism as combining social liberalism with support for social justice and a mixed economy.[347] According to the site, the leading liberal President of the United States, John F. Kennedy, defined a liberal as:

"...someone who looks ahead and not behind, someone who welcomes new ideas without rigid reactions, someone who cares about the welfare of the people—their health, their housing, their schools, their jobs, their civil rights, and their civil liberties— someone who believes we can break through the stalemate and suspicions that grip us in our policies abroad, if that is what they mean by a 'Liberal', then I'm proud to say I'm a 'Liberal'."[348]

"Yet Kennedy cut capital gains taxes as President, in what would hardly be seen as a liberal position today, and famously justified the cuts by stating "a rising tide lifts all boats."[349]

The conservative author and icon William F. Buckley, Jr. once said, "[l]iberals, it has been said, are generous with other peoples' money, except when it comes to questions of national survival when they prefer to be generous with other peoples' freedom and security."[350]

California Governor Jerry Brown, commonly classified as a liberal politician,[351] is perhaps the most successful elected official in California state government's history. His long engagement in politics reveals plenty of examples of his own liberal political philosophy. In a 1995 Pacifica Radio interview Brown provides a decidedly

---

347 http://en.wikipedia.org/wiki/Modern_liberalism_in_the_United_States

348 Id., citing Authur M. Schlesinger, Jr., *A Thousand Days, John F. Kennedy in the White House*, "On issues he showed himself a practical and moderate liberal...", (City: Mariner Books, 2002), 99.

349 http://www.usingenglish.com/reference/idioms/a+rising+tide+lifts+all+boats.html

350 http://www.goodreads.com/author/quotes/16697.William_F_Buckley_Jr_

351 http://usliberals.about.com/od/stategovernors/p/Profile-Of-Jerry-Brown-of-California.htm

liberal view on the role of government. He said, "(t)he conventional viewpoint says we need a jobs program and we need to cut welfare. Just the opposite! We need more welfare and fewer jobs. I'm talking about welfare for all."[352] However, as liberal as Jerry Brown may be, or have been, California's problems today weren't created by him alone. To the contrary, California's problems today have been created by an entrenched structure of liberal special interests and politicians that have wielded practically total control in the state for the last few decades, and Brown is simply a facet of, and his policies usually reflect, this controlling liberal elite.

It is liberalism's reflexive embrace of more and more government spending and regulation to address perceived societal ills that have posed the worst policy results for California. Liberal advocates simply disregard the negative impact on jobs and the economy that their interventionist policies create. These liberals diminish the role of the individual in creating wealth, jobs, and prosperity, in favor of more government regulation of markets, more government programs, union monopoly of labor, more government jobs, more welfare, and the confiscatory taxes the liberals need to pay for it all.

In California liberalism is not characterized either by Kennedy's description or his policies as President, but by a more radical rhetoric coming from the California Democratic Party, the SEIU, and the CTA. This is especially true of issues affecting children and families. Democrats in the legislature recently pushed through a "transgender bathroom" bill.[353] The bill requires schools to allow children and teenagers who consider themselves "transgender" to participate in sports and use bathrooms based on the gender they prefer to identify with, and not

---

352 http://nation.foxnews.com/jerry-brown/2010/10/14/ jerry-brown-flashback-we-need-more-welfare-and-fewer-jobs

353 "California Gov. Brown signs transgender-student bill,"Fox News, August 13, 2013.

their sex.[354] According to a USC Dornsife/*Los Angeles Times* poll, 46 percent of registered voters and 52 percent of parents said they opposed the measure. [355]

The California Democratic Party published its 21-page platform in 2012. The policies advocated are a blueprint for liberal intervention in the economy and justification for big government spending, higher taxes, and even class warfare. The party supports "universal healthcare… through a single payer plan"; "restoration of appropriate regulation and elimination of corporate personhood," and "requiring millionaires [to] pay their fair share."[356] It seems stuck in another century with support for "the investigation of the viability of creating a State owned bank."[357] Here are just a few of the verbatim policy planks affecting Californian's economy:

- Withdraw the profit motive from healthcare delivery, imprisonment, and war;
- Provide new funding mechanisms and legislative support for the promotion of progressive big businesses to foster the legitimate democratic aspirations of individual investors and employees to build strong, profitable corporations with elected accountable leadership, separation of powers, checks and balances, and other tools of an economically democratic society;
- Boycott employers who have permanently replaced strikers and protect the collective bargaining rights of workers in

354 http://news.yahoo.com/calif-lawmakers-pass-k-12-transgender-rights-bill-000619167.html

355 *LA Times*, June 6, 2013, http://www.latimes.com/news/local/political/la-me-pc-california-transgender-students-20130604,0,2428085.story

356 California Democratic Party Platform, The final Platform was adopted at the State Convention on February 12, 2012. http://www.cadem.org/admin/miscdocs/files/2012-CDP-Platform-Final.pdf

357 California Democratic Party Platform, The final Platform was adopted at the State Convention on February 12, 2012. http://www.cadem.org/admin/miscdocs/files/2012-CDP-Platform-Final.pdf

both the public and private sectors; and support binding arbitration for police and firefighters who are not authorized to strike [358]

The various planks of the California Democratic Party platform reveal a philosophy that is radical in nature and hostile to the more moderate viewpoints of most Californians. The Democrats' program is distinctly anti-capitalist and oriented to "class warfare" to address policy issues. California Democrats are also out-of-touch with most mainstream Californians in terms of their rigidity of views, such as banning all new oil exploration. A slight majority of Californians oppose fracking, according to a July 2013 Public Policy Institute of California poll.[359] That seemingly puts Californians in line with Democrats on the issue. However, public opinion changes dramatically when respondents are told that fracking could lower energy prices. According to a poll conducted by USC/Dornsife College of Letters, Arts and Sciences and the *Los Angeles Times* in June 2013, 56 percent of voters said fracking should be legal in California if the additional oil and gas was used to reduce energy and gas prices.[360] It is a sad state of affairs but the truth is the Democrats' platform reflects ideas that are out-of-step with most Californians. Yet their ideas are not just influencing policy in California, but they have controlled it for some time, and the result has been fiscal disaster.

When California's liberals see what they perceive to be a problem, often their reflexive reaction is to make it a problem for everybody else too. They use state power to pass a law about it, rather than looking to the marketplace to self-regulate, considering all the data, or allowing people to just take personal responsibility. And their

---

358 California Democratic Party Platform, The final Platform was adopted at the State Convention on February 12, 2012. http://www.cadem.org/admin/miscdocs/files/2012-CDP-Platform-Final.pdf

359 http://blogs.kqed.org/newsfix/2013/07/31/105239/

360 http://dornsife.usc.edu/usc-dornsife-la-times-poll-fracking-june-2013/

favored device in the realm of state power is to outright ban things the liberals don't like, for them and for everyone else. In California liberals have banned a lot of things, and these laws are often self-involved, costly, irrational, and harmful to personal liberties. Here are just a few of their kookier laws banning and regulating things, which serve more to erode personal responsibility and limit choices and freedom of all Californians than to accomplish anything truly meaningful:

Foie Gras. This classic French delicacy is made from the liver of a specially fattened goose or duck. In the United States, the foie gras produced in New York's Hudson Valley is particularly delicious. It is often prepared in the form of a paste, and can be enjoyed in its *torchon* form spread on crackers or toast points, seared and served on its own, or used as part of a recipe with other ingredients, such as chef Julia Child's "Roast Goose with Prune and Foie Gras Stuffing."[361]

Unfortunately, preparing Julia Child's roast goose according to her own recipe and serving it in one of California's fine dining establishments is now illegal in California. In mid-2012 a law promoted by liberal Democrats in the legislature went into effect that bans this ancient staple of French cooking from consumption in California's restaurants.[362] California's ban means one now has to look outside the state for a taste of foie gras. While California restaurants can be prosecuted and fined $1,000 per day for offering the dish,[363] locations in neighboring states can offer it without penalty. Regarding the ban in California, "to chefs around the world, they think it's ridiculous, " said Greg Daniels, a restaurant owner in Pasadena, "it's the stupidest thing that Californians could ever do, and it just proves

---

361 Julia Child, *Mastering the Art of French Cooking*, Volume I, (City: Alfred A. Knopf, updated 1997), 284.

362 http://www.huffingtonpost.com/2012/07/01/california-foie-gras-ban_n_1638380.html

363 http://lagunabeach.patch.com/articles/caught-serving-foie-gras-amar-santana-backs-down

that Californians are stupid."[364] Not all Californians are stupid, but the liberals who enacted this ban during an economic downturn for the restaurant industry surely are.

Shark Fin Soup. California's regulation of gastronomy isn't limited to classic French cuisine, but also classic Chinese culinary dishes. The main ingredient in Shark Fin soup is also banned in California.[365] Enacted in 2012, California's ban on "shark finning," where sharks are caught, their fins removed and the fish is returned to sea, has the purported aim of protecting shark conservation and reducing human risk in potential mercury exposure. But in a confounding twist for liberals, a group of Chinese-Americans has filed a Federal civil rights action against the state, alleging racial discrimination in enacting the ban because shark fin soup "is a cultural delicacy" that is a centerpiece of Chinese celebrations and " a traditional symbol of respect, honor, and appreciation" served at special occasions.[366] After the district court refused to issue an injunction, the Federal 9th Circuit Court of Appeals in San Francisco ruled in the Plaintiffs' favor and ordered further proceedings by the lower court. If Chinese-Americans win their case, their soup rights will be restored under the Federal Civil Rights Act, and they will be able to successfully sue the state for their attorney fees as well.

Plastic bags. The ban on these useful grocery market items calls to mind the sad opening lyrics of one of Katy Perry's inspirational songs:

> *"Do you ever feel, like a plastic bag,*
> *Drifting through the wind, wanting to start again?"*

Regardless, there are going to be a lot fewer plastic bags to contemplate, and the utility and convenience that goes with them, as

---

364 http://www.huffingtonpost.com/2012/07/01/california-foie-gras-ban_n_1638380. html

365 http://www.sfgate.com/science/article/Shark-fin-ban-stands-while-opponents-challenge-law-4765894.php.

366 http://www.courthousenews.com/2013/08/15/60329.htm

California implements bans against them up and down the state.[367] Already big cities such as Los Angeles and San Francisco and smaller Watsonville have banned use of plastic bags in local supermarkets, and soon the bags will even be banned in Santa Barbara,[368] home to Katy Perry herself, who was born and grew up there.[369]

Liberals say that one-use plastic bags are bad for California because they do not biodegrade as quickly as paper bags. (Of course, they mean recycled, biodegradable paper.) But recycling of plastic bags is the rational environmental policy.[370] The liberals don't consider the unintended consequences of these bans, which in the case of plastic bags have been shown to raise the overall costs of garbage collection. In one study of locations where plastic bags were banned in grocery stores, consumers actually ended up using more plastic for their garbage disposal at home.[371]

Foam take-out food containers. These useful items are now banned in San Jose and Hermosa Beach as a result of leadership by liberals on those city councils.[372] Presumably citizens are allowed to bring their own non-lead metal buckets when picking up Chow Fung at the local Chinese take-out. But the legislature is expected to continue statewide efforts during the current legislative session to ban Styrofoam, which is inexpensive and reusable.[373]

Lead Bullets. A bill banning lead bullets passed two-to-one on partisan lines in the State Assembly, ending the use of lead ammunition

367 http://dailycaller.com/2012/05/18/california-is-leading-the-nanny-state-trend/

368 http://www.huffingtonpost.com/2013/06/26/los-angeles-plastic-bags-banned_n_3500576.html; http://www.noozhawk.com/article/santa_barbara_council_adopts_plastic_bag_ban_20131015

369 http://www.biography.com/people/katy-perry-5626/8?page=2

370

371 http://www.cga.ct.gov/2008/rpt/2008-R-0685.htm

372 http://dailycaller.com/2012/05/18/california-is-leading-the-nanny-state-trend/

373 Id.

when hunting wildlife in the state.[374] The reason for banning lead bullets is to prevent exposing animals who are wounded but not killed to the bullets deadly toxins. "We're hoping we have a more vibrant and plentiful wildlife population in the state" said the bill's author.[375] But there is no guarantee that copper or other bullet replacements will offer any better treatment to wounded animals. Even union leaders have expressed opposition, calling it a "bad law."[376]

Beach fire pits. The South Coast Air Quality Management District proposes to override local government control and ban all fires in long-established public fire pits built on beaches in Orange and Los Angeles counties.[377] Beach fires at night are a tradition in southern California and as one Orange County Supervisor said, "(o)utlawing fire rings is like banning mother and apple pie."[378]

Passive religious symbols. California is a markedly religious state with a strong presence of all dominations. Surveys indicate at least 45% of Californians affiliate with a religion.[379] Almost 28% are Catholic, 12.5% are another Protestant Christian faith, 2% are Latter Day Saint, and 0.58% are Jewish.[380] Catholic higher education, bible colleges, parochial school systems, and values-based homeschooling are evident throughout the state.

But liberals have spawned a type of "political correctness" in state institutions that has sadly operated to deny religious Californians their fundamental rights to practice and express their religion even in the most innocuous ways. For example, a policy initiated by

---

374 http://touch.latimes.com/#section/-1/article/p2p-75943061/

375 Id.

376 http://www.foxnews.com/politics/2013/09/23/
unions-now-back-opposition-to-calif-bill-to-ban-lead-bullets-for-hunters/#ixzz2fjlN6I4J

377 http://abclocal.go.com/kabc/story?section=news/local/orange_county&id=9078370

378 Id.

379 http://www.bestplaces.net/religion/state/california

380 Id.

the Chancellor of Sonoma State University in northern California recently resulted in a 19-year old student helping at freshman orientation being ordered to remove a small cross necklace she was wearing "because it might offend others, it might make incoming students feel unwelcome."[381] After the student's supervisor told her "hide the cross under her shirt or remove it," she quit the job. "I was very hurt and felt as if the university's mission statement—which includes tolerance and inclusivity to all—was violated," the student said.[382] The Chancellor is reportedly rethinking the policy as a result of the incident.

There are some things that liberals care about that they don't want to ban, but rather legalize, like marijuana. But sometimes California liberals' self-indulgent enthusiasm for making bad things legal gets the best of them. The city of Berkeley, with a population of 113,000 and the site of the University of California, is already home to three locations where marijuana can be legally purchased for "medical" purposes. Three locations to legally buy weed in Berkeley should be plenty. However, the city council wants to approve a fourth pot shop.[383] The potential location has been temporarily put on hold due to objections by the Federal government, since the site is located within 600 feet of not one, but two preschools.[384] While the Obama Administration's Justice Department has announced it will not challenge states that have legalized use of small amounts of marijuana or medical marijuana, it nevertheless requires strict local measures to keep the drug away from

---

381 http://radio.foxnews.com/toddstarnes/top-stories/university-tells-student-to-remove-cross-necklace.html

382 "Calif. Univ. Officials Apologize After Student Told to Remove Cross Necklace", The New American, July 4, 2013, http://www.thenewamerican.com/culture/faith-and-morals/item/15898-calif-univ-officials-apologize-after-student-told-to-remove-cross-necklace

383 Eli Wolfe, "Berkeley delays decision on 4th cannabis dispensary," September 20, 2013, http://www.berkeleyside.com/2013/09/20/berkeley-again-delays-decision-on-4th-marijuana-dispensary/

384 http://www.berkeleyside.com/2013/06/13/berkeley-delays-fourth-cannabis-dispensary/

minors.[385] One of those measures is that pot not be sold anywhere near children. Berkeley, whose city policy appears to favor the interests of drug users as opposed to exposure of the drug to minors, has voted to sue the Federal government over the matter.

In the meantime, across the Bay in regulatory San Francisco, the highly charged left-wing political environment has been focused on new rules purportedly protecting dogs rather than drug users. The City's Board of Supervisors decided that "professional dog walkers" should register with the city and apply for a permit.[386] Under the new rules, a dog walker for hire needs to have $1 million in liability insurance, and must have their vehicles inspected. Something called the "San Francisco Dog Walkers Association" says nearly 300 walkers will have to register and be regulated. Initial fines start at $50 and will likely escalate.[387]

This arrogance of one-party, liberal control is now thoroughly working itself into policy in the state in some rather obvious ways. For example, California enacted a relatively modest "enterprise zone" law 30 years ago, and maintains a $700 million program, which manages a few geographic areas where businesses can receive tax breaks for hiring disadvantaged workers in locations where high-unemployment is persistent. One of the earliest historical supporters of "enterprise zones" nationally was former conservative Republican Congressman and Vice-Presidential candidate Jack Kemp.[388] Enterprise zones are a good idea to give incentive to businesses to build new investments and bring value into communities that would not

---

385 http://www.usatoday.com/story/news/nation/2013/09/04/
marijuana-drug-use-survey/2760061/

386 http://blog.sfgate.com/cityinsider/2013/07/15/professional-dog-walkers-reigned-in/

387 Dan Francisco, "Permit Required Under New Law For Some SF Dog
Walkers," CBS, July 5, 2013, http://sanfrancisco.cbslocal.com/2013/07/05/
permit-required-under-new-law-for-some-sf-dog-walkers/

388 Jason DeParle, "How Jack Kemp Lost the War on Poverty," New York Times,
February 28, 1993, http://www.nytimes.com/1993/02/28/magazine/how-jack-kemp-
lost-the-war-on-poverty.html?pagewanted=all&src=pm

otherwise receive attention, because of the high costs associated with doing business in, for example, a high crime neighborhood. Emboldened by more recent electoral gains, the California Labor Federation, which despises the program, now argues that 61 percent of the program's credits go to very large corporations, and therefore it should be "reformed."[389]

The alleged "reform" of the enterprise zone law offers California's liberal Democrats and their union allies two inter-related targets of political opportunity: 1) raising California's minimum wage statewide, and 2) using that effort to also kill off enterprise zones in minority communities, by raising the minimum wage in those economically disadvantaged areas to an untenable $16 per hour. The Obama Administration and national labor organizations are also lobbying to raise the Federal minimum wage, which is currently $7.25. However, California already has established a higher minimum wage at $8 per hour. California's liberal Democrats in the state legislature don't see the obvious "job-killing" effect of raising the minimum wage. Their efforts coincide with labor's national efforts to organize fast food workers. But the rush to raise the minimum wage in California and nationwide is not without criticism, even from a writer that usually agrees with the liberal Democrats in control. Sandy Banks, a columnist for the *Los Angeles Times* who grew up in urban Cleveland and is a single mom with three daughters with two of them in college, writes "How do you justify paying $15 an hour for someone to bag fries? That's almost on a par with the average hourly wage of a paramedic, whose job involves saving lives?"[390] Banks understands that artificially lifting wages to unrealistic levels can not only have bad economic repercussions, but also can undermine the incentive of young people to seek a better education. In opposing

---

389 http://www.bizjournals.com/sacramento/news/2013/04/16/labor-wants-to-reform-enterprise-zones.html?page=all

390 http://www.latimes.com/local/la-me-0910-banks-labor-unions-20130910,0,4841593.column#axzz2lgPXG7w3

such a steep hike in the minimum wage, Banks writes "[l]et's prepare this next generation so McDonald's won't have to be a career, but a stop en route to better things."[391]

But the liberals in the legislature don't share Bank's viewpoint. The California Legislature approved a new bill that was rushed through the last few days of the 2013 legislative session that would raise the minimum wage 25 percent, making it the highest minimum wage in the country.[392] The state's minimum wage will rise from $8 to $9 an hour next July.[393] Then in January 2016, it will rise again to $10 per hour, effectively killing off the incentive for companies to invest in blighted communities—which is inherent in the idea behind enterprise zones in the first place! Governor Jerry Brown has promised to sign the bill and is credited with rescuing it at the last minute from the legislative graveyard. The fact that liberal Democrats are moving on a strict party-line voting[394] to raise California's minimum wage, already one of the highest in the nation, to what would be the highest in the nation at $10.00, shows how out-of-touch the state's liberals really are.[395] The California Chamber of Commerce calls the effort to raise the minimum wage in a time of recession "a job killer."[396] One can therefore easily imagine what both the Chamber and any potential business investor would have to say about a $16 per hour minimum wage in South Central Los Angeles or Hunter's

---

391 Id.

392 Josh Richman and Mike Rosenberg, "California Legislature approves raising minimum wage to $10—the highest of any state," *San Jose Mercury News*, September 13, 2013, http://www.mercurynews.com/politics-government/ci_24083554/california-legislature-poised-raise-minimum-wage-from-8

393 http://online.wsj.com/news/articles/SB1000142412788732475510457907318275698 4074

394 http://www.dailybreeze.com/news/ci_23323718/bill-raise-californias-minimum-wage-goes-assembly-floor?source=rss&utm_source=feedly

395 http://articles.latimes.com/2013/sep/12/business/la-fi-minimum-wage-20130913

396 http://www.latimes.com/business/la-fi-capitol-business-beat-20130429,0,2131702.story?track=rss&utm_source=feedly

Point in San Francisco, where unemployment is at chronic levels.

Craig Johnson, president of the California Association of Enterprise Zones, claims the zones have created 124,000 jobs in the state.[397] But the California Labor Federation apparently doesn't like those *types* of jobs, so they are more than happy to sponsor job-killing legislation, regardless of unemployment statistics showing that among black teenagers the unemployment rate is growing, is up to 43.1 percent nationally,[398] and is even worse in California. The California Labor Federation's attitude on enterprise zones is one that would not be lost on economist Walter E. Williams, who has observed, "(l)abor unions have a long history of discrimination against blacks," and "(t)o the detriment of their constituents, black politicians give support to labor laws pushed by unions and white liberal organizations."[399]

California is truly a unique state that is entitled to revel in its differences with the rest of the country and in what makes the state the special place it is, be it its exceptional natural beauty; its beaches, rivers, mountains and lakes; its hip culture; or its diversity. The state is entitled to its kooky eccentricities. But its leaders are not entitled to also perpetuate kooky policies that keep its citizens unemployed, underemployed, and overburdened by taxes and regulations.

---

397 Id.

398 http://www.huffingtonpost.com/2013/03/08/black-teen-unemployment_n_2836816.html

399 http://townhall.com/columnists/walterewilliams/2013/04/10/black-unemployment-n1561096/page/full/

ENERGY AND ENVIRONMENTAL POLICY AND CALIFORNIA'S PERSISTENT HIGH UNEMPLOYMENT PROBLEM

CALIFORNIA'S ENERGY AND ENVIRONMENTAL laws are complicated, duplicative, and anti-growth. They're routinely used by business and labor interests for non-environmental purposes to delay legitimate development. California's over-regulation of businesses depresses employment in the state; however, the energy industry is especially on the wane at the same time that availability of energy is becoming more expensive and not always reliably available. The biggest obstacle to reforming these laws is the liberal Democrats in the state legislature.

A widely accepted tenet among liberal politicians, political science academics, and the media in California is that no development at all is a good thing. This is especially the case with the state's abundant mineral resources. Professor Gerson, an often quoted professor of political science at San Jose State University, reflects this misguided, job-killing viewpoint widely accepted among liberal elites in California when he writes:

"There is a bit of light in California's dark tunnel—environmental management. As mentioned earlier, ever since the 1969 Santa

Barbara oil spill, residents and elected officials alike have been united in opposing offshore drilling."[400]

At a time of deep recession, massive public over-spending, debt problems, and high unemployment in the state; given that both oil extraction and environmental protection technology have greatly advanced in the last 45 years; and in view of the immense untapped mineral reserves laying underneath California and its shores, one would think that there might be a deeper inquiry by rational policymakers into how California might make use of the resources, even in a "green" manner for the greater benefit of society. Texas, for example, has had a booming economy throughout the recession precisely because it maintains a balanced "environmental management" policy that allows for extraction of minerals while at the same time giving considera-tion to the environment. Its environmental policy keeps Texas wealthy with employment up through energy-related jobs, keeps taxes low, and insures Texas public employee pensions are adequately funded. "What would Texas do?" with California's natural resources is a fair question to ask. The answer to that question is Texas would not allow California's vast resources to have become immobile and useless to the state for 45 years because of one unfortunate spill.

But in California, the response is to do hardly anything about outdated energy and environmental laws that stifle the economy, and that attitude has greatly harmed the state. Some of California's anti-business rules have simply defied sanity.

The California Environmental Quality Act:

Even Jerry Brown has said that needed changes to the California Environmental Quality Act (CEQA), one of the most significant

---

400 Larry N. Gerston, *Not so Golden After All, The Rise and Fall of California*, (Boca Raton: CRC Press, 2012), 14.

state environmental laws, won't happen anytime soon, because reforming the Act "is stronger among groups outside the state Capitol than among Democratic lawmakers, who control the legislature."[401] According to the Associated Press, critics of the 40-year-old CEQA say it is being used "by unions, activist groups, and rival developers to delay or stop projects they don't like, often at great legal expense to the developers."[402]

The CEQA was first adopted in 1970 as policymakers nationwide started to become more focused on issues raised by the environmental movement. The law's purpose, "[t]o take action to provide the people of this state with clean air and water," is a goal everyone can agree with. But the problem is that over the years, liberal Democrats and their environmental lobby allies have used the law to stifle rational development projects. Even developers have turned against themselves to gain economic advantage, to the disadvantage of jobs and economic progress.

For example, technology giant Google, based in Silicon Valley, is interested in making an $82 million privately funded expansion of the San Jose Airport to accommodate private aviation. The city processed paperwork to allow for construction of the new airport facilities with the selected contractor, but a business rival has filed a lawsuit saying the city did not properly fulfill its CEQA obligations when it approved the expansion, and progress on the expansion is halted.[403] "It underscores the need for CEQA reform," said San Jose's city attorney, "(y)ou have a competitor who loses out on the competition, who now files a case under CEQA to try to stop the project."

And in an interesting twist, CEQA, henceforth considered an iconic liberal environmental achievement, has even been used to slow down and gain concessions from the construction of a multibillion dollar

401 Associated Press, "Brown says environmental law overhaul unlikely." April 16, 2013.

402 Id.

403 Donato-Weinstein, Nathan. "San Jose hit with CEQA suit over Google airport." *Silicon Valley Business Journal*, May 9, 2013

liberal pet public works project (and financial nightmare for the rest of California), the California High-Speed Rail project, commonly referred to as the Bullet Train. Perhaps all the CEQA problems that are slowing down and increasing the construction costs of the Bullet Train have opened the eyes of some liberal Democrat lawmakers in Sacramento about the need for CEQA reform. The authority that controls the project had $9 billion in state funding and $3.5 million in matching Federal grants in 2010, and announced it was going to start building the first leg of the system from quiet Merced in the Central Valley to Fresno,[404] which is California's fifth largest city.[405] This stretch, referred to as the "railroad to nowhere" by one critic, must be completed by September 2017 to assure federal participation in the project.[406] But construction hasn't even started, thanks to lawsuits initiated by the rural agricultural counties of Merced and Madera, the small city of Chowchilla, and a group of farmers, farm bureaus, and property owners, all of whom are claiming that the project has not properly received its CEQA approvals,[407] and that the "environmental impact report" required by the statute is flawed, resulting in claims of destruction or interference with farms, wildlife habitat, roads, water systems, and home developments. "These suits run up the costs of projects astronomically and impose time delays that are measured in years—or even decades," said the CEO of the Los Angeles Area Chamber of Commerce.[408]

Liberal Democrats who control the legislature recently beat back a reform proposal to modernize the law from their super-minority Republican colleagues as "too broad and comprehensive

---

404 *California Lawyer Magazine*, May 2013, 20.

405 http://en.wikipedia.org/wiki/Fresno,_California

406 *California Lawyer Magazine*, May 2013,. 20.

407 Id.

408 Id., p. 21.

a change."[409] Democrats instead offered a weak bill they claim will speed up processing of construction permits that are lucky enough to get approved. But the focus of the bill has been criticized by Republicans for a loophole for one special project: construction of a basketball arena in Sacramento as an amenity to try to keep the Kings professional basketball team in the State Capitol, where presumably the same legislators could watch the games.[410] Such obvious favoritism in how the liberal Democrats enact laws in California is sad commentary for all the other businesses, large and small, that don't get such a fair deal on their projects. "It's clear the legislature is interested in tinkering around the edges but not in enacting real reform," observed one Republican State Senator.[411]

California Coastal Act:

As high-minded as the California Coastal Act is intended, to protect and allow public access to California's coastal zone, the reality of its administration has been a nightmare for some developers, including Manhattan real estate mogul Donald Trump and his modest attempts to invest in California. Trump simply wanted to place an American flag over his new resort on the beautiful Palos Verdes Peninsula south of Santa Monica Bay, but the bureaucratic wrangling to do so took years and costs tens of thousands of dollars.

In Trump's case, his organization made an application for his 300-acre Trump National Golf Course, a potential gem for regional tourism, to the city of Rancho Palos Verdes to build a Driving Range on his site and to situate a flagpole next to it. The application languished with the city for over a year as the city staff considered the implications of the

---

409 Van-Oot, Torey, "Bill to change California's environmental review law advances." *Sacramento Bee*, May 1, 2013.

410 Id.

411 http://capitolweekly.net/ceqa-fight-modernize-mantra-spin/

flagpole and range to the environment.[412] An element of the Coastal Act is that development requires duplicative approvals, from both city and Coastal Commission approval. Trump's business couldn't wait, and he could not imagine that the process would result in a long process or rejection of his organization erecting a pole to display the American flag on his lovely coastal property. The pole was erected, the American flag was hoisted, and eventually Trump received retroactive approval from the city, but that was not enough to make the flagpole legal—he needed explicit approval from the Coastal Commission. However, the filing fee to erect the pole with the Coastal Commission was $10,000, and the fee is intended to allow the Commission staff to evaluate the impact on the environment of the pole, which had already been done by the city.[413] Trump submitted the application without the filing fee, but no Commission approval was forthcoming. But the issue did not end there. In 2012 a bill was introduced in the California Legislature by a Republican Assemblyman, to exempt flagpoles from the Coastal Commission's jurisdiction.[414] However, the Coastal Commission responded by officially opposing the bill and committing staff time and resources to lobby against it. According to the Coastal Commission's analysis, the bill "could result in a proliferation of flag poles" in coastal areas which could impact "wetlands" and views of the American flag could result in "adverse visual impacts."[415] The bill was defeated.

Sadly, Trump's problems with the irrational Coastal Commission did not end there. In 2007 Trump's organization also made a separate application for approval of two rows of ficus hedges planted on the golf course. One row was 5' 6" in height to screen the driving range from existing neighboring homes. The other row included a

---

412 Rancho Palos Verdes City Staff Report, January 17, 2012,

413 Kim, Victoria, "Stern agency meets unflappable mogul." *Los Angeles Times*, February 7, 2008.

414 AB 2178 (Jones), Committee Analysis.

415 California Coastal Commission Bill Analysis, April 2012.

12' high row on the other side of the driving range. In a 20-page analysis of Trump's ficus plants, the city rejected his application for the 12' hedge row.[416] Trump asked a *Los Angeles Times* reporter, "Do we need permission to plant bushes?"[417] After a four-year process of considering the ficus plant applications, numerous public hearings and staff reports consumed with the height of the plants, the City Council rejected the Trump application because they determined the proposed hedges might impair some views and that the ficus species "was not consistent with the project's plant palette that focuses on the use of native and drought tolerant plantings."[418] Not to be stopped, Trump eventually won a new application to the city to plant a row of trees in place of the ficus plants, after five years of tangling with the city and the Coastal Act,[419] but that approval is still pending with the Coastal Commission itself.

Given these Trump examples, clearly the regulatory hurdles in the coastal zone in California placed on even the simplest types of development—such as erecting a flagpole or planting a row of bushes - are unreasonable and unjustifiable in terms of time, expense, and deployment of government resources. These rules, and the precious time and resources they waste, are a product of liberalism and an element of that political philosophy's ongoing destruction of California's economy.

Clean Air Act:

Perhaps one of the biggest successes of environmental regulation has been the dramatic reduction of smog in the Los Angeles basin. Los

---

416 Rancho Palos Verdes City Staff Report, January 17, 2012,

417 Kim, Victoria, "Stern agency meets unflappable mogul." *Los Angeles Times*, February 7, 2008.

418 Rancho Palos Verdes City Staff Report, January 17, 2012,

419 Agostoni, Kristin. "Trump wins right to plant trees at driving range in Rancho Palos Verdes," January 18, 2012, *Daily Breeze*.

Angeles was at one-time known for its persistent smog. First recognized in 1943, in October of that year the Los Angeles County
government appointed a "Smoke and Fumes Commission" to study
the dense smoke on the Los Angeles basin.[420] Both the state and city
of Los Angeles joined the county over the next years in establishing
review boards and new rules to attempt to control sources of air pollution, caused primarily by automobiles. Smog reached its highest
levels in 1974, when ozone was recorded at 0.51 parts per million in
southern California, and reached its highest level of alert, a so-called
"Stage Three" smog alert. Governor Reagan urged residents at the
time to "limit all but absolutely necessary auto travel" and recommended people drive slower to reduce emissions.[421]

Since that time, air pollution in Los Angeles has steadily decreased.
Most of the smog in Los Angeles was caused by automobile emissions, and over time efforts to reduce such emissions by local agencies were joined by the Federal government in the form of strict
emission standards and mandated longer-term anti-pollution goals,
and also by the state in various programs, including the California
Clean Air Act. The Act allowed for the creation of regional "air
quality management districts" which over time implemented regulations across the state (including Los Angeles) to attack problems
like its persistent smog by regulating emissions from, for example,
polluting factories. By 1984 a separate "Smog Check" program to
identify highly polluting automobiles was implemented statewide.
In time, Stage One ozone episodes plummeted from 121 in 1977
to just 7 in 1996.[422] Cleaner burning cars helped make 1997 in Los
Angeles a "landmark for the fewest ozone and health warnings in
memory."[423] By 2010, automobile pollution decreased 99% from

420 "History of Smog," LA Weekly, September 22, 2005.

421 Id.

422 http://www.aqmd.gov/news1/Archives/History/marchcov.html#After%2050%20
Years,%20How%20Close%20Are%20We%20to%20the%20Goal?

423 Allen, Jane. "L.A., Cleaning Up Its Act, Sees Smog Level Plummet." Associated
Press, December 30, 1997.

where it was in 1960, and vehicle related air pollution was down 85% since 1975.[424] There is no doubt that combined Federal, state, and local efforts have greatly reduced air pollution in Los Angeles from its primary source: automobile emissions. Without the state doing much of anything more, the future looks even better as newer "smart cars," hybrids and non-polluting electronic vehicles increasingly enter the California vehicle market.

But while California's and the nation's efforts to reduce polluting emissions from automobiles and factories have indeed had significant success over the last decades, enforcement of the rules has also been characterized by some irrational regulatory excess. The Federal government has done most of the heavy lifting in reducing air pollution in California through its own regulations and mandates in automobile pollution. Meanwhile California vigorously extends its regulations whenever a liberal politician senses a headline can be grabbed from liberal allies in the media. A ood, and rare, accidental fire at a Chevron oil refinery, for example, which inconvenienced neighbors but resulted in no deaths, is being used as a platform by a Democratic State Senator from Berkeley to increase the fine for such an accident by 10-fold, to $100,000, regardless of the magnitude of chemicals released or the number of people affected.[425] The California Chamber of Commerce calls the bill a "job killer."[426] But this harsh regulatory environment extends far beyond refineries, automobiles, and polluting factories to cover hair spray, floor polish, lighter fluid, wood burned in fireplaces, and aerosol underarm deodorants.[427] And there is no better example of excessive regulation than the state's efforts to shut down bakeries that emit the smell of baking bread, which under California law is considered a noxious pollutant.[428]

---

424 Hsu, Tiffany. "California cars 99% cleaner than in 1960s, but smog levels still high, study says." *Los Angeles Times*, November 16, 2010.

425 Quinton, Amy. "Bill To Increase Fines for Big Air Polluters Moves Forward." *Capitol Public Radio*, August 12, 2013.

426 Id.

427 http://www.csmonitor.com/1991/0111/aroma.html

428 http://www.csmonitor.com/1991/0111/aroma.html

In 1991 the South Coast Air Quality Management District (AQMD), a unit of the state AQMD, adopted a regulation limiting emissions from bakeries in Los Angeles, and banning the building of any new bakery unless the bakery complied with a strict emission control system.[429] As the *Christian Science Monitor* observed at the time, "many of the rules are pushing the battle against air pollution to frontiers never before explored."[430] The target was the ethyl alcohol formed when bread leavens, which is emitted in the aroma of hot, baking bread. Since 1991 California's air pollution enforcers have continued their jihad against bakeries. More recently, in 2012, Cottage Bakery of the modest Central Valley community of Lodi agreed to pay $1.3 million in fines and to install mandated equipment on their ovens.[431]

While air pollution in Los Angeles has dramatically decreased since the adoption of "Air Regulation Rule 1153, Commercial Bakery Ovens" in 1991, commercial bakeries nevertheless remain subject to a ban on the emissions of the aroma of their baking bread unless they have installed expensive devices intended to almost completely eliminate particulate emissions. Home food makers were exempted from the rules in 2013,[432] but not commercial bakers. California's current rules regulating the aroma of baking bread are outdated, have been overtaken by events, and ought to be repealed.

California's outdated and obsessive air pollution rules include fines on homeowners who burn wood in fireplaces or at outdoor sites on days it deems "high-pollution days" in colder winter months.[433] In one

---

429 http://www.aqmd.gov/rules/reg/reg11/r1153.pdf

430 http://www.csmonitor.com/1991/0111/aroma.html

431 http://www.centralvalleybusinesstimes.com/stories/001/?ID=21348

432 "California eases regulations on homemade food businesses, boosting startups," Fox News, January5, 2013, http://www.foxnews.com/us/2013/01/05/california-eases-regulations-on-home-made-food-businesses-boosting-startups/#ixzz2VwDSMt5d

433 "Pollution rules will put a damper on fireplace use," LA Times, March 08, 2008, http://articles.latimes.com/2008/mar/08/local/me-fireplace8

rare intelligent move, the South Coast AQMD rejected a request to require fireplaces in southern California homes to be replaced before all new real estate transactions were completed.[434] But wood burning nevertheless remains banned when the AQMD says so. "You're not going to regulate my chimney," said one San Bernardino resident at a government hearing.[435] But enforcement officials said they would count on watchful neighbors as a "front line in enforcing" the ban on burning wood in fireplaces, with inspectors responding to phone complaints to issue fines as high as $500 per violation.[436]

Energy Policy:

Under political pressure from California's liberal Democratic Senator Barbara Boxer, [437]on June 7, 2013, Southern California Edison, one of the state's biggest utility companies, announced it was closing for good its two reactors at the San Onofre Nuclear Power Plant, because of problems in its steam generator systems. [438] The plant had provided electricity to about 5% of the state,[439] for 1.4 million households. Edison had already laid off 730 workers the previous August, and announced plans to eliminate another 600 shortly after the closure with an additional cut of 1,500 more jobs in 2014.[440] Job

---

434 Id.

435 Id.

436 Id.

437 http://www.guardian.co.uk/environment/2013/jun/07/
san-onofre-nuclear-reactors-shut-down

438 http://articles.latimes.com/2013/jun/07/local/
la-me-ln-edison-closing-san-onofre-nuclear-plant-20130607

439 http://www.sacbee.com/2013/06/16/5500147/dan-walters-californias-big-power.
html

440 http://labusinessjournal.com/news/2013/jun/26/edison-plans-600-lay-offs/ Also
see http://www.nytimes.com/2013/07/26/us/californians-consider-a-future-without-a-
nuclear-plant-for-a-neighbor.html

losses could eventually impact as many as 5,500 workers according to the plant's labor representative.[441] The closure of the facility leaves just one operational nuclear power facility in the state, the Diablo Canyon Power Plant in San Luis Obispo County. As a result of the closure and increases at the same time in the cost of natural gas, which is used to generate replacement power for San Onofre, wholesale energy prices rose 59% during the first half of 2013.[442]

Sadly, reductions in California's available sources of energy have been on the downswing for some time. And during this decade, California's attitude toward energy needs has become even more highly eccentric as a result of AB 32, known as "The Global Warming Solutions Act of 2006," passed by the liberal Democrats and signed into law by Governor Schwarzenegger. The law seeks to fight climate change through "comprehensive programs" designed to reduce carbon-polluting emissions from virtually all sources state-wide.[443] But the reality is that fulfillment of AB 32's lofty goals has been overplayed at the expense of economic well-being and jobs growth; served to limit available energy resources to Californians; and damaged California's economy. In some instances it has caused rationing of power and raised the cost of energy to consumers, even though polluting emissions have already been reduced dramatically throughout the state over the last decades.

Pursuant to the policy behind AB 32, which does not have California's real energy needs much in focus, in 2007 the California Energy Commission banned energy acquisition from coal-fueled power plants.[444] Coal is considered a "dirty" fuel under AB 32. Earlier in that year, liberals in the legislature, supported by Governor Schwarzenegger, also enacted a ban on state utility investment in

---

441 http://www.scpr.org/blogs/economy/2013/06/09/13929/
san-onofre-plant-closure-will-mean-hundreds-layoff/

442 http://www.scpr.org/news/2013/07/24/38334/
california-power-prices-up-59-percent-after-san-on/

443 http://www.c2es.org/us-states-regions/action/california/ab32

444 "State Acts to Limit Use of Coal Power," *Los Angeles Times*, May 24, 2007.

traditional coal-fired plants anywhere, even out-of-state, that provided energy to the state.[445] State government has been in jihad against coal ever since. More recently, San Francisco State University decided to even divest endowment investments in fossil fuels companies.[446] Calls for further carbon cuts at power generation plants globally by the Obama Administration, and an executive order to back up that goal nationwide,[447] do not portend well for increased availability of abundant, lower-costing power to Californians of all income levels, but especially its poorest citizens.

When also considering that any new offshore oil and natural gas drilling has essentially been banned for the last four decades, it should come as no surprise today that energy outages, shortages, rolling-blackouts and emergencies have become fairly commonplace. It is not uncommon in southern California for "the lights to go out" unexpectedly for three or four hours during summer months, rendering havoc to food storage and home computer sys tems. Such black-outs disrupt not only residences but businesses that depend upon reliable electricity, such as supermarkets, whose losses as a result of refrigeration interruption can be substantial, while also posing health and safety hazards to the public. Energy prices, both from electric utilities and at the pump, have never been higher for Californians, and one report claims California's misguided liberal energy policies are responsible for raising costs to the consumer by 33% more than need be.[448] California increasingly has come to rely on one major source of energy: imported natural gas.[449] But in yet

---

445 http://www.marketwatch.com/story/
california-moves-quickly-to-block-new-coal-fired-power-plants

446 http://www.mercurynews.com/business/ci_23443908/
san-francsico-state-university-votes-divest-investment-coal

447 "Obama to call for carbon cuts at power plants," *USA Today*, June 25, 2013, 5A.

448 http://dailycaller.com/2013/01/24/
report-costly-state-energy-policies-to-raise-california-power-costs-by-33-percent/

449 http://www.reuters.com/article/2013/06/09/
us-utilities-sanonofre-natgas-analysis-idUSBRE95802620130609

another twist of liberal illogic, California state policy will not allow for new drilling for natural gas. Though natural gas is abundant in California and nationally, it is also more expensive than other sources of energy,[450] and 85% of it has to be imported from other states[451] because of various bans on extraction in California itself, adding to the expense to California consumers. Thus natural gas, which at one time was considered a cheap source of fuel, is getting more and more expensive to Californians.[452]

California has done an abysmal job exploiting its energy resources, which should be used to increase economic growth and employment. Crude oil production has actually fallen steadily and drastically over the last decades, and this persistent reduction in production coincides with California's statewide economic decline. According to state government statistics, statewide oil production in November of 1995 was at 971.3 thousand barrels per day[453]; but by November 2012 production had dropped to 536.3 thousand barrels per day[454], a loss of 46% annually.

Table on Oil Production

Oil Production (Mbbl per day)

	Nov-12	Oct-12	Sep-12	Aug-12	Jul-12	Jun-12
State Onshore	499.6	501.2	496	498.4	501.2	503.6
State Offshore	36.6	37.7	37.8	37.2	36.8	35.3
Total	536.3	539.0	533.8	535.6	538	538.9

---

450 Id.

451 http://www.energy.ca.gov/lng/

452 http://www.scpr.org/news/2013/07/24/38334/
california-power-prices-up-59-percent-after-san-on/

453 ftp://ftp.consrv.ca.gov/pub/oil/monthly_production_reports/1995/nov95/NOV95.TXT

454 ftp://ftp.consrv.ca.gov/pub/oil/monthly_production_reports/2012/Latestprod.pdf

	Nov-95	Oct-95	Sep-95	Aug-95	Jul-95	Jun-95
State Onshore	714.4	714.6	709.5	709.2	703.7	710
State Offshore	55	55.9	56	55.2	54.7	53.7
Federal OCS	201.9	198.1	191.9	204.1	196.1	203
Total	971.3	968.6	957.4	968.4	954.5	966.7

Offshore Oil:

California needs to change the way it regulates businesses for environmental issues for many reasons. But in particular it is time to get over the unfortunate Santa Barbara spill of 1969, an event that occurred before most of today's California residents were even born. California possesses huge offshore oil and gas resources that could be put to work through safe extraction technologies to expand the economy and create jobs. As for offshore extraction, there are currently 30 operating platforms, mostly off the coasts of Santa Barbara, Los Angeles, and Orange County that date back to before the Santa Barbara spill, and which have been operating safely without any major environmental issues for decades. But different Federal and state bans on further drilling as a result of the Santa Barbara spill have cut-off establishing new rigs for drilling and new exploration for the last four decades. Offshore oil extraction now accounts for only a little more than 7% of total statewide production per day,[455] significantly below capacity.

Since the 1969 Santa Barbara oil spill, California has responded by imposing an across-the-board ban on any development of new offshore oil leases. Liberals in the legislature codified the policy and added new prohibitions against new leasing in additional offshore areas in 1994 with the passage of the California Coastal Sanctuary Act. The Act states "*The legislature hereby finds and declares that offshore oil and gas production in certain areas of state waters poses an*

---

455 ftp://ftp.consrv.ca.gov/pub/oil/monthly_production_reports/2012/Latestprod.pdf

unacceptably high risk of damage and disruption to the marine environment of the state.[456]

At the time of passage, legislators were warned that the law was "unwise fiscal policy to take a significant source of potential revenue and lock it away through a permanent statutory ban."[457] The legislation created a de facto prohibition on all new leases in state coastal waters, but provided an arcane method to obtain a lease pursuant to application to the State Land Commission, where the lease was deemed "in the best interests of the state." The State Land Commission has not approved a new lease since 1968. During the past decade, the commission has adopted numerous resolutions opposing new leases in coastal waters.[458]

In 2008 President George W. Bush lifted an executive ban the White House had on further drilling off the California coast, a small step forward.[459] But opening up the coast for such exploration would require Federal and state cooperation. Republican Governor Schwarzenegger, rather than embracing the opportunity Bush's move presented, slammed it in the press while attending a climate change conference in Florida organized by then Republican Governor Charlie Crist.[460] Schwarzenegger said of ending the offshore drilling ban, "anyone who tells you this will lower our gas prices anytime soon is blowing smoke."[461] He confirmed to a local reporter in Florida that he was opposed to offshore oil drilling. The small

---

456 PUBLIC RESOURCES CODE , SECTION 6240-6244

457 State Senate Floor Analysis, August 23, 1994.

458 Legislative Analyst's Office Report, Presented to: Senate Budget and Fiscal Review Committee Hon. Denise Moreno Ducheny, Chair, "Tranquillon Ridge Offshore Oil and Gas Lease Agreement January 21, 2010,

459 Brennan, Pat. *Orange County Register.* "Bush lifts ban on new oil drilling off California." July 14, 2008.

460 http://abcnews.go.com/blogs/politics/2008/06/schwarzenegger-7/. Crist famously left the Republican Party and registered as a Democrat a few years late to run for U.S. Senate in Florida, in a race he lost.

461 Id.

door to economic expansion that George W. Bush opened was not completely closed in California until the rejection of the Tranquillon Ridge project and the terrible news of the British Petroleum spill in the Gulf of Mexico.

Despite the restrictions of the Coastal Sanctuary Act, the Tranquillon Ridge project was an initiative by the Houston-based Plains Exploration and Production Company for approval of a new gas and oil lease offshore from Santa Barbara County. The plan, which developed during 2008-2009, called for use of one of the pre-existing offshore platforms, known as Platform Irene, in so-called "Federal waters," to slant drill 14 wells into the coastal area controlled by state law, in order to access and recover an estimated 40 million to 90 million barrels of oil over a 14 year period.[462] Remember, under the Coastal Sanctuary Act, the state could approve the new leases if it determined it was in "the best interests of the state."[463] The Tranquillon plan was subject to an Environmental Impact Report that was prepared for the liberal Santa Barbara County government and the report estimated that, in the unlikely event of a spill, under the proposal the potential worst-case scenario would be less than 8,000 barrels. [464] In comparison, the 1969 Santa Barbara spill was estimated to be more than ten times as much, at 80,000 to 100,000 barrels as a result of a wellhead blowout.[465] Clearly, in the last 45 years, aspects of oil spill risk have declined as a result of technical advancements that increase the safety of oil production and improve oil spill prevention.

---

462 January 21, 2010, Legislative Analyst's Office Report, Presented to: Senate Budget and Fiscal Review Committee Hon. Denise Moreno Ducheny, Chair, "Tranquillon Ridge Offshore Oil and Gas Lease Agreement

463 PUBLIC RESOURCES CODE, SECTION 6240-6244 http://www.leginfo. ca.gov/cgi-bin/displaycode?section=prc&group=06001-07000&file=6240-6244

464 January 21, 2010, Legislative Analyst's Office Report, Presented to: Senate Budget and Fiscal Review Committee Hon. Denise Moreno Ducheny, Chair, "Tranquillon Ridge Offshore Oil and Gas Lease Agreement

465 Id.

Tranquillon's good environment impact report gained it some support from the Schwarzenegger administration and even the Environmental Defense Center, which won some environmental concessions from the developer during the review process. The State Senate even voted to approve the project. Nevertheless, in January 2009 the State Lands Commission rejected the application by a vote of 2-1, with Lieutenant Governor John Garamendi and Controller John Chiang opposing it, while the Department of Finance representative on the panel voted in favor.[466] After passage in the State Senate, in July 2009, the Assembly rejected approval of the project on a largely party-line vote, 43-30, even though estimates were that the project would not only help address persistent unemployment, but would generate $100 million a year for 15 years in oil royalty payments to the state.[467] Tranquillon was dead-in-the-water at that point, but the final blow occurred in May of 2010 when Governor Schwarzenegger, responding to news of the British Petroleum spill in the Gulf of Mexico, announced "[t]hat will not happen here in California, and this is why I am withdrawing my support for the T-Ridge project."[468] "The governor reacts impulsively to short-term events," said John Pitney, Jr., professor of American Politics at Claremont McKenna College. "If we had just had a gasoline shortage and a fire in a state park, these decisions would have come out the other way."[469]

Technology has dramatically transformed how oil and natural gas are found and produced. According to the industry, "Advances in computing power, miniaturization, and robotics in the past 10 to 15 years have given the industry the tools for recovering the national valuable oil and natural gas resources while enhancing efficiency,

---

466 Roberts, Jerry. "Key Schwarzenegger Aide: Governor's Offshore Plan Not An End Run," *Calbuzz.com*. May 15, 2009.

467 Woodall, Bernie. "California kills offshore oil lease project," Reuters, July 24, 2009.

468 Wood, Daniel B. *Christian Science Monitor*, "Citing BP oil spill, Schwarzenegger drops offshore drilling plan." May 4, 2010.

469 Id.

safety, and environmental protection."[470] And even since the British Petroleum spill in the Gulf of Mexico, improvements have been made in well-control technology, so-called "downhole" pressure management, and installation of "blowout" preventers and other equipment (such as frequently inspected pressure sensors) that are assuring unusual conditions can be quickly addressed. [471]

New technologies combined with active regulatory oversight for safety do make offshore extraction happen safely. Stringent regulatory oversight assures protection of the environment, and offshore operators are generally required to obtain 17 major federal permits and comply with 90 sets of federal and state regulations to operate, including frequent inspections by regulators.[472]

Rice University is at the forefront of research and development of even more early spill detection technologies. Rice is proposing a novel infrared sensor that has the potential to achieve unprecedented detection sensitivity. Such a system can be very low-cost and robust for automated outdoor operations, leading to massive offshore deployment.[473]

There is no question that the right technology now exists for "green," spill-free extraction of California's offshore oil if the state's policymakers can have the will and foresight to allow it. One such newer technology is directional or "slant" drilling, which is considered less risky than drilling through the sea floor from a platform in the water.[474] When combined with state-of-the-art automated systems that can shut off quickly in the event of a blow-out or spill, risks become so minimal that ignoring the economic benefits and not

470 http://www.api.org/~/media/Files/Policy/Exploration/environment/070319_Environmental_Harmony_Offshore.pdf

471 http://www.api.org/~/media/Files/Policy/Exploration/environment/Oil_Spill_Preparedness.pdf

472 American Petroleum Institute, http://www.api.org/environment-health-and-safety/clean-water/oil-spill-prevention-and-response/gulf-of-mexico-offshore

473 http://www.caam.rice.edu/tech_reports/2010_abstracts.html

474 Mai-Duc, Christine. Los Angeles Times. "Hermosa knows this drill." July 22, 2013.

allowing oil extraction simply becomes irrational. In the case of the small coastal community of Hermosa Beach in Los Angeles County, allowing a proposal for offshore oil drilling by the slant method will generate a huge $500 million windfall in tax revenue over 30 years and an additional $11.7 million for its school district,[475] not to mention the new jobs the project would create. Hermosa Beach citizens voted to approve new drilling more than 30 years ago but development became mired in legal controversy. A legal settlement with the developer may allow for the re-authorization of the proposal, with the state also benefitting from tax revenues for coastal improvement projects. In a cash-strapped economy, voter approval of the project could boost both interest in and prospects from renewed offshore oil exploitation statewide.

But in rejecting the Tranquillon Ridge project, a project that would have generated $1.5 billion in royalty revenue for the state over 15 years and expanded the economy while broadening the tax base, California's liberal policymakers chose to once again ignore the quite obvious economic benefits presented by an important development project in favor of doing nothing. It is this type of flawed decision-making, which is definitely not in the best interests of the state, and has contributed mightily to California's decline, its unnecessarily high unemployment, and its need to maintain taxes on its citizens at the very highest rates in the nation.

Fracking:

Californians and their policy makers need to throw off this liberal cloak of inaction and begin listening to the science that tells us that energy is and can be extracted safely. Allowing safe extraction could completely turn around California's financial problems and in short time. This not only includes lifting the ban on offshore oil drilling,

---

475 Id.

but also allowing for development by use of "fracking," immense shale deposits in California's Central Valley, away from the coast.

Fracking uses water and chemicals to shatter rock formations and release oil or gas. It involves pumping chemicals into wells to melt rocks and other impediments to oil flow. In the past, companies have not been required to "report" when they frack. In essence, new proposed regulations would require the companies to publicly report when and where they are fracking.[476]

According to a recent study by the University of Southern California, use of advanced oil-extraction technologies such as fracking in California, without a tax increase, could jump-start California's economic growth by 14.3%, grow state and local government revenues by $24.6 billion, and increase personal incomes up to 10%. Up to 2.8 million new jobs could be created in the state.[477] The USC study, titled "Powering California: The Monterey Shale & California's Economic Future," a joint project of the University's Public Policy and Engineering schools in association with The Communications Institute, identifies the shale in California's Central Valley as containing "vast reserves of oil,"[478] and concludes that "the prudent development of the Monterey shale could add hundreds of thousands of new jobs to California over the next decade while stimulating economic growth and generating significant new state and local tax revenues."[479]

California possesses a gigantic and almost entirely untapped resource in the 15.4 billion barrels of shale oil reserves lying under the 1,752 square mile Monterey shale deposit. The shale formation is unfortunately misnamed and has nothing to do with pristine Monterey Bay, stretching from inland Modesto in California's Central

---

476 http://www.reuters.com/article/2013/05/28/
us-california-oil-insight-idUSBRE94R0CO20130528

477 http://www.vcstar.com/news/2013/apr/14/
george-runner-a-severance-tax-will-cost-jobs/

478 http://gen.usc.edu/assets/001/84787.pdf

479 Id.

Valley south to Bakersfield, and includes only a limited coastal area in the Santa Maria Basin south of San Luis Obispo County. Based on a geological study by the U.S. Energy Information Administration (EIA), this region of California represents 64% of all shale oil reserves in the nation. To put this in perspective, according to EIA data, California's shale reserves in this region alone could conceivably feed the American oil appetite for roughly 2.2 years.[480] In the meantime, other states like Texas, North and South Dakota, Pennsylvania, and Ohio "are witnessing powerful economic revivals stimulated in part by a boom in oil and gas production."[481] According to Ohio Congressman Bob Gibbs, who chairs the House of Representatives Subcommittee on Water Resources and the Environment:

"in Pennsylvania alone, employment is projected to expand by over 180,000 jobs during 2012 in the Marcellus Shale region of the state,... and in my state of Ohio, activities associated with energy production from the Utica Shale will be responsible for generating more than 204,000 jobs and $12 billion in wages by 2015. In addition to the clear economic benefits of energy production through fracking, there is a national security benefit as well. Making greater use of domestic sources of energy reduces our dependence on foreign energy sources that are often unstable and unfriendly."[482]

North Dakota has done especially well exploiting shale deposits with newer extraction technologies, and the unemployment rate there is just 3.2%, the lowest in the nation, as a result. Back in Ohio, lawmakers have seen exploitation of the large Utica shale deposit as an important new way to improve employment in the state, and

---

480 Carson Bruno, *Advancing A Free Society.* "Sacramento Spotlight: A Cornucopia of Fracking Legislation," April 4, 2013,

481 http://gen.usc.edu/assets/001/84787.pdf

482 November 16, 2011, Subcommittee Hearing Focuses on Ensuring Regulatory Approaches to Hydraulic Fracturing that Will Help Protect U.S. Jobs; House Transportation and Infrastructure Committee News Release

have ensured that the state Department of Natural Resources can assist industry in obtaining needed land leases and help even reluctant landowners in obtaining fair compensation for below surface drilling with no rigs or equipment above land, including payment of 100% of the value of the oil and gas once a drilling company recovers twice its costs to drill the well.[483]

There are many good reasons for allowing California to join with other states in approving safe oil extraction through fracking, not the least of which is contributing to America's energy security. However, jobs and economic growth at a time of high unemployment are among the best reasons to free California's shale deposits to extraction.

The idea of developing California's shale deposits is actually receiving some positive attention. Veteran columnist Daniel Weintraub has written that the traditional powers of California's economy—technology, trade, and tourism, have not rendered much by way of high-paying jobs and tax production for Central Valley residents, and that unlocking California's oil shale could be an important way to achieve a much better economy in the Valley and throughout the state in future.[484] Weintraub acknowledges that "environmental protection is one of California's passions"[485] and that might cause liberal policymakers to reflexively stop what would otherwise be a very rational decision to help elevate the state from its economic problems. And Weintraub says, "Gov. Jerry Brown, who all his life has straddled the line between environmentalists and the business world, seems eager to see fracking move forward in California, if he can be assured it can be done safely."[486] If Weintraub is correct, on shale, Jerry Brown would prove himself to be hardly the reflexive liberal that Arnold Schwarzenegger was in rejecting

---

483 "State Forces Fracking on Some Owners," *Columbus Dispatch*, May 25, 2013, A12.

484 http://www.ocregister.com/articles/oil-507858-california-state.html

485 Id.

486 Id.

efforts to open California's coasts to more drilling. Time will tell, but the real problem is that liberal Democrats in the legislature are predictably doing exactly the opposite of what is needed in the state. They have predictably attempted to enact legislation placing a moratorium on all fracking in the state,[487] which could last until 2019. Both new offshore oil drilling *and* fracking would be banned in the meantime. Industry spokespeople have provided the liberal Democrats with testimony that hydraulic fracking has been used successfully in California in at least nine counties for many years, is not destructive, and has never been associated with environmental harm.[488] But such facts have had little influence on California's liberal Democratic lawmakers, who are content to keep unemployment high and economic development low in the state. They ignore these glaringly obvious solutions to job creation while unemployment continues to be endemic, at 9.6% in early 2013, well outpacing the national unemployment rate of 7.6%, and placing California in the dubious distinction as having the third highest unemployment of any state in the Union.[489] Though there are reports of jobless claims starting to drop across the country as the recession in the rest of the nation eases, California is moving in exactly the opposite direction and is still seeing the largest increases in such claims in the nation.[490] California desperately needs to do something about joblessness, and fracking can be an answer for hard-hit Central Valley residents.

California already has about 50,000 producing oil and gas wells scattered throughout the state, of which about 750 (or 1.5%) already use hydraulic fracturing. But while fracking has been used safely in

---

487 Herdt, Timm. *Ventura County Star.* "Assembly committee passes three bills to impose fracking moratorium." April 29, 2013.

488 Bacher, Dan. California Progress Report. "California Anti-Fracking Bills Move Forward, Now Face Appropriations Vote." May 24, 2013.

489 *Los Angeles Times,* April 20, 2013, B1. http://articles.latimes.com/2013/apr/19/business/la-fi-mo-california-jobs-unemployment-20130419

490 Wiese, Melissa. LA Business Journal. "California jobless claims jump by 8,000." June 6, 2013.

California for more than 60 years, the state is now giving greater focus to regulations and legislation to govern the drilling practice,[491] presumably because it has finally caught the attention of environmental advocates looking for more to regulate in California's economy.

Voters in California are still deciding what they think about fracking as the issue comes more to the public policy forefront. The same USC that issued the report on the significant economic benefits of fracking in California, recently conducted a poll on voter attitudes about the environmental and health impacts, and found that 46% of voters supported a ban on the use of fracking that could only be lifted by the legislature, while 42% opposed such a ban. [492] However, voter support for fracking increases when potential economic benefits are explained, with more than 56% of California voters supporting it if it results in lower oil and gas prices.[493] Clearly, the more information that California voters have about fracking's benefits, the more they support it.

Some environmental groups have been at work for a long time helping to develop regulation templates for states that allow for the public disclosure of fracking sites. Earthjustice, a San Francisco nonprofit that acts as a law firm for the Sierra Club and other major environmental groups, led D.C.-based Earthworks and four other environmental groups in negotiations with industry officials and state regulators in Colorado. According to a news release, Earthjustice was "instrumental" in a "positive outcome" that requires "full disclosure of the substances used in the fracking process" in that state.[494] An Earthjustice attorney even told The Associated Press that the Colorado rule provides "a full picture of what's in that fracking

491 Carson Bruno, "Sacramento Spotlight: A Cornucopia of Fracking Legislation," April 4, 2013, http://www.advancingafreesociety.org/eureka/sacramento-spotlight-a-cornucopia-of-fracking-legislation/

492 http://dornsife.usc.edu/usc-dornsife-la-times-poll-fracking-june-2013/

493 http://dornsife.usc.edu/usc-dornsife-la-times-poll-fracking-june-2013/

494 http://earthjustice.org/news/press/2011/colorado-adopts-new-fracking-disclosure-rule

fluid." Meanwhile, Earthworks called the Colorado rule a "victory" that "elevates the community right-to-know principle (disclosure) above the narrow economic principle of protecting corporate property." As for other green groups, the Environmental Defense Fund called the negotiations in Colorado "an example of how government and industry and the environmental community can work together," and Colorado Conservation Voters declared: "The clear winners of the rule-making today are the citizens of Colorado."[495]

The new public notice rules for California essentially mirror those in Colorado, but now the same environmental groups have teamed up to actually oppose their implementation in California, in a blatant flip-flop, to now put focus on the actual types of chemicals used in the process. Like California's proposed rules, Colorado's existing regulations require the composition of hydraulic fracturing fluids to be disclosed, with protections for trade secrets and provisions to ensure regulators and health professionals have full access to all the information they need. But while industry appears willing to follow the rules and make public disclosures about the chemicals they use, they are understandably not willing to disclose processes they have invested in that are trade secrets. It is insistence of disclosure of such trade secrets, and nonscientific-based concerns about the fracking process by the environmental lobby and their liberal Democratic allies that threatens progress on developing the Central Valley shale, and the tremendous boost to California's economy it offers.

California is capable of addressing reasonable concerns about fracking. Democratic State Senator Fran Pavley has told State Legislators that Californians should have nothing to fear from so-called "acidization" in the fracking process and has introduced a bill to allow fracking and regulate it.[496] But that has not stopped lathered environmental protestors, lead by the hard-left wing political action

495 Dave Quast, "Fracking rule proposal in California is like Colorado's," *San Jose Mercury News*, January 14, 2013.

496 Herdt, Timm. Ventura County Star. "State Regulator Says Oil Industry's Use of Acids to Unlock Shale Reserve Is Safe." June 18, 2013.

committee MoveOn.org, from staging protests against the bill and fracking at her district office in Calabasas.[497]

The Heritage Foundation has published a report that clarifies that in California, drilling permits may not be issued unless chemical disclosures, source of water used in the process, and analysis of drilling injection fluid are disclosed with monthly updates. Permits require reports on groundwater protection and include mandates for protection of aquifers. The process requires onsite approvals of state drilling experts. Wastewater must be properly disposed of through a plan that meets strict State Water Resources Board requirements under the direction of state regulators.[498] Representatives of oil companies including Chevron and Los Angeles-based Occidental Petroleum Corp., the largest oil producer in the continental U.S., have said they support the disclosure rules. "We think it's an appropriate framework to provide people the confidence that oil is produced prudently and safely and under stringent oversight by the state of California," said Hull, a spokesman for the Western States Petroleum Association.[499]

According to Bloomberg News, Kern County produces more than 80 percent of California's oil and gas of which roughly 600 of its 50,000 active oil wells are already hydraulically fractured each year.[500] "We don't have any evidence that there's impact on ground water from hydraulic fracturing in Kern County," Lorelei Oviatt, director of the county planning department, told a reporter. "I don't want to leap to conclusions that will put 15,000 to 20,000 people out of work."[501]

---

497 http://calabasas.patch.com/groups/around-town/p/
activists-protest-pavleys-compromise-bill-to-regulate-hydraulic-fracturing

498 Nicolas D. Loris, "Hydraulic Fracturing: Critical for Energy Production, Jobs, and Economic Growth," Backgrounder No. 2714, August 28, 2012.

499 Alison Vekshin, "California Fracking Fight Has $25 Billion Taxes at Stake," *Bloomberg*, March 17, 2013.

500 Id.

501 Id.

Nevertheless, liberal Democrats have been intent on urging a complete ban on fracking. Three bills introduced in 2013 would all institute an immediate moratorium on the procedure pending commissioned scientific studies. While not an overt moratorium, the intent of Democratic Senator Hannah-Beth Jackson's SB 395, which would broadly define "produced water" and classify it as a hazardous waste material, is to effectively ban the fracking process.

Even worse, after the San Onofre closure, a bill by Assembly Speaker John Perez would alter California's energy policy to give state preferences to solar, wind, and geothermal power instead of energy efficiency and energy generated from clean fossil fuels such as natural gas.[502] Yet a state commission, known as the Little Hoover Commission, has called for a "timeout" on new green energy mandates because of the energy crisis the state faces.[503] Perez's bill demonstrates that the liberal Democrats in control of the state simply do not grasp the magnitude of the sorrow they inflict on residents of the state by their Pollyannaish attitude about power generation in the state.

Misguided liberal policies on the environment have added insult to injury in attempts to develop so-called "clean" sources of energy, such as solar and wind power, with the cancellation of a proposed massive 500-megawatt Rio Mesa solar energy project in the southern California desert, because of concerns for fossil deposits, the effect of "solar flux" on birds, and conflict with local native tribes.[504] Likewise, when six golden eagles were found dead in the Tehachapi Mountains in 2011, also in southern California, and their deaths were attributed to a nearby windmill farm owned by the Los Angeles Department of Water and Power, concerns of environmentalists were

---

502 Lusvardi, Wayne. *CalWatchdog.com.* "New bill would short-circuit Hoover call for green power 'timeout'" June 11, 2013.

503 Id.

504 Clarke, Chris. *KCET.* "Another Large Solar Power Project Canceled in California." July 3, 2013.

raised about wind power.[505] As a result, a proposed 84 megawatt windmill farm between Barstow and the Lucerne Valley that "had been in the works for over a decade" and would have sold power to Southern California Edison was cancelled by the developer because of environmental regulation.[506] If both of the highly touted energy alternatives, solar and wind projects, are to be added to the list for cancellation for environmental concerns, then the energy policy the liberal Democrats have put in place in California leaves the state almost completely at the mercy of one increasingly expensive source of energy: imported natural gas.[507]

California needs an energy policy that not only provides a reliable source of inexpensive energy, but that also creates jobs. It can be done by allowing regulated "green" offshore drilling again and opening the Central Valley shale deposit to development through fracking. These steps would turn on an economic dynamo that would revive growth and Jobs in the oil industry, in every sector up and down the supply chain, and increase income and consumer spending. California would gain new skilled workers and the state unemployment rate would fall significantly and for a sustained period of time. It is time for California to emerge out of its "no development" box when it comes to energy resources and allow the private sector to revive the California Dream by fast-tracking approval of development of the Central Valley shale.

---

505 http://articles.washingtonpost.com/2011-08-28/
national/35269438_1_wind-turbines-wind-farms-wind-power

506 http://www.kcet.org/news/rewire/wind/another-desert-wind-project-dropped.html

507 The extreme emphasis that California's environmental activists put on the environment above rational public works development extends beyond just energy issues. A concern for disturbing some cranes in the Sacramento Delta by tunneling under an island they inhabit for a needed $15 billion tunnel to move fresh water has stalled and set-up a big and distracting public policy battle. http://www.modbee.com/2013/09/01/2896227/new-water-tunnel-route-sets-up.html

LIBERALISM IS BANKRUPTING CALIFORNIA

CALIFORNIA AND ITS LOCAL governments are at least $648 billion in debt and depending upon how public employee pension liabilities are calculated, the debt could be as high as $1.1 trillion.[508] Such a high level of "red ink" by public agencies is simply unsustainable in the future for California.

Yet, speaking to the California Democratic Party state convention in 2013, State Senate President Pro Tem Darrell Steinberg summed up the substance of liberal fiscal policy for the state: "No more cuts to education, to healthcare, to public safety, or help to those in need."[509] Clearly, in the depth of fiscal crisis and saddled with among the highest sustained unemployment rates in the country and highest tax rates in the nation, Steinberg and his liberal brethren do not consider taxpayers as among "those in need," when they continue their out-of-control spending policies. They should, for the sake of California's future.

---

508 http://blogs.sacbee.com/capitolalertlatest/2013/04/california-governments-could-be-11-trillion-in-debt.html

509 http://www.breitbart.com/Big-Government/2013/04/15/CA-Sen-President-no-more-cuts

California state government is in crisis because liberals like Steinberg, who are firmly in control, refuse to stop taxing and spending. But this liberal "blank check" philosophy on public spending, which has gotten the state government into so much fiscal trouble, isn't limited to the State capitol. Sadly, the liberal spending spree runs up-and-down the state, as local elected offices have been dominated by union-controlled politicians, or officials have simply failed to have the political will to stand up to their public employee unions.

There is no more important problem in the state of California than its public employee pension system, which is far too generous, and greatly underfunded to meet future obligations. According to CalPERS own data, there are now 14,763 retired public employees in California earning pensions of $100,000 or more per year.[510] California has seen an increase of 700% of such $100,000-plus pensions in less than a decade. "Unbelievable!" said the head of the California Foundation for Fiscal responsibility.[511] Some pensions that have been set in the current unsustainable system are more than unbelievable. A city manager of tiny Vernon in Los Angeles County who was paid an incredible $911,000 a year before being convicted of misappropriating funds, left his job with a pension in the CalPERS system that topped $500,000 annually. In the wake of press accounts of local bankruptcies and reports of pension abuses, even CalPERS took action to reduce the 78-year-old retiree's annual pension to $115,000, claiming he fudged what he was entitled too when he retired.[512] The pension reduction is now mired in litigation, but even at a reduced $115,000 annually, the retired public employee still enjoys a benefit well above the average annual salary of his fellow Californians.

Stockton, with a population of nearly 300,000, is the county seat

---

510 http://www.ocregister.com/articles/city-515888-100k-club.html

511 Id.

512 http://articles.latimes.com/2013/jul/23/local/
la-me-ln-la-now-live-vernon-pension-lawsuit-20130723-dto

of San Joaquin County, an important Central Valley location south of Sacramento known for its leadership in agriculture, manufacturing, and transportation. Stockton itself is among the larger cities in the state, ranked at 13th largest. It sits on a plain where California's major north/south highways, Interstate 5 and State Route 99, intersect. The area was once populated by the Yokut and Miwok Indians who lived among the nearby rivers and Sacramento delta's waterways, and it grew out of a Mexican land grant known as the Rancho Campo de los Franceses, or French Camp, referring to French-Canadian fur trappers who wintered there. Stockton developed with the Gold Rush and incorporated as one of California's oldest cities in 1850. It thrived after the Gold Rush as well, as settlers introduced mechanization to the agriculture industry, spawning companies such as the Holt Manufacturing Company, whose first workable tractors came to be known as Caterpillars.[513]

Today Stockton boasts a developed downtown area with moderate high rise buildings, ample public art, a yacht marina, sports facilities, museums, and an important deep-water port in the heart of Central California. This port is connected to the San Francisco Bay through a 78-mile channel of the San Joaquin River, which allows for economic shipping of agriculture production. Stockton is also home to the charming undergraduate campus of the University of the Pacific, founded in 1851 and California's first chartered university.[514]

Stockton has always been a culturally diverse city. In 1870 the Census Bureau reported a significant Asian population of 10.7%, a remnant of the Gold Rush and expansion of railroads with Asian labor.[515]

Can there be any better proof of the failure of liberalism in California when the city of Stockton, with all it has going for it, had its

---

513 Ralph Lea, "Ben Holt pioneered tractors for farming, construction, war," Lodi *News-Sentinel*, February 16, 2008, Retrieved February 27, 2008.

514 http://www.pacific.edu/Admission/Undergraduate/Pacific-At-A-Glance.html

515 "California - Race and Hispanic Origin for Selected Cities and Other Places: Earliest Census to 1990," U.S. Census Bureau.

new City Hall building foreclosed on and repossessed by the bank because the city couldn't afford to make its bond payments?[516] The bank had already repossessed three downtown parking garages the city had owned but defaulted on, and those losses helped prompt the city to seek bankruptcy protection. It filed its petition for bankruptcy protection under Chapter 9 in July 2012.[517] Until Detroit's recent filing, it was the largest city in American history to declare bankruptcy.[518] The Stockton bankruptcy is especially important because, along with smaller San Bernardino's similar bankruptcy application, the issue of whether these city governments' greatly underfunded public employee pension liabilities are considered ordinary debts that can be discharged in bankruptcy or deserve special privileges in bankruptcy court, will be decided, with "incalculable impacts" for other massive pension underfunding throughout the rest of California.[519]

Stockton seems to be trying to shield its pension liability from discharge in bankruptcy and shed other debts. According to a published account, Matthew Walsh, attorney for National Public Finance Guarantee Corp., stated that Stockton acted in bad faith when it sought "no concessions" from its obligations to CalPERS while refusing to negotiate with the creditors that issued bonds for the city's $68 million downtown arena.[520] Perhaps Stockton's eminent failure could have been predicted, as such collapses don't just happen overnight. Indeed, in the 2000s, Stockton policy-makers started to rapidly accumulate public debt.

---

516 http://latimesblogs.latimes.com/lanow/2012/05/bank-repossesses-near-bankrupt-stocktons-new-city-hall-building.html

517 "Stockton bankruptcy talks may soon be made public," In reuters.com. July 7, 2012, Retrieved February 16, 2013.

518 http://www.sacbee.com/2013/03/28/5298519/judge-to-rule-monday-on-whether.html#mi_rss=Capitol%20and%20California

519 http://www.sacbee.com/2013/09/16/5738629/dan-walters-bankruptcy-confronts.html

520 Id.

The multimillion dollar arena that attorney Walsh complained of was completed in 2005 as a hockey arena,[521] but with no professional hockey team committed to play there. Also in 2005, a minor league baseball team began playing in another taxpayer-financed stadium.[522] As the storyline goes, the city intended by these expensive amenities to woo Bay Area residents seeking lower home prices, but recession hit, and the city went bust.[523]

Yet that is not the whole story.

From 2000-2005, the city's population grew by 20% and real estate grew steadily in value. But by 2006 home prices were dropping, and dropping sharply.[524] Still, Stockton didn't stop the public spending. In 2008 the city had accumulated almost $1 billion in public debt on civic amenities, such as the unused professional hockey arena and the minor league baseball park, as well as unfunded liabilities for public employee pensions and healthcare. In the meantime, consistent with California's changing demographics, Latino and Asian families continued to drive Stockton's further growth, and by 2012 more than 40% of the city's 300,000 population was Latino, and 21.5% was Asian.[525]

In 2012 Stockton was ranked the 10th most dangerous place in the nation, and the second most dangerous place in California, just behind Oakland.[526] Stockton today ranks fourth in the nation for the highest rate of automobile theft per resident.[527] It was also

---

521 http://www.azcentral.com/news/free/20130324california-stockton-bankruptcy court-economy.html; Associated Press report, March 24, 2013.

522 Id.

523 Id.

524 Id.

525 http://www.usa.com/stockton-ca.htm

526 Abby Rogers, "The 25 Most Dangerous Cities in America," Finance.yahoo.com, November 1, 2012. Retrieved February 16, 2013.

527 http://www.centralvalleybusinesstimes.com/stories/001/?ID=23728

ranked in 2013 as one of the most illiterate places in the country.[528] Even Stockton's 35-parish Roman Catholic Diocese is broke, financially reeling from sex-abuse lawsuits[529] and headed to bankruptcy court.[530] The acquisition of such negative distinctions just doesn't happen overnight. And with respect to its financial collapse, Stockton had been ramping up for some time, and it has been caused by liberal spending policies and catering to public employee unions.

There is disagreement about whether bankruptcy court is even a good idea for overspending cities like Stockton. One observer argues that granting Stockton bankruptcy protection will allow that city and others in the future to offload debt on bond insurers and bondholders without having to confront the main reason for such bankruptcies in the first place, which he states is "union greed."[531] According to Steven Greenhut, public services and taxpayers suffer first, while union members and public retirement systems are protected in bankruptcy.[532] Greenhut's position has merit, especially because the city has refused to cut pensions to trim its budget. Greenhut well understands how Stockton came to its is bankruptcy and cites the court testimony of City Council member Kathy Miller who stated, "In the 1990s, Stockton granted its employees some of the most generous and unsustainable labor contracts in the State of California. . . . Safety employees could not retire at the age of 50. . . . Many safety retirees today earn 90 to 100 percent of what they made when they were still on the job."[533]

The road to disaster included much more according to council

---

528 http://homes.yahoo.com/news/america-s-most-and-least-literate-cities-224612878.html

529 http://sanfrancisco.cbslocal.com/2013/06/15/stockton-bishop-diocese-broke/

530 http://www.capradio.org/9942

531 Steven Greenhut, http://www.utsandiego.com/news/2013/mar/30/stockton-bankruptcy-unions-lessons/

532 Id.

533 Id.

member Miller. "Stockton went even further . . . and granted unlimited vacation and sick time that could be cashed out when an employee retired. . . . Our public safety employees were costing us on average more than $150,000 a year each. That's three times more than most of us in Stockton make in a year."

Stockton has since won some concessions on salaries from its public employee unions so that essential public services can continue while its bankruptcy is worked out in a long contentious process. Riddled with crime, the city has been able to hire a few more police officers to address its burgeoning crime problem, due to a concession averaging 23% in pay by current city employees.[534] But the sad reality is, given its crime problem and history of poor financial management, Stockton will not be receiving any new investments by the business community or the new private-sector jobs they bring for some time.

An editorial in the *San Diego Union-Tribune* brings even more clarity to the Stockton financial disaster. Among Stockton's creditors is CalPERS, but the city is not seeking to discharge those debts citing a state law giving priority to such pensions. At the time of its bankruptcy filing, Stockton owed CalPERS $900 million making it the city's biggest creditor.[535] The Wall Street firms that funded the bonds, such as for the little used hockey arena and the baseball stadium, stood to lose as much as $165 million. But the city and the pension fund have argued in bankruptcy court that under California laws the funds owed to CalPERS should take precedence over other creditors.[536] In other words, the people who loaned the city money for its own public works spending spree should take the hit before the pensions created by the city's decision to provide lavish

534 http://www.sacbee.com/2013/04/03/5311792/next-steps-in-stockton-will-be.html#mi_rss=Opinion

535 http://www.utsandiego.com/news/2013/apr/02/stockton-calpers-bankruptcy-pensions-chapter-nine/

536 Id.

retirement benefits to its employees. CalPERS' actuary has more recently called for a formula that includes public employees actually contributing to their own retirement system to help solve the problem. But the *Union-Tribune* writes that public employee unions reject that idea because they feel it will make pay increases less likely. The newspaper calls that mindset "daffy, greedy, destructive (and) incoherent..."[537] yet the unions remain adamant in their position and the case remains in bankruptcy court, with taxpayers ultimately on the line for the losses.

In the meantime, Stockton predictably is considering tax increases to cover its awful financial decisions, including a sales tax increase,[538] which will hit lower income families with high unemployment the hardest.

The Stockton bankruptcy does not stand by itself as an example of the dire consequences of runaway spending and imprudent fiscal policies among California cities. San Bernardino, a city about two-thirds the size of Stockton and located in southern California, also followed Stockton into bankruptcy court. San Bernardino's bankruptcy is a little different though. In its case the city completely stopped making its CalPERS pension contribution payments as well as stiffing bond sellers and insurers in favor of funding other city services like police, and CalPERS opposed the San Bernardino bankruptcy application for that reason.[539] The city simply ran out of money and stopped making their pension contributions to CalPERS and the accumulated debt over time has grown to more than $12 million.[540] Now San Bernardino intends to resume its contributions to the pension fund but whether CalPERS will do a "work-out" for the unpaid contributions is a major bone of contention, because it

537 Id.

538 http://www.reuters.com/article/2013/06/21/
usa-stockton-bankruptcy-budget-idUSL2N0EX1DU20130621

539 http://www.sbsun.com/opinions/ci_22928797/
bankruptcy-ok-would-apply-san-bernardino-well?source=rss

540 http://calpensions.com/2013/05/06/calpers-wont-refinance-san-bernardinos-debt/

could set a precedent with other local governments who might seek an exit for some of their own liabilities to the fund. So far CalPERS is taking a hard-line with San Bernardino. "California law provides for statutory interest, penalty interest, penalties and costs of collection, all of which are accruing and will continue to accrue until the past due amounts are paid in full," said CalPERS spokeswoman Amy Norris.[541] Nevertheless, a U.S. Bankruptcy Court judge ruled San Bernardino was eligible for Chapter 9 bankruptcy, over the objections of CalPERS, even though it had stopped making $1.2 million bimonthly payments for pensions.[542] Some of the city's pension obligations therefore may ultimately become discharged in bankruptcy court, with huge implications for other California cities.

With pressure from creditors like CalPERS, San Bernardino has moved more aggressively to cut some city employee benefits, and that has irked the public employee unions. San Bernardino maintains a rare city policy that seemingly puts its public safety employee salary and benefits before taxpayer interests. That is because the City Charter of San Bernardino contains a provision that can only be changed by a vote of the people, requiring police and fire salaries to be adjusted each year based on the average pay of 10 similarly sized communities, regardless of the City's actual ability to pay those rates.[543] This policy stands in contrast to what most California Charter Cities do, which is to negotiate periodic contract renewals with the police and fire unions. "It's clearly outside what most professional managers consider good practice," said Kevin Duggan, West Coast regional director for the International City/County Management Association.[544]

Stockton and San Bernardino may not be California's only

541 Id.

542 http://www.californiacitynews.org/2013/08/san-bernardino-eligible-chapter-9-bankruptcy.html

543 http://www.sbsun.com/opinions/ci_23037613/san-bernardino-charter-puts-public-safety-salaries-ahead?source=rss

544 Id.

bankrupt cities. *USA Today* has predicted 10 more cities in California are candidates to declare bankruptcy and they include major population centers such as, San Jose and Fresno, as well as smaller cities like Compton, Monrovia, and Azusa.[545] Potential bankruptcies are threatening government units both large and small. The city council of Adelanto, a small desert community in San Bernardino, declared a "fiscal emergency" because its annual tax revenues of $4.5 million are not enough to cover its $7 million annual police and fire personnel costs. And according to a consultant to the California State Treasurer, the Foothill-Eastern Corridor Agency, which operates 39 miles of toll highways in Orange County, is at risk to default on $2.4 billion in accumulated bond debt.[546]

Oakland's public employee unions, specifically the SEIU, and the International Federation of Professional & Technical Engineers (IFPTE), threatened a strike because the city is broke and can't offer their members significant raises,[547] and followed through on their threats with a general strike of all city workers, including transit workers, for one-day during negotiations with the city officials.[548] "[T]he working class in Northern California are mad as hell, and we're not going to take it anymore," said one union representative to cheers at a union rally before the strike. [549] But the average SEIU employee already costs the city $87,514 in salary and pension benefits, while the average IFPTE worker costs the city $133,825 per year,[550] and both

545 http://www.californiacitynews.org/2013/05/more-california-cities-may-face-bankruptcy.html

546 http://www.businessweek.com/news/2013-09-11/california-road-near-biggest-default-since-detroit-muni-credit#p1

547 http://www.insidebayarea.com/breaking-news/ci_23388933/oakland-unions-threaten-strike

548 http://www.sfgate.com/bayarea/article/Oakland-city-workers-to-strike-on-Monday-4637160.php

549 http://www.sfgate.com/bayarea/article/Oakland-city-workers-to-strike-on-Monday-4637160.php

550 http://www.insidebayarea.com/breaking-news/ci_23388933/oakland-unions-threaten-strike

salary levels already well-exceed all standard definitions of "working class." Such well-paid public employees contrast greatly with the rest of Oakland's population, which suffered the highest homicide rate in the state in 2012 at 130—90% gun-related;[551] where the average per capita worker income is just $30,671, (and more in line with what "working class" means) and 18.7% of the city's population, estimated at 71,599 individuals, live in poverty.[552]

In sunny San Diego County, the cost of its public employee retirement system has grown by 37% since 2010, rising over $100 million and hitting $418 million in 2013, according to a study by the San Diego County Taxpayers Association.[553] An official of the Association said that the increases in pension costs "lead to increased costs to residents, and they see declined services because their tax costs are going to pension costs as opposed to the normal day-to-day services government should be providing."[554]

Even in the verdant, rolling hills in the heart of California's picturesque and relatively wealthy wine country, Sonoma County is financially struggling with an inability to care for 1,400 miles of largely worn-out roads that will require $1.6 billion to repair— money that the County simply doesn't have largely because of public employee pension costs.[555] "[A] toxic combination of inflated public employee salaries and pensions, combined with reckless financial decision-making and the 2008 housing market crash and subsequent recession have stripped that financial cupboard bare" states one news story about Sonoma's financial problems. This has drastically reduced road maintenance budgets so the county can afford

---

551 http://articles.latimes.com/2013/sep/14/local/la-me-oakland-gun-law-20130914; http://www.sfgate.com/crime/article/Crime-up-in-Oakland-much-of-Bay-Area-4573391.php

552 http://www.bayareacensus.ca.gov/cities/Oakland.htm

553 http://www.utsandiego.com/news/2013/jun/07/county-pension-costs-rising-sdcta/

554 Id.

555 http://www.reuters.com/article/2013/05/29/us-usa-pensions-sonoma-idUSBRE94S0GP20130529

to spend money on public employee pensions which have grown 400% since 2000.[556] Sonoma County does not pay into CalPers; it is one of the few government entities that have established their own pension system. However, with an annual budget of just about $1 billion, unfunded pension liabilities from too generous salary and pension decisions in the past could reach $527 million in 2013, not including the $489 million that will be paid to workers in the same year, and the $46.5 million the county must pay to service its acknowledged pension debt of another $619 million.[557] Of course there is no money to pay for road maintenance, or any other public service in the county, as funds are completely committed to public employee salaries and benefits, and that scenario could very well lead to bankruptcy for lovely Sonoma County.

Chico, located in northeastern California where rice is a huge agricultural export for the state, is $24.3 million in debt,[558] even after cutting its annual budget by close to 30% from 2013 to 2014 to $105,000,000.[559] "Although we have made a lot of cuts, it remains to be seen if we have cut enough," said the city's administrative services director.[560]

Some cities that are in the CalPERS system have considered leaving it to get better financial control of their own pension systems, but the price-tag to do so is usually too high to enable reform. In financially troubled Modesto, voters passed three nonbinding public employee pension reform proposals in 2011 which called for the city to replace its defined-benefit plan with CalPERS with a 401(k)-style

---

556 Id.

557 Id.

558 http://www.chicoer.com/news/ci_23781312/
city-chicos-capital-projects-fund-carries-2-5

559 http://www.chico.ca.us/finance/documents/2013-14CityAnnualPROPOSED-
Budget.pdf

560 http://www.chicoer.com/news/ci_23781312/
city-chicos-capital-projects-fund-carries-2-5

plan that would require some employee contributions.[561] But when Modesto asked CalPERS for an estimate of what it would cost the city to severe their retirement plan, CalPERS said it would need to be paid between $1.1 billion and $1.26 billion, almost one billion dollars more than the city had expected.[562] With a $11.8 million general fund shortfall this fiscal year,[563] Modesto can neither afford to reform its public employee system by severing from CalPERS, let alone pay for the underfunded retirement plan it currently has with CalPERS. The result is to cut public service positions like firefighters. But even in lowering overall payroll, bitter consequences have resulted in salaries skyrocketing for the remaining employees because of overtime. One engineer who kept his job with the city saw his base pay more than double from $83,173 to $171,708 for the year.[564] Stuck with an inability to reform its pensions, Modesto has little alternative but to drastically scale back the services it is expected to provide, while doubling salaries of remaining employees. It is an obviously unsustainable scenario.

Bankruptcies are threatened not only in California's cities and counties, but also its school and public safety districts. The troubled Inglewood Unified School District is mired in more than $17 million of debt in the most recent school year, and it is currently in state-run receivership, the ninth such school district in California's history to do so.[565] Administrators plan to lay off 177 employees of the school district in all employee categories to make ends meet.[566]

---

561 http://www.modbee.com/2013/01/16/2535858/leaving-calpers-would-cost-modesto.html

562 Id.

563 http://www.modbee.com/2013/06/08/2754136/18-million-shortfall-projected.html

564 http://www.modbee.com/2013/06/08/2754136/18-million-shortfall-projected.html

565 http://www.dailybreeze.com/news/ci_23346852/inglewood-unified-school-district-at-risk-being-vaporized?source=rss

566 Id.

According to the Administrator, the Contra Costa County Fire Protection District, the biggest such district in San Francisco's East Bay, will be bankrupt in 2016 without changes or more money to solve its underfunded pensions problem.[567] According to a news report, a generous pension plan adopted by the county Board of Supervisors in 2002 has "driven the district to the financial edge" with more than 25% of its annual fire safety budget now being gobbled up for its rapidly growing pension payment obligations. To make ends meet, the district has already closed 28 fire stations. But more firings and less fire protection services are in store as the district's available fire safety funds become more and more consumed by pensions.

The sad case of local governments drowning in pension obligations and even teetering on bankruptcy because of poor decisions on public employee salaries, benefits, and pension management repeats itself again and again in localities where government officials simply gave in to public employee union demands which they simply could not afford. In otherwise conservative Orange County, the unfunded public employee pension liability has skyrocketed due to generous benefit increases put in place by Republican supervisors in 2000, another enhancement in 2004, and actuarial changes and investment losses.[568] Estimated at $1 billion in 2004, the unfunded liability, or long-term gap between pension obligations and revenues in Orange County government, is currently estimated at $5 billion.[569] In San Mateo County, a residential suburb just south of San Francisco on its peninsula, a grand jury investigation and report determined that the unfunded liabilities of the San Mateo County Employees' Retirement Association were understated by nearly $1 billion by the Association, which was criticized for using unrealistic assumptions about the rate of growth of investments. "The problem is huge," said

567 http://www.contracostatimes.com/daniel-borenstein/ci_23976160/
daniel-borenstein-pensions-driving-east-bays-largest-fire

568 http://www.voiceofoc.org/county/article_a1a60910-1a22-11e3-9d02-
0019bb2963f4.html

569 Id.

jury Foreman Timothy Johnson, Jr.[570] With unfunded liabilities near $2 billion, the grand jury "excoriated" the San Mateo County Board of Supervisors for failing to properly monitor the investments, said the elected officials should have supported larger contributions to the pension fund they approved in order to reduce the shortfall, and said the County must look for more substantive ways to reduce employee retirement costs going forward.[571]

In nearby San Jose, in June of 2012 nearly 70% of voters approved a city-sponsored ballot initiative known as Measure B, reducing pensions for new public employee hires and requiring current employees to pay more of their own pensions or accept a lower benefit formula. Of course, the city's unions are fighting the needed reforms in court, and the case exemplifies just how difficult it is for local governments that mistakenly agreed to too generous retirement plans to change them, short of going bankrupt. One of the biggest issues to be decided is whether the pension offered public employees at the date of hire is a "vested" right that cannot be reduced for them in future.[572] Pension costs will exceed 25% of San Jose's annual general fund by the 2017-18 fiscal year, said Mayor Chuck Reed, unless Measure B is fully implemented.[573] The average San Jose police officer or firefighter who retired in the last ten years and worked for 26 years receives an annual pension from San Jose of $100,000,[574] a level city officials say is simply unsustainable into the future. In the meantime, the city council, which has sought to reduce and terminate future pension benefits to new elected officials in the city as a gesture in support of overall reforms, has expressed surprise that CalPERS says it needs an additional $5 million payment for

---

570 http://californiacountynews.org/2013/04/grand-jury-says-san-mateo-pension-liability-a-serious-concern.html

571 Id.

572 http://calpensions.com/#sthash.VfoU9YUF.dpuf

573 http://calpensions.com/#sthash.VfoU9YUF.dpuf

574 http://www.reuters.com/article/2013/07/22/us-san-jose-pensions-trial-idUSBRE96 L11720130722?feedType=RSS&feedName=politicsNews

underfunded liabilities just to dump the plan for its small group of politicians.[575]

From a public policy standpoint, if the courts resolve under Federal bankruptcy laws that retirement agencies like CalPERS must be treated just like any other creditor, it would have huge implications for the public employee retirement systems throughout the state. CalPERS reportedly manages $260 billion in retirement funds,[576] and administers 450 pension accounts for California's local governments.[577] Unfortunately, according to Daniel Borenstein, a staff columnist at the *Contra Costa*, for years CalPERS has used "accounting gimmicks" that have kept the actual amounts that local governments have contributed to the retirement system "artificially low."[578] CalPERS admits that its unfunded pension liabilities are about $80 billion,[579] but critics say the unfunded liability is much more. Its optimistic presumption that it can make a 7.5% return over the next twenty years on investments has been criticized as part of the "underfunding" problem.[580] Ron Seeling, a former CalPERS chief actuary, said as early as 2009 that in his personal view, CalPERS was headed for "unsustainable pension costs" "without a significant turnaround in assets."[581] Pension reporter Ed Mendel has written that while CalPERS has taken steps to increase minimum contributions from local governments, the "official CalPERS view ignores the

---

575 http://www.contracostatimes.com/breaking-news/ci_23071124/
calpers-5-7-million-end-san-jose-council?source=rss&utm_source=feedly

576 http://www.riabiz.com/a/5270811782938624/a-careful-look-into-whether-calpers-
is-ticking-along-or-a-ticking-time-bomb

577 http://www.contracostatimes.com/daniel-borenstein/ci_23056266/
daniel-borenstein-city-pension-hypocrisy-reaches-absurd-level

578 Id.

579 http://www.riabiz.com/a/5270811782938624/a-careful-look-into-whether-calpers-
is-ticking-along-or-a-ticking-time-bomb

580 http://www.riabiz.com/a/5270811782938624/a-careful-look-into-whether-calpers-
is-ticking-along-or-a-ticking-time-bomb

581 http://calpensions.com/2013/04/22/
how-much-can-pensions-squeeze-other-programs/

possibility that the big rate increase could squeeze funding for other programs enough to trigger a backlash. . ."[582]

California simply has a gigantic underfunded public employee pension liability. CalPERS recent actions to require localities to contribute more to their pension plans may help, but those contributions will not make the long-term problems go away in communities that need funds for essential public services but have been squeezed because of pensions. In those cases, through bankruptcy, big underfunded pension liabilities could be wiped clean for local agencies that had, along with CalPERS, mismanaged their own retirement plans. The clean slate would be a relief to taxpayers and consternation to public employees who had counted on more generous pensions. The bankruptcy option for pensions will be a "day of reckoning," opening the door for resolution of underfunded pension liability throughout the state,[583] not just for cities, but also county governments, school districts, and other of the hundreds of local agencies throughout California. Provision of essential public services could continue. But if CalPERS is found to have a priority as a creditor that allows cities like Stockton to force all the burden of bankruptcy to fall on its investors, bond holders, and insurers, there is no question that municipal bonds will become much harder to sell in California in the future, making it more expensive to finance public works and infrastructure projects. Under that scenario, many cities would be forced to just stop servicing infrastructure, such as road building and repair, as available tax revenues would simply be gobbled up by public employee retirement obligations.

Concern about the "day of reckoning" on California's too generous public employee pensions has rightly prompted CalPERS to

---

582 Id.

583 http://www.voiceofsandiego.org/government/article_c0a7ba8c-9bd0-11e2-beed-0019bb2963f4.html?utm_source=feedburner&utm_medium=feed&utm_campaign=Feed%3A+voice-of-san-diego-all-articles+%28All+articles+voiceofsandiego.org+--+full+feed%29

take some actions itself to protect pension benefits. It is intent on accounting changes that would raise the minimum employer contributions by 20% on average for the next six years.[584] But such action to improve the actuarial tables may be too little, too late for some of California's big-spending localities, as pension cost hikes in general could hit 40 to 50% by 2020, and the state's contribution may climb from $5.1 billion to $7.4 billion.[585]

Agencies that rate pensions such as Moody's and the Government Accounting Standards Board have reviewed California's soaring retirement costs and are implementing new accounting rules that, according to one report, could "double California's unfunded liabilities to $328.6 billion" and cause more cities to approach bankruptcy.[586] Moody's in particular thinks government retiree costs have been improperly reported nationwide. The problem is particularly acute in California, where underfunded liabilities exist on top of overly generous defined-benefit retirement plans. Fox Business cites the example of one retiree in troubled Sonoma County, which does not have funding to fix its road system, who receives $371,000 a year in retiree pay.[587] A retired librarian in San Diego is being paid $234,000 annually; a 51 year-old retired lifeguard in Newport Beach is making $108,000 per year and nearly 12,200 retired public employees statewide are being paid more than $100,000 a year.[588]

Public employee pension funding problems have become particularly acute in cities like Sacramento and Los Angeles. Sacramento paid $51 million of a total of $60 million in pension contributions

---

584 http://www.sacbee.com/2013/04/13/5338325/day-of-reckoning-is-coming-for.html#mi_rss=Opinion

585 Id.

586 http://www.foxbusiness.com/government/2013/06/11/california-on-brink-pension-crisis/

587 http://www.foxbusiness.com/government/2013/06/11/california-on-brink-pension-crisis/

588 Id.

to CalPERS in 2012-13 [589] out of its general fund budget of $365 million.[590] That's almost 14% of Sacramento's current general discretionary funds being eaten up by pensions, and not counting any underfunded liability that CalPERS is also carrying. In the same year, Sacramento's proposed budget projected a nearly $16 million deficit that the Mayor blamed on "increases in contracted employee salaries" and a decline in property tax revenue, "the City's single largest discretionary source."[591] Property tax increases are limited to no more than 2% annually under Proposition 13, and will only further increase if the economy improves and the tax base is expanded to include newly built homes or if property values increase and existing homes are turned over. That isn't happening in Sacramento as well as it should because of the endemic crime and poor public services that make the city a poor choice to live for many young families The handwriting is very clear for a city like Sacramento: cutting public employee pensions will reduce its liabilities to CalPERS, reverse its current deficit problems, and free up general funds for other public services, like fighting crime and repairing infrastructure, regardless of a slightly declining property tax base. The question is will Sacramento's liberal politicians ever have the courage to stand up to the public employee unions?

The city of Los Angeles has faced recurrent overall deficits in its fiscal years over the course of the last several years, and as the causes of the deficits come into focus, there is little question that contributions to still underfunded pension plans for public employees have choked off the major portion of overall spending, thus contributing to throwing the city into "red ink" again and again. During its most recent fiscal year, Los Angeles spent about $1.3 billion on pensions, about 18% of total expenditures of $7.2 billion for all

---

589 http://www.sacbee.com/2013/04/13/5338325/day-of-reckoning-is-coming-for.
html#mi_rss=Opinion

590 http://www.cityofsacramento.org/finance/budget/proposed-budget-2012-13/01_
Budget_Message.pdf

591 Id., "Mayor's Budget Message" dated May 1, 2012.

citywide services.[592] Pension costs have risen at a rate of 25% a year for the past decade and outpace spending growth in every other category of spending in the city's budget.[593] According to one report, and because prior payments were not based on realistic expectations of return, Los Angeles' contributions to its two pension plans have increased 140% since 2005.[594] The city's own administrative office acknowledges that pension contributions will grow another 50% by 2017, becoming more than 25% of the overall city budget.[595] Worse, the unfunded liability of the pension plans has grown by $1 billion a year over the last seven years.[596]

And to be sure, other California cities are teetering on the brink of bankruptcy as well as a result of lax fiscal policies. Compton, for example, had by 2011 built up a $40 million general fund deficit because "for years, officials had raided the city's water, sewer, and retirement funds when the general fund ran short on cash."[597] To deal with the deficit, the city laid off 15% of its employees and cut back on city services like street maintenance and eliminating pervasive graffiti throughout the city.[598] Nevertheless, Compton, a city of just 97,000, did not cut back on its $60,000 salary to its largely ceremonial mayor.[599] By comparison, the mayor of Republican voter-rich Newport Beach, just down the 405 Freeway in Orange County, presides over a comparable-size and similarly organized city

---

592 http://www.publicceo.com/2013/03/
los-angeles-city-pension-costs-grew-25-annually-over-last-decade/

593 Id.

594 http://www.citywatchla.com/
lead-stories-hidden/4795-the-unholy-alliance-becomes-more-unholy

595 Id.

596 Id.

597 http://articles.latimes.com/2013/apr/06/local/la-me-compton-election-20130406

598 Id.

599 Id.

of 87,000,[600] and has not complained in any press accounts about his modest annual salary of $20,491 for the part-time position. In contrast, Los Angeles, with a population approaching 13 million, pays its full time mayor a little more than $230,000 per year,[601] while the Mayor of San Francisco, a smaller but important city, receives $272,103.[602] In San Jose, California's fourth largest city, the mayor's full-time salary is set at $114,000 and city council members receive $81,000,[603] for what some critics say are really part-time jobs.

The salaries elected officials such as mayors and city council members receive may be subject to more press attention and public scrutiny, however, disclosures of compensation agreements between cities and their key, non-elected professional managers have also raised eyebrows in recent years. In May 2010 it was disclosed that the City Manager of Laguna Hills, a community of 34,000 in Orange County, was paid close to $400,000 a year. Despite controversy surrounding the revelation of comparable high city manager salaries in nearby cities, the new City Manager of Santa Ana, also in Orange County, will be paid more than $500,000 annually for his first year of work in the city of 330,000 residents.[604] According to a news report, Indian Wells, near Palm Springs in Riverside County with a population of just 5,073,[605] in one year paid its city manager $677,172.[606]

Overgenerous compensation agreements negotiated between liberals managing California's governmental units and their key employees and especially public employee unions plague taxpayers as cash-strapped agencies have little left for improving services and

600 http://quickfacts.census.gov/qfd/states/06/0651182.html

601 http://projects.scpr.org/salaries/list/mayor

602 http://www.mercurynews.com/bay-area-news/ci_23039067/san-jose-residents-say-mayor-council-overpaid-but?source=rss

603 Id.

604 http://articles.latimes.com/2013/aug/07/local/la-me-0808-santa-ana-phoenix-20130808

605 https://www.google.com/search?q=indian+wells+population&ie=utf-8&oe=utf-8&aq=t&rls=org.mozilla:en-US:official&client=firefox-a

606 http://articles.latimes.com/2013/aug/07/local/la-me-0808-santa-ana-phoenix-20130808

infrastructure after the unions and administrators gobble up most of the limited revenue. Such irrationality is at its zenith at the Bay Area Rapid Transit District (BART). BART reached its previous four-year agreement with its principle unions, the SEIU, the AFSCME, and the Amalgamated Transit Union, in 2009.[607] By the last year of the agreement, one of BART's top-paid station agents, whose job is to simply sit in a fare booth watching fare gates for "jumpers" and answering patrons' questions, was paid $167,784 in total salary, overtime, and benefits.[608] The top train operator received $193,407, and an employee responsible for controlling traffic in the train storage and maintenance yards received an eye-popping $271,458.[609] According to a study of employee payroll data by the *San Jose Mercury*, BART employees are the highest paid transit operators in the state and paid the most money on average of the 25 largest government agencies in the Bay Area.[610] BART's highest paid janitor received $82,752 while the same custodian in the swanky Hillsborough City School District was paid $59,360.[611] An electrician at BART made $149,957, twice that of a similar employee for the bus company serving BART's routes.[612]

Should it come as a surprise that BART has the same fiscal problems as most other troubled agencies in the state, including unfunded liabilities for pension and health benefits? BART's payments to CalPERS were $3.1 million for public employee pensions in 2002, but those payments have jumped to $50 million in 2013 and are expected to grow 7% a year for the next four years.[613] According to

---

607 http://www.bart.gov/news/articles/2009/news20090714a.aspx

608 http://www.contracostatimes.com/daniel-borenstein/ci_23217899/
daniel-borenstein-prepare-long-hot-summer-bart-negotiations

609 Id.

610 http://www.mercurynews.com/bart/ci_23742276/
bart-workers-paychecks-already-outpace-their-peers?source=rss

611 Id.

612 Id.

613 http://calpensions.com/2013/08/12/public-pensions-become-issue-in-labor-strikes/

reporter Daniel Borenstein, BART faces a $3 billion shortfall in the next ten years, even if it does not increase salaries further and does increase fares.[614] Borenstein says, "(l)ook to BART to turn to voters for a tax increase to offset" some of the shortfall.[615] But voters in the BART district make annual salaries on average of only a fraction of what BART pays its public employee union workers.

Rationality calls for managers to make better sense of employee pay by using comparable pay data, reducing overtime, and reforming pension and healthcare benefits in negotiating contracts, and not taking the reflexive liberal position of simply giving the unions everything they want and then just raising the tax burden yet again on the public. That strategy will eventually bankrupt not only the taxpayers, but also the district, and given the stark disparity between what BART's public employees are paid and what the community it serves is paid, BART managers shouldn't just count on winning a vote on more taxes to solve their spending problems.

Yet BART's managers need only look to themselves and the culture of overspending they create as leaders to confirm the gross mismanagement of taxpayers' funds at the agency. BART's current General Manager took home $318,000 in annual pay last year not including all benefits, and her predecessor, Dorothy Dugger, received payouts of $330,000 in "vacation pay," without having to show up at work once after she retired, according to one news report.[616] BART's elected board and the public are calling for an investigation into pay practices but the current General Manager has referred to the "vacation pay" for Dugger as "a nice reward."[617] It is hard to imagine a rational manager looking at billions of dollars in financial deficits and facing

---

614 http://www.mercurynews.com/bart/ci_23742276/
bart-workers-paychecks-already-outpace-their-peers?source=rss

615 Id.

616 http://www.mercurynews.com/breaking-news/ci_23447131/bart-chief-policies-behind-predecessors-330-000-vacation?source=rss&utm_source=feedly

617 http://www.mercurynews.com/breaking-news/ci_23447131/bart-chief-policies-behind-predecessors-330-000-vacation?source=rss&utm_source=feedly

wage negotiations with an aggressive union representing clearly over-paid line workers referring to a $330,000 executive "vacation pay" payout as "a nice reward." But even worse, a subsequent study by the *Oakland Tribune* found that the same "nice reward" of vacation pay for Dugger actually amounted to a $558,000 windfall collected during 2012 including management bonuses and vacation pay, even though she had resigned in May *2011*.[618] BART's "vacation time" piggybank allows executives to stay on the BART payroll even after they retire and start receiving some retirement benefits, and now amounts to some $7.8 million.[619] One such employee, ironically a labor relations specialist, had his last day of work in March 2011, but continued to collect full salary through the summer of 2013 at $98,000 per year, by tapping into his BART "vacation bank."[620] "You can't make this up," said the President of the Washington, D.C.-based Citizens Against Government Waste.[621] When BART's unions went on strike in the summer of 2013, lead by the SEIU, they said it was about "healthcare and pensions," but the reality is that the employees pay nothing for their ample pension benefits and just $92 a month for health insurance under their 2009 contract, on top of their big salaries, reported the *San Francisco Chronicle*.[622] And the newspaper added in the same piece, "[t]hat doesn't evoke much sympathy for many workers in the Bay Area who are finding their healthcare costs are rising and pensions are evaporating."[623]

BART's overspending on executive and front-line worker sala-ries while it is deeply in debt contrasts sharply with how the agency treats its passengers and employee safety. The SEIU has claimed that

618 http://www.insidebayarea.com/breaking-news/ci_23562408/
barts-top-level-employees-vacation-bank-tops-69?source=rss

619 http://www.insidebayarea.com/breaking-news/ci_23562408/
barts-top-level-employees-vacation-bank-tops-69?source=rss

620 Id.

621 Id.

622 http://blog.sfgate.com/cwnevius/2013/07/03/bart-workers-overplay-their-hand/

623 Id.

lighting in tunnels and a substandard electrical system pose a public safety threat so bad that train operators can't see fellow employees doing repair work.[624] It is hard to pay for infrastructure safety when all the money in the enterprise is going to salaries, benefits, and $330,000 "vacation pay" packages.

Despite it all, BART's unions are asking for even more. Given BART's shabby financial condition, an awful economy, and a recession that has left many in the Bay Area jobless, one newspaper report has asked the question of whether the unions are engaging in "delusional tactics" that are "out of touch with economic reality."[625] It is a fair question.

Not just overspending, but outright greed, has sadly been another fiscal problem plaguing California's localities. In Los Angeles County alone, there are more than 80 smaller cities and hundreds of single-purpose governmental units like water, parks, recreation, and fire protection districts, and it has been estimated that they spend as much as $100 billion a year.[626] Corruption and mismanagement has taken its toll on some of them. In the small community of Bell in the county, city manager Robert Rizzo was finally fired in 2010 when his astounding $800,000 annual salary and benefits package was disclosed, along with other corruption involving the city council.[627] Bell also illegally overcharged its residents $800,000 for sanitation services and took $3 million more illegally in inflated property tax collections from property owners and businesses.[628] Now owing residents and property owners tax refunds, Bell is on the brink of

---

624 http://www.sfexaminer.com/sanfrancisco/
bart-employees-might-vote-next-week-to-strike/Content?oid=2473440

625 http://www.mercurynews.com/breaking-news/ci_23611642/
bart-strike-illustrates-heated-debate-over-public-sector?source=rss

626 http://www.sacbee.com/2013/06/23/5517246/dan-walters-corruption-flourishes.
html

627 http://www.latimes.com/news/local/la-me-0403-rizzo-20130403,0,5020731.
story?track=rss

628 http://www.latimes.com/news/local/la-me-0523-bell-20130523,0,1062047.story

fiscal disaster with a negative balance of more than $1 million in its general fund and $4 million more in unpaid legal bills associated with the Rizzo corruption scandal.[629] In nearby Compton, the Los Angeles County District Attorney has recently demanded documentation of all files relating to car allowances, inspired most likely by a news report regarding "questionable expenditures, big loans that haven't been paid back, and council members making up to $1,500 per hour."[630] The news report revealed a questionable $3.1 million city loan to a construction company that appeared to be largely forgiven.[631] The Federal Bureau of Investigation is conducting an audit of financial records of the Central Basin Water District in the county's San Gabriel Valley, and the investigation has included a raid of the capitol offices of a Democratic State Senator and claims of special financial favors to his family members.[632] In the meantime, just to the south, a study by the *Orange County Register* found that in 2011 and 2012, five governing board members and eight staff members of the Mesa Water District spent $170,000 on conferences, food, and travel, including a $144 steak dinner for two in Palm Springs while attending the Urban Water Institute Conference, which included as a topic, "explaining to constituents why water rates are going up while water use is down."[633]

The statewide spending spree doesn't exclude California's professedly cash-strapped top public institutions of higher education. While University of California officials in 2011 publicly claimed they were experiencing "the worst financial crisis in history," $140 million that had been raised from increases in student tuition fees was used to

---

629 Id.

630 http://www.citywatchla.
com/8box-left/5022-is-inglewood-ca-planning-a-retirement-party-soon

631 Id.

632 http://www.latimes.com/news/local/political/la-me-pc-ron-calderon-fbi-central-basin-water-district-tom-calderon-water-20130605,0,2842227.story

633 http://www.ocregister.com/articles/district-515008-water-board.html

grant high-income faculty members raises.[634] President Obama's former Secretary of Homeland Security, Janet Napolitano, will be paid $570,000 annually to take over the position of Chancellor of the University of California at Berkeley, plus an auto allowance of $8,916, and a $142,500 one-time "relocation fee." Napolitano also will live rent-free in a home to be provided by the University and receive "standard health and retirement benefits." Her immediate predecessor, Mark Yudof, was paid $847,149 in total pay with a base salary of $591,084 after five years on the job, the eighth highest paid public university leader in the nation.[635] And top administrators are not the only well-paid employees at the University of California. At the University of California--Davis, the position of "associate chancellor for strategic communications" has been created and a new administrator hired for the position at a salary of $260,000 per year.[636] The job description includes responsibility for "improving the university's image."

Some of California's many obscure agencies are awash in too much cash, and these hoards of funds have caught the attention of grand juries. In Orange County the grand jury has issued a report critical of special districts governing water and sewage infrastructure that have accumulated as much as $860 million in "unrestricted reserves" of taxpayer funds that have been accumulated without reference to any standards and can be spent at the complete discretion of the agencies.[637] Agencies may argue they need their piles of cash to protect against expensive emergencies, but the grand jury found the amassing of taxpayer funds was "excessive," and in one case

634 http://www.sfgate.com/education/article/Cash-strapped-UC-hands-out-millions-in-raises-2334427.php

635 http://www.sfgate.com/education/article/Janet-Napolitano-tapped-as-UC-president-4661685.php

636 http://www.kcra.com/news/local-news/news-sacramento/uc-davis-adds-highly-paid-official-to-boost-image/-/12969376/21336268/-/gpao8m/-/index.html

637 http://www.voiceofoc.org/oc_coast/article_0c0e8582-9ba4-11e2-8758-0019bb2963f4.html

amounted to 40% of capital assets, a high bar. Returning such excessive funds back to the taxpayers, or lowering tax rates, has apparently not occurred to the government agencies in question, which include the Mesa Water District, which actually raised its water rates in 2009 despite sitting on a mountain of cash.[638]

In Los Angeles, nearly $43 million in taxpayer funds "piled up unnoticed in a (city) Department of Transportation fund" over a period of years, and city employees could not explain why the treasure trove was not audited or examined, or ever disclosed for budget purposes prior to finding the account.[639] And now investigative reports are emerging that claim there are as many as 700 "special funds" and that some of them may be wrongfully hiding troves of the taxpayer funds in Los Angeles.[640]

Cash-strapped California itself mismanages revenue programs or has funds stuffed away from public view. The state Department of Toxic Substances Control has spent $100 million on cleanups of some 1,700 contaminated properties in California over the last 26 years, but has failed to send bills to the polluters to reimburse the state, as required by law, including to major corporations such as Chevron, Boeing, and Aerojet who can afford to pay.[641] Not too long ago, it was learned through an Attorney General's office review that managers "at the highest levels" of the California Department of Parks and Recreation had intentionally kept secret over a period of years more than $20 million in taxpayer funds hidden in a special fund account.[642] Funds were apparently not pilfered for private gain,

---

638 Id.

639 http://articles.latimes.com/2013/may/14/local/la-me-ln-oversight-special-funds-20130514

640 http://www.scpr.org/blogs/politics/2013/05/15/13675/
la-budget-officials-don-t-know-how-much-money-may/

641 http://www.sacbee.com/2013/05/30/5457371/california-agency-failed-to-collect.
html

642 http://www.huffingtonpost.com/2013/01/04/california-parks-officials_n_2413036.
html

but intentionally kept secret from the state to avoid it being taken away in the face of budget deficits. The long term Parks Director and an aide were fired over the incident, which has done little to build confidence in taxpayers that Sacramento is handling their money wisely. The State Auditor found that a special license plate program in the Department of Motor Vehicles failed to collect as much as $22 million from sales of the plates, and overcharged the state $2.1 million for overhead.[643]

There are solutions available to correct the liberal excesses that threaten California's economic future. Government can and should change the way it deals with public employee salaries to make them more rational and reasonable. The city of Carlsbad in lovely coastal San Diego county is leading the way by reaching an agreement with its public employment union to end automatic annual pay increases to its staff, and instead dedicate the same amount of funds to a "merit pay poll" that will be distributed to employees based on performance on the job.[644] "When I hear that employees will get raises based on performance, I say, 'Welcome to the real world,'" said Kris Vosburgh, executive director of the Howard Jarvis Taxpayers Association. "It would be nice if other cities around the state followed suit."[645] Though it was narrowly defeated on the ballot in Fresno in June of 2013, efforts to allow private contractors to assume certain services for municipalities, like trash hauling, can improve local services at lower costs and greatly reduce exposure to the looming threat of California's underfunded public employee pension liabilities.[646] Rational local policymakers should continue to pursue such transitions in the way they do business. Nevertheless, the biggest

643 http://www.arc.asm.ca.gov/BudgetFactCheck/?p id=477

644 http://www.utsandiego.com/news/2013/jun/22/carlsbad-merit-pay-government-step-increases/

645 Id.

646 http://www.fresnobee.com/2013/06/14/3344320/measure-g-vote-has-been-certified.html

solution is for government officials to reign in the tax-and-spend policies that have allowed the cost of government and unfunded pension liabilities to reach untenable levels. Their failure to do so is precipitating the eminent economic collapse of not just Stockton or San Bernardino, but the entire state.

ARNOLD SCHWARZENEGGER'S FAILURE TO REFORM CALIFORNIA

THE HISTORIC RECALL OF Democratic Governor Gray Davis in 2003 and the election of Republican Arnold Schwarzenegger as the replacement candidate on the same ballot were supposed to reverse California's decline. The causes of Davis' recall were surely rooted in voter dissatisfaction with Davis' performance in office, which was characterized by a poor business climate and Davis enacting an unpopular tax increase on the high-profile "car tax." In his re-election in 2002, Davis only was able to gather 47% of the vote against a stiff Republican, Bill Simon, Jr., and a surprisingly strong Green Party candidate that polled 5% of the vote. Fueled by a monumental petition signature-gathering effort generously funded by Congressman Darrell Issa, himself briefly also a Gubernatorial replacement candidate, Arnold won election as a populist reformer who would "blow up the boxes" in state government. But after winning re-election in his own right in 2006 and serving close to seven years as governor, Schwarzenegger failed to "blow up the boxes" and a fair question is: Why did he fail? Despite his populist rhetoric and early charm offensive with California's special interests, he fell victim to those same special interests that continue to control and mismanage the state today. His accomplishments never matched his rhetoric, and when his term ended, no boxes were blown up.

In *"The People's Machine,"* author and columnist Joe Mathews meticulously assembled the insiders' accounts of Arnold's first term. But, even without reading Mathews' outstanding work, Californians instinctively know that something went wrong. Too many Californians, especially Republicans, originally fell under Arnold's spell. "Let's make this clear: I'm a Republican, I'm a proud Republican from the first day I came to this country," Schwarzenegger told conservative talk show host Eric Hogue during the recall campaign. "I'm a Republican, and I'm running as a Republican to be the next Republican governor."[647] Of course, Republicans come in many different shades. Arnold's rhetoric wasn't in pale pastels, at least not in the early days. "I'm a conservative because I believe communism is evil and free enterprise is good," Schwarzenegger told cheering delegates at a lunchtime speech during the California Republican Party's 2003 Fall Convention. "I'm a conservative because Milton Friedman is right and Karl Marx was wrong. I'm a conservative because I believe the government serves the people; the people don't serve the government. I'm a conservative because I believe in balanced budgets, not budget deficits. I'm a conservative because I believe the money that people earn is their money, not the government's."[648] One dyed-in-the-wool conservative Republican who was present when Arnold addressed the convention was Jon Fleischman, a former Executive Director of the California Republican Party, one-time President of the California Republican Assembly volunteer group, and the publisher of FlashReport.org, the leading center-right news aggregation and political opinion website. Fleischman supported Arnold in 2003, but today regrets his decision. "I remember listening to this speech and getting so very excited, as a conservative. It had

---

647 http://www.nytimes.com/2003/08/27/national/27RECA.html

648 Joe Mathews, *The People's Machine: Arnold Schwarzenegger and the Rise of Blockbuster Democracy*, (New York: Public Affairs, 2006), 172.

been so long since I had heard a candidate saying those things that I thought could win the office of Governor," said Fleischman.[649] "Speeches like this one, and others with him holding up a broom and talking about 'sweeping out the special interests' caused me to back Schwarzenegger even though my close friend Tom McClintock was also in the race. I think I have subsequently apologized to Tom a dozen times."[650]

On the campaign trail, Arnold repeatedly alluded to the 1.6 million people that had signed the recall petition that he had not funded, rather that Darrell Issa had made possible by donating $1.7 million of his own funds to get the recall on the ballot.[651] Arnold even harkened back to the rhetoric of legendary tax-fighter Howard Jarvis by repeating the 1970s property tax mantra that was borrowed from the film *Network*. "We are mad as hell and we're not going to take it anymore," Arnold repeated from Jarvis, who borrowed it from fictional character Howard Beale.[652] All of Arnold's rhetoric helped reassure conservative Republicans who had signed the recall petitions.

And many Republicans believed that Arnold would correct the state's problems and usher in a new era of limited government and fiscal responsibility. "Every governor proposes moving boxes around to reorganize government. I don't want to move the boxes around; I want to blow them up," he vowed in his first State of the State address. "We have multiple departments with overlapping responsibilities. I say consolidate them. We have boards and commissions that serve

---

649 Interview with the author September 22, 2013.

650 Id.

651 "Legacy of Gov. Gray Davis' recall endures," *San Francisco Chronicle*, April 14, 2013. http://www.sfchronicle.com/politics/article/Legacy-of-Gov-Gray-Davis-recall-endures-4432913.php

652 Joe Mathews, *The People's Machine: Arnold Schwarzenegger and the Rise of Block-buster Democracy*, (New York Public Affairs, 2006), 139.

no pressing public need. I say abolish them."[653] The governor's solution came in the form of the California Performance Review, the largest and most ambitious reorganization of state government since the 1960s. The document recommended "consolidating 11 agencies and 79 departments into 11 major departments while eliminating 12,000 state jobs." [654] By the end of year, the state's political observers were drawing comparisons between Schwarzenegger and another Republican governor from Hollywood, Ronald Reagan. There was even talk of amending the U.S. Constitution to enable a presidential run. "Amend for Arnold" was one 2004 slogan that received support from several members of Congress.[655]

But what happened? To most observers, Arnold's term of office ended in disaster. "The Californian dream has faded, if not died, on this governor's watch," the British newspaper *The Telegraph* observed in 2010. "That matters for the rest of the world - if it was a country, the 37 million residents of America's most populous state would be in the G8 grouping of the eight richest economies. And it also matters deeply to the American psyche."[656] In July 2010 during Arnold's last summer in office, his approval ratings reached an all-time low for any governor in California history with just 22% of voters approving of Arnold's performance as governor, while an astounding 70 percent disapproved, according to a survey by the Field Poll.[657] These

653 "Schwarzenegger Promise To Blow Up Boxes Fizzled," Associated Press, December 28, 2010, http://losangeles.cbslocal.com/2010/12/28/schwarzenegger-promise-to-blow-up-boxes-fizzled/

654 "Schwarzenegger Promise To Blow Up Boxes Fizzled," Associated Press, December 28, 2010, http://losangeles.cbslocal.com/2010/12/28/schwarzenegger-promise-to-blow-up-boxes-fizzled/

655 John Wildermuth, "'Amend for Arnold' campaign launched, Web site, TV spot promote change to Constitution," *San Francisco Chronicle*, November 18, 2004, http://www.sfgate.com/politics/article/Amend-for-Arnold-campaign-launched-Web-site-2635267.php

656 http://www.telegraph.co.uk/news/worldnews/northamerica/usa/7945915/How-Arnold-Schwarzeneggers-California-dream-soured.html

657 "Schwarzenegger Approval Rating Hits Gray Davis Lows," *Huffington Post*, July 14, 2010, http://www.huffingtonpost.com/2010/07/14/schwarzenegger-approval-r_n_646244.html

ratings matched the Field Poll's low for Gov. Gray Davis, just prior to his recall.[658]

How could Arnold's popularity fall to the same all-time lows of his disgraced and recalled predecessor? Ronald Reagan was able to transform his executive leadership from Sacramento to Washington; couldn't Arnold Schwarzenegger do the same? Was Arnold secretly a liberal just like his failed predecessor Gray Davis, but hiding in conservative clothing? Or, did Arnold simply change in office? Conventional wisdom, or at least the version that gives Arnold the benefit of the doubt, is that the Terminator genuinely believed he could change government. He campaigned as a fiscally conservative Republican and governed as a fiscally conservative executive during his first two years in office. In 2005 the governor proposed a wide-ranging reform package to fix state government, a package that was embraced by the state's fiscal conservatives, and placed the package before voters in a special election. It failed. After voters defeated his measures, Arnold changed course, jettisoned promoting conservative solutions and embraced the same big government liberalism of his failed predecessor, perhaps in a desperate effort to mollify the special interests that could stand in his way for re-election in 2006. This conventional wisdom views Arnold Schwarzenegger's tenure as governor as the greatest missed opportunity for even moderate reforms to fix California.

The problem with this version of history is that it doesn't line up with all of the facts. Schwarzenegger didn't veer off course from his conservative beliefs following the 2005 special election. Despite his conservative rhetoric in the early years, the facts show that Arnold was never a deeply committed conservative. For example, during his transition in 2003, he first suggested that his administration have co-chiefs of staff, one Republican and one Democrat, which would undercut conservative initiatives. Arnold offered the jobs to former Democratic Speaker of the Assembly Bob Hertzberg

---

658 Id.

and his eventual Republican chief of staff Pat Clarey.[659] Privately, Schwarzenegger openly mocked and insulted Republicans. He called them "foreheads," "the wild bunch," or "out there."[660] As early as the recall campaign, Arnold's team was considering whether he should re-register as an independent. The campaign even polled whether a party change would bolster his candidacy. Sixty percent of voters said that his party affiliation didn't matter to them. [661]The polling never stopped. His ideology seemed defined by what's best for his own approval rating. Above all else, in place of political philosophy or partisan constituencies, Arnold's governing style appeared animated by his desire to be liked.

Arnold, who'd proven adept at sweet-talking the public, had endeared himself especially to Republicans at a crucial time, when Californians were demonstrating an embrace of limited government, having recalled Davis. He came to power because of conservative rhetoric associated with the Davis recall; a prerequisite to him winning a vote for Governor. But, after his election, Republicans proved unable to hold him to those promises. Perhaps the most prescient observations about Arnold's leadership style came in 2004 from two individuals that couldn't be further apart on the ideological spectrum. "Arnold is a very seductive individual," Stephen Moore, then president of the conservative Club for Growth, said of the Terminator. [662] The notion of Arnold as the seducer was echoed by his liberal gubernatorial rival, Arianna Huffington. "What we've seen in Arnold is an alternation of the seducer and the bully," Huffington said in the summer of 2004, when Arnold's popularity was soaring.

659 Joe Mathews, *The People's Machine Arnold Schwarzenegger and the Rise of Blockbuster Democracy,* (New York: Public Affairs, 2006), 197,.

660 Joe Mathews, "Arnold Considered Party Switch," Daily Beast, http://www.thedailybeast.com/articles/2009/02/23/arnold-considered-party-switch.html

661 Joe Mathews, *The People's Machine: Arnold Schwarzenegger and the Rise of Blockbuster Democracy,* (New York: Public Affairs, 2006), 125.

662 Joe Mathews, "Arnold Considered Party Switch," Daily Beast, http://www.thedailybeast.com/articles/2009/02/23/arnold-considered-party-switch.html

"Seduction worked for a while because he's a very charming man and the people were so relieved to be rid of Gray Davis and have someone entertaining in his place." [663] And Huffington observed that eventually Arnold would change. "When the seduction doesn't work anymore, the bully comes out," she said. [664] Republicans in California were largely seduced by Arnold in the early days. Eventually, Arnold came to bully the state's Republicans. He famously declared himself "post-partisan," campaigned for tax increases, and repeatedly criticized Republican officials in the mainstream press.

Arnold's aspiration to become a reform governor was compelled by equal parts naiveté and a gross misrepresentation of who he was as a leader. Case in point: his doomed courtship with the CTA, which, according to conventional wisdom in the capitol, is "the most politically powerful organization in California."[665] Joe Mathews observes in his book, *The People's Machine*, CTA's unprecedented influence over the movie star governor. "No relationship would be more important to Schwarzenegger's political career than the one with the California Teachers Association," Mathews writes. "The state of the bond between the star and the CTA would become the most reliable barometer of his standing with the public."[666] The CTA allowed Arnold to play both roles as Governor: a tough-talking outsider who governed by initiative, as well as the consummate wheeling-dealing insider who would reach secret agreements with the state's biggest lobby. But, Arnold made a gross miscalculation with the CTA. He believed that his charm offensive that worked so well with the public and California Republicans would also be effective with an entrenched special interest group. The CTA spent millions of dollars in union-funded advertisements against the 2005 reform package.

---

663 http://www.nytimes.com/2004/07/19/national/19arnold.html

664 Id.

665 Joe Mathews, *The People's Machine: Arnold Schwarzenegger and the Rise of Blockbuster Democracy*, (New York: Public Affairs, 2006), 88.

666 Id., 90.

His inability to charm the CTA resulted in his reform measures being defeated.

The CTA's relationship with Arnold had been forged years earlier when he first used an afterschool initiative as a trial balloon for his gubernatorial candidacy. In the fall of 2001 at the urging of his political consultants, Arnold met with the CTA at their offices in Sacramento. The goal of the meeting was to find a way for the teachers union to support his afterschool initiative. Although Arnold had in the past supported afterschool programs through his charity work, the initiative was designed entirely as a feel-good policy to increase his policy credentials for an eventual gubernatorial candidacy. All of the CTA's top brass would be introduced and have some input on Arnold's initiative. John Mockler, the then-head of the CTA, set up a meeting with John Hein, who was brought in to provide expert analysis on the policies that would best aid the union. In turn, Hein asked his preferred ballot lawyer to review the afterschool program proposal. The CTA's lawyers worked alongside Arnold's own advisors in reviewing a dozen drafts.[667] By intimately involving the CTA in his campaign, the union had gained crucial access to the soon-to-be governor and learned how to influence him on the important fights to come. As Mathews describes it, "Hein also saw that a deal would allow CTA to build a relationship with a future Republican leader."[668] The CTA received control of Arnold's initiative and in exchange merely provided the CTA's endorsement of Arnold's feel-good measure. It's no wonder that Arnold embraced the CTA. Like Schwarzenegger, the CTA was heavily dependent on polling, reportedly spending a million dollars per year to take the pulse of the public in the early 2000s.[669] The CTA had a similar affinity for ballot measures, having spent $45 million from 2000- 2004 on contributions to initiative campaigns.

---

667 Id.

668 Id,91.

669 Id., 90.

Arnold therefore started his road to the governorship by secretly kowtowing to the state's most powerful public employee union. They returned the favor by publicly opposing the recall election that would bring him to power.[670] Although the CTA was among the long list of labor unions that opposed the recall election, it was not the most passionate union involved in defending Gray Davis, who had offended the union by demanding more campaign funds in a policy meeting. The teachers union's internal polling showed that the Davis recall was popular and that only Senator Dianne Feinstein or Leon Panetta, a former White House chief of staff, had the gravitas and public approval to unite the Democratic Party.[671] Despite its polling, the CTA was caught off guard by the recall election. "I don't think anyone believed the election would take place as soon as October," then CTA president Barbara Kerr said in the summer of 2003. [672] Kerr also revealed what may be an Achilles heel of the teachers union's political influence: timing. "Unfortunately, we're at the end of our fiscal year, and most teachers don't get paid from June 30 to Oct. 1. So it's not the best time to pass the hat."[673]

The CTA may have been caught off guard by the speed of the recall, but its leaders would not repeat the mistake during Arnold's transition. Predictably, the liberal mainstream media was busy hyping Arnold as a conservative. News accounts of the transition put special emphasis on the business executives, well-known GOP politicos, and taxpayer advocates on Schwarzenegger's transition team. For example, Jon Coupal of the Howard Jarvis Taxpayers Association earned a prominent mention in the first few paragraphs of news reports. In contrast, the CTA quietly made sure that its political

---

670 "Leaders of California's Largest Union Vote to Raise Large Amounts to Defeat Davis Recall," *New York Times,* August 27, 2003.

671 Joe Mathews, *The People's Machine: Arnold Schwarzenegger and the Rise of Blockbuster Democracy,* (CityNew York: Public Affairs, 2006), 132.

672 "For California Democrats, Recall Strategy Is Up for Grabs," *Sacramento Bee,* August 17, 2003.

673 Id.

director, John Hein, was also named to Arnold's November 2003 transition team.[674] Hein was a liberal's liberal and also had a relationship directly with Arnold from the afterschool program initiative. He had a record of being an effective organizer and skilled activist. Speaking about Hein the following year, Rep. Robert Matsui, D-Sacramento, praised Hein for his work to block school vouchers and his "vital role in the successful effort to reduce the vote threshold for local school bonds from two-thirds to 55 percent." Matsui's praise, which was recorded in the congressional record, concluded, "Time and time again, John has proven that he is one of the greatest friends of public education in California."[675]

With Hein's spot on the transition team, the CTA had a seat at the table in picking Arnold's advisers and guiding his initial agenda, despite opposing his election. The teachers union also had a means for testing its strategy for persuading the novice politician. The first major test came before Arnold took office. In November 2003, before he was sworn in as governor, Schwarzenegger announced that former Los Angeles Mayor Richard Riordan would serve as the state's education secretary. The Associated Press reported, "Shortly after Schwarzenegger announced Riordan's appointment, the California Teachers Association said that one of its officials, John Hein, had withdrawn from the Schwarzenegger transition team." [676] Riordan, who is considered a moderate Republican, is hardly a partisan. However, he had gone toe-to-toe with the teachers union in the past over campaigns for the Los Angeles Unified School District.[677] It was,

---

674 John Wildermuth, "Eclectic transition group is selected / S.F. mayor, HP leader, Wilson aides to help," October 10, 2003, http://www.sfgate.com/politics/article/Eclectic-transition-group-is-selected-S-F-2583583.php

675 Congressional Record, Volume 150 , number 51 pages e546extensions of remarks, April 20, 2004, Rep. Robert T. Matsui, http://capitolwords.org/date/2004/04/20/E546_tribute-to-john-hein/

676 "Schwarzenegger names Arduin to finance, Riordan to education post," The Associated Press, November 3, 2003.

677 "Gov.-Elect Picks Two For Team," *San Jose Mercury News*, November 4, 2003.

however, surprising for the CTA to make Riordan's nomination an absolute make-or-break issue. Kerr even admitted to the AP that the union had no current problems with Riordan. [678]

Why then would the CTA's political director resign his position in the new governor's kitchen cabinet over an appointment of a moderate Republican with whom the CTA "had no current problems"? The most credible explanation is that the union wanted to test Schwarzenegger and evaluate the most effective ways to influence him. "We at this point feel this decision shows we're not being listened to," CTA president Kerr said of the Riordan appointment kerfuffle. "We're not going to be a doormat and merely lay down and say, 'OK'." [679] The teachers followed up Hein's resignation with another shot across Arnold's bow. In December 2003 the teachers union criticized Arnold's proposed spending cap, which was a central platform of his gubernatorial agenda. "It dramatically undermines education funding for the state and future funding," Kerr told the press. Arnold responded to the threat by giving the CTA president 90 minutes for a lengthy discussion about the spending cap proposal. After the meeting, Kerr alone played good-cop, bad-cop. "What I'm saying is from the tone of what he said to me is that he does support public education and we're going to do everything we can to work it out," she said. "If we don't, then there will be a different side to the CTA."[680] By the end of 2003 the teachers' union was talking "almost daily with the administration."[681] That's what the union wanted all along, direct talks with the governor in order to negotiate its own deal for the looming budget cuts. It was a deal and special treatment that no other legislative leader or special interest group would

678 "Schwarzenegger names Arduin to finance, Riordan to education post," The Associated Press, November 3, 2003.

679 "Gov.-Elect Picks Two For Team," *San Jose Mercury News*, November 4, 2003.

680 "Critics Say Gov. Schwarzenegger's Spending Cap Undermines California Schools," *San Jose Mercury News*, November 27, 2003.

681 "Governor Stumping For Budget Plans," San Jose Mercury News, December 3, 2003.

receive. Hein said later that he told Schwarzenegger, "I think you'll find that the organization is awfully good at solving problems when you talk to us early in that way."[682] Meanwhile in public appearance and media interviews, Arnold was seducing conservatives with what now can be seen as empty rhetoric. Arnold appeared on CNN in mid-December and floated the idea of suspending Proposition 98, the teachers' union sacrosanct measure that guarantees schools receive the bulk of the state's resources.[683] Prop 98 had never been suspended and was considered a third rail of state politics.

By January the teachers' union had cut a deal with Arnold that would preserve their state funding and avoid any cuts to public education. The *New York Times* observed of Arnold's first budget, "There was little evidence of a major restructuring in the budget blueprint presented on Friday. Some analysts called it a moderate document that could have been prepared by Mr. Davis, whom Mr. Schwarzenegger replaced in November." [684] In typical fashion, the CTA sold the deal to the public as accepting a cut. Educators had "agreed to accept $2 billion less next year than they are owed," the Associate Press claimed. [685] However, in reality, the deal was a $2 billion net increase for K-12 spending, which translated into $200 more per-pupil. [686] The CTA's representatives happily stood behind the governor at a budget press conference. CTA president Barbara Kerr, explained that "working, being part of the solution, is a lot

---

682 Joe Mathews, *The People's Machine: Arnold Schwarzenegger and the Rise of Blockbuster Democracy*, (New York: Public Affairs, 2006), 208.

683 "California Governor Hints School Funding May Be Targeted in Budget Crisis," *Sacramento Bee*, December 10, 2003.

684 Broder, John. "Governor Seeks Big Cuts In California's Spending." *New York Times*, January 10, 2004

685 "Schwarzenegger cuts deal to trim billions from education," Associated Press, January 8, 2004.

686 Broder, John. "Governor Seeks Big Cuts In California's Spending." *New York Times*, January 10, 2004

better than being on the sidelines."[687] By its own admission, the CTA had received an unprecedented seat at the budget table. "The way he involved us in this budget proposal is a first, and we appreciate it," Kerr said.[688] In other reports, Kerr described the interactions by saying, "It wasn't contentious. It was, 'We're going to work to get this done.'"[689]

In just two months the CTA had figured out how to influence Arnold. The CTA's deal spared it from any budget sacrifices, while every other department faced record budget cuts. Even one of Sacramento's most respected liberal newspaper columnists, Peter Schrag, called out the sweetheart deal for the teachers union. Kerr, according to Schrag, looked "like the cat that swallowed the canary," he wrote. "Her description of the deal her union made with the governor as 'fair' immediately became a candidate for understatement of the year." According to Schragg, the agreement didn't just add money to the state's education budget, it did so by enriching the teachers. Instead of block grants, the governor's deal "put $1.7 billion more on local districts' salary bargaining tables than for the current year. That's in addition to increases in the cost of living and enrollment."[690] In exchange for a collective bargaining giveaway to the teachers union, Arnold received the union's support for his two ballot measures, Propositions 57 and 58. The first measure, Prop. 57, was a $15 billion economic recovery bond to help "temporarily" bail out the state, while Prop. 58 was the spending cap that Arnold repeatedly promised would prevent future budget deficits. "If this recovery package does not pass in March, the prospect of brutal cuts to education, healthcare and local police and firefighting is real and too painful to imagine," Kerr said in

---

687 "Schwarzenegger cuts deal to trim billions from education," Associated Press, January 8, 2004.

688 "Budget fix includes cuts, fee increases," *San Bernardino Sun*, January 8, 2004.

689 "Schwarzenegger's rising credibility," *Christian Science Monitor*, March 2, 2004.

690 Peter Schrag writes for the Sacramento Bee, "Did teachers' group eat Arnold's lunch—and the kids', too?" *Alameda Times-Star*, February 1, 2004.

explanation of the CTA's support. [691] By the end of spring, the CTA had also dropped its plans to back a $6 billion tax increase. The CTA had drafted an initiative that would have instituted a split-roll property tax system, applying higher taxes to commercial properties. [692] It's not clear why the initiative was dropped.

Arnold didn't know it, but the deal with the teachers union in January 2004 likely sealed his fate as governor. In one month, he had given away his negotiating strategy. But, even worse than tipping his hand for future negotiations, Arnold cut a deal that was unsustainable. Mathews describes the deal as "Schwarzenegger's political Waterloo: his education funding deal with CTA."[693] He had promised the teachers union more money in the future, when the economy turned around. In exchange for this future boon, the teachers had agreed to a $2 billion increase in the current year. The union got a good deal: a future hike in exchange for a current hike. The teachers union had given up nothing and received a future windfall. By the end of 2004, his administration was accused of reneging on its deal with the teachers' union precisely because the state could not afford to spend more. The state's independent Legislative Analyst's Office (LAO) warned in November that the state's fiscal outlook was not good with an expanding budget deficit. "The size and persistence of this shortfall, even in the face of an expanding economy and strengthening revenues, underscores a critical point that we have made in the past—namely, it is unlikely that California will be able to simply 'grow its way out' of this shortfall," the LAO wrote. [694]

Throughout the spring, Arnold demonstrated that the CTA

---

691 "Teachers Union Backs $15 Billion Bond Issue," *San Jose Mercury News*, January 27, 2004.

692 "Calif. teachers drop school tax initiative," United Press International, April 9, 2004.

693 Joe Mathews, *The People's Machine: Arnold Schwarzenegger and the Rise of Blockbuster Democracy*, (New York: Public Affairs, 2006), 387.

694 November 2004, LAO, California's Fiscal Outlook, http://www.lao.ca.gov/2004/fiscal_outlook/fiscal_outlook_04.htm

would receive special attention. "When Barbara Kerr, the president of the CTA, sent a message one morning in late April that she was unhappy about something, Schwarzenegger called her up within two hours and invited her to lunch that day," according to Mathews. [695] Meanwhile, conservative Republicans, namely John Campbell, an Orange County Assemblyman and the budget lead for his caucus, were given excuses. "What he said back to me was, 'Look, John, I probably should have done something different. I've been on this job three weeks, and I made some mistakes here.'"[696]

Similarly, Arnold's political naiveté and reluctance to confront the Democrats who controlled the legislature and their special interest allies doomed his "California Performance Review," a detailed program that offered real hope for reform, but which Schwarzenegger fairly quickly abandoned as governor. Joel Fox, an early Arnold supporter and member of his policy team during the campaign for Governor, recalls working with former Governor Pete Wilson and Carl De Maio, among others, on building a framework of reforms for the state during the campaign.[697] Once Arnold was elected, those policy ideas were taken up by Arnold's administration and developed more and more, incorporating the advice of senior civil servants. A full-fledged commission was created to formally develop the ideas as official recommendations and Fox was appointed a member. Staff working on the California Performance Review took over two floors of an office building in Sacramento, not too far from the Capitol Building, and began earnest work on a reform agenda. A goal of the commission was to endorse a program to refashion state government out of a 19th century model and into the realities of the new century. Or, to use Schwarzenegger's shorthand for the project: "To blow up the boxes."

---

695 Joe Mathews, *The People's Machine: Arnold Schwarzenegger and the Rise of Block-buster Democracy*, (New York: Public Affairs, 2006), 256.

696 Id. 207.

697 Author's telephone interview with Joel Fox, August 16, 2013.

The Report of the California Performance Review was developed over five months with the assistance of 275 volunteers.[698] It included 1,200 recommendations involving restructuring of government, health and human services, education, infrastructure, conservation, and public safety that identified $32 billion in savings over a five year period if implemented by the state.[699]

Fox believes that if the Commission's recommendations were pushed by Arnold and adopted by the state, that better government would have been the result with billions of dollars saved. Though Arnold submitted a reorganization plan calling for the elimination of 88 boards and commissions, hardly any of the recommendations of the California Performance Review were actually pushed by the Governor and adopted into law. Why? Fox says he thinks the Governor became convinced the legislature was going to make it very difficult for him to push through the reform package. "I'm putting it temporarily on the shelf" Arnold told Fox. But all the work just died away.

Known for his one-liners, Arnold added to the list in the summer of 2004. When legislators dragged their feet on a state budget deal, Arnold infamously accused Democrats of being "girlie men." Speaking at a budget rally organized at a Southern California shopping mall, the governor said that Democrats "should get back to the table and they should finish the budget."[700] The comment was an expression of Arnold's frustrations with his inability to work with the legislature. Obviously, the comment only made that task more difficult because it allowed far left liberals to characterize Arnold as a sexist leader. Yet, the war of words between Arnold and liberal Democratic legislators was not his biggest problem. Arnold's 2004 budget problems stemmed from his deal-making with the teachers'

---

698 http://cpr.ca.gov/cpr_report/

699 Id.

700 "Schwarzenegger Calls Budget Opponents 'Girlie Men'," *The New York Times*, July 19, 2004.

union. "By brokering the behind-the-scenes deal with the California Teacher's Association - and then doing the same thing with several other key interest groups - Schwarzenegger had appeared to be paving the way to a budget," the *Christian Science Monitor* observed. "In reality, the opposite occurred. Among legislators, both Republican and Democrat, the subject stings." [701] One liberal Democratic state Senator specifically identified those outside deals as the source of the governor's legislative problems. "Up until the point that he cut those outside deals, we had a good working relationship with him," Sen. Sheila Kuehl said. "Then it became difficult for him to come to us and say, 'Here's the deal: Rubber-stamp it.'" [702] The deals, which were with Democratic interest groups, left the party outside looking in. "They were a sign of disrespect to Democrats." [703] Democratic legislators' frustrations were a cost of doing business. The CTA was now an instrumental component of his political strategy. Mathews claims that combined with his celebrity and reliance on direct democracy, the protection of the CTA was the third leg of his political effectiveness.[704]

Despite the rhetoric and "show" to the contrary, Arnold never really addressed the systemic problems in California government. In January 2004, his first budget and State of the State Address, he promised change. But, that same year, his budget included "little evidence of a major restructuring in the budget blueprint," according to the *New York Times*. Thus, when the CTA and Arnold cut their budget deal, it was only delaying the day of reckoning. Even the CTA knew that their budget demands were untenable. In the fall, representatives of the CTA and the California School Boards Association reached out to the governor's office to find out whether

---

701 http://www.csmonitor.com/2004/0722/p02s01-uspo.html/

702 Id.

703 Id.

704 Joe Mathews, *The People's Machine: Arnold Schwarzenegger and the Rise of Blockbuster Democracy*, (New York: Public Affairs, 2006), 317.

the deal was still in place. They were told that there was nothing to worry about. Inside the horseshoe, the term used by insiders as a euphemism for the governor's office, the governor's office was quietly preparing its budget that would not meet the CTA's demands. One of the governor's top advisors wrote in a December 9 memo, "We are going after CTA with a vengeance." A week later, the war had begun. "Our students and public schools sacrificed this year with the promise that if the economy improved, they would get their fair share of any additional revenues," Barbara Kerr, president of the California Teachers Association, told the press in mid-December 2004. "We expect the governor and the legislature to honor that agreement. Our students are counting on it."[705] In truth, "our students and public schools" had sacrificed nothing. The schools had fared better than any other department, agency, or interest group in the 2004 state budget. Yet, they were adamant that they didn't get enough. The CTA, after all, was and remains unto this day the most powerful special interest group in Sacramento. They wanted more and they were willing to fight to get it. Mathews writes that a group of conservative leaders were advising against a direct confrontation with the powerful union. "We weren't going to do this because we weren't going to take on the teachers' union directly," Assemblyman John Campbell said.[706]

In his 2005 State of the State address, Gov. Schwarzenegger offered a reform platform that Republicans could only dream of. One press report that summarized many of the time, began with this opening sentence: "Gov. Arnold Schwarzenegger set the stage for what could be a bare-knuckle brawl with organized labor this year as he attempts to overhaul California government with changes that appear aimed directly at some of the most powerful unions in the state," the

705 Jill Tucker, "School groups want gov. to pay up," *The Oakland Tribune*, December 10, 2004.

706 Joe Mathews, *The People's Machine: Arnold Schwarzenegger and the Rise of Block-buster Democracy*, (New York: Public Affairs, 2006), 326.

United Press International wrote on January 6, 2005.[707] "Any time you try to remove one dollar from the budget, there are five special interests tugging on the other end," the governor explained in his annual address. "Any time you try to make something more efficient, there are a half-dozen special interests trying to prevent it."[708] Special interest groups, including the CTA, didn't appreciate being directly attacked by the governor. "I'm feeling a little chilly right now," Kerr said in response to the gubernatorial address. In some respects, the governor had already lost the public relations battle. The CTA in the first round of news stories had convinced the press to characterize Arnold as "breaking last year's deal." [709] Privately, Kerr emailed her board with a clear message of her 2005 strategy. "I guess I'm a wartime president," she wrote. [710] Within days, the CTA was assembling its army of paid political consultants, polling firms, and public relations experts. Over the Martin Luther King Jr. holiday in 2005, the top CTA political operatives secretly met in Sacramento to plot against Arnold's reforms. [711] Arnold's team, which wasn't aware of the meeting, had never faced the teachers union head-on, and thus didn't know the full extent of what was to come. One aide reportedly said of the CTA's State of the State response, "Can you believe CTA? They're going ape shit." Arnold, too, was naïve to the CTA's wartime posture. The governor ran into one of the CTA's leaders after the budget speech. When the CTA's representative expressed misgivings, the governor reportedly expressed surprise, "What are you talking bout?" Arnold said. "I love teachers."

Almost immediately, the CTA isolated Arnold from his Democratic allies. State Senate President Pro Temp Don Perata initially

---

707 "Commentary: Union battle ahead for Arnold?" UPI, January 6, 2005.

708 Id.

709 "Help me change it," Orange County Register, January 6, 2005.

710 Joe Mathews, *The People's Machine: Arnold Schwarzenegger and the Rise of Block-buster Democracy*, (New York: Public Affairs, 2006), 331.

711 Id. 335.

expressed some interest in working with the governor on his reform package. Just the willingness to engage the governor drew an attack from the CTA. In mid-February, Perata's district received 50,000 pieces of mail about how the state Senator wanted to cut funding for schools. These mailers were paid for by the ABC Alliance, an unprecedented coalition of the state's leading unions. Each union was required to contribute a minimum of $500,000 in order to join the coalition. It was, without a doubt, the single biggest special interest operation in California's history. Never before, and likely never again, had all the unions combined forces and worked together to stop a common enemy.

The CTA, along with the other ABC unions, also didn't have to struggle with the state's campaign finance laws. The CTA raised its dues by $60 per year, and immediately had more than $50 million in its coffers.[712] The union coalition also took their message to a willing press. Any move or policy decision, no matter how small or insignificant, was an opportunity to weaken Arnold.

The press reveled in a teachers-versus-Arnold storyline. In April, when Arnold appointed Alan Bersin, a former San Diego schools superintendent as his state education secretary, the media framed the move as a deliberate shot at the teachers union. "The appointment of Alan Bersin as California's next education secretary sent a strong signal Friday that Gov. Arnold Schwarzenegger remains committed to the notion that the chief ill of public schools is an entrenched, tenure-based hierarchy that rewards time over achievement among teachers," read the opening line of a press report in the *San Francisco Chronicle*. The press was playing along or being played by the CTA, who sent out a release claiming that the appointment "divided the community, hurt teacher morale, and failed to significantly improve student learning."[713]

712 Joe Mathews, *The People's Machine: Arnold Schwarzenegger and the Rise of Block-buster Democracy*, (New York: Public Affairs, 2006), 339.

713 http://www.sfgate.com/education/article/Schwarzenegger-has-new-man-same-message-on-2676343.php

By the end of spring, Arnold's popularity had plummeted and his staff began to realize the true strength of the entrenched special interest group they were at war with. But it was too late. The war had begun and the unions would accept nothing less than total surrender. In late May the Schwarzenegger administration sat down for peace talks with the CTA. The negotiations held secretly in Sacramento didn't result in any settlement. The CTA knew that their millions of dollars in negative political ads were working. All told, the unions spent $164 million attacking Arnold Schwarzenegger and his four reform proposals.[714] Not surprisingly, facing such a well-funded opposition, all of his measures were defeated. In 2005, an off-year election, special interest groups had spent more than $325 million in campaign spending on just eight ballot measures. "At $238 million, the total spending on the governor's four measures was greater than the domestic box office gross of any Schwarzenegger movie," Mathews writes in his book on Arnold's time in Sacramento. "*Terminator 2* came closest with $204 million." [715] Arnold's naïveté included assuming when he became governor that he would have all the power he needed to push "reforms" because of his popularity. He made an attempt with his initiatives but still fumbled. It's difficult to determine whether the outcome would have been different if Arnold waited until a normal election year. If it had been on the regular election ballot, maybe the outcome would have been different. After all, Ronald Reagan similarly lost a special initiative election in 1973 on his Prop. 1.

Whatever the cause of Arnold's special election defeat, the outcome was devastating on Arnold's resolve to fight the liberal special interest groups, the groups directly responsible for California's rapid decline. His accomplishments surely did not match the rhetoric of his early years. His secret promises to the CTA eventually doomed him. Within days of the special election defeat, Arnold settled a

---

714 Joe Mathews, *The People's Machine: Arnold Schwarzenegger and the Rise of Blockbuster Democracy*, (New York: Public Affairs, 2006), 392.

715 Id.

bitterly-contested lawsuit with the California Nurses Association about the staffing ratios in hospitals. That fight had been one of the first and most public spats between Arnold and the unions. [716]

Arnold also made major changes to his staff. The more conservative members of the Governor's staff were sent packing, while he brought in liberal replacements. The most substantial new staff member was Susan Kennedy, a Democratic activist and former Gray Davis advisor, as his new chief of staff. Republicans were furious with what was perceived as a deliberate snub. [717] The conservative California Republican Assembly volunteer organization (CRA), once dubbed by Reagan as the conscience of the Republican Party, said that the GOP should consider pulling Arnold's endorsement. [718] "The problem is a very partisan Democrat chief of staff will still be directing all these people on Schwarzenegger's staff," Mike Spence, president of the CRA, told reporters. [719] According to FlashReport. org's Jon Fleischman, "Schwarzenegger's appointment of Kennedy was a body blow to Republicans. Not only had she been Deputy Chief of Staff to recalled Democrat Governor Gray Davis, but she had served as Executive Director of the California Democratic Party. I got to know Kennedy a bit, and found her to be wicked smart. I know that she got 'inside of the head' of Republican legislative leaders in 2009 and it resulted in a budget deal with, at the time, the largest tax increase in California history." [720]

California Republican Party Chairman Duf Sundheim immediately defended the governor after a quick meeting with some of the party's leaders. "He addressed all the issues that were raised,"

---

716 "Governor expected to move back to center in 2006," Associated Press, December 28, 2005.

717 http://indian-valley.vlex.com/vid/schwarzenegger-aguiar-hed-taps-69356757

718 "Schwarzenegger, GOP try to move past Kennedy controversy," Associated Press, December 16, 2005.

719 *Monterey County Herald*, December 10, 2005.

720 Interview with the author, September 23, 2013.

Sundheim said of Arnold's meeting with Republicans. "He reaffirmed his commitment to be a strong fiscal conservative, and everybody in that room is totally committed to his re-election in 2006."[721]

The state's business community released a statement praising Kennedy. "I have the highest respect for Susan and know that she will be a terrific asset to Governor Schwarzenegger's administration," said California Chamber of Commerce President Allan Zaremberg. "Throughout her career in government, Susan has always sought to improve California's economy."[722] But perhaps the Chamber was simply trying to make the best of a bad situation. Kennedy's time as deputy chief of staff to the previously recalled governor included raised taxes, a bungled energy crisis, and a workers' compensation reform crisis. Kennedy's appointment by Arnold signaled that he was going to give-in to the very same political forces he claimed to have opposed in his first run for Governor. Yet again, so much for "blowing up the boxes."

Kennedy's biography also showed the way forward for a new liberal Schwarzenegger. Kennedy was forced to resign as a member of the state's Public Utility Commission to take her new position with Arnold. At the PUC, she had developed a very liberal record on environmental issues.[723] Arnold would rely on Kennedy's guidance to shepherd his crowning achievement and most questionable anti-business boondoggle through the legislature, AB 32.

California's experiment with Arnold Schwarzenegger as governor demonstrated that regardless of reform rhetoric, an angry and motivated public demanding change, and the popularity of a wealthy Hollywood mega-star, liberal Democrats and their public employee union allies could still run the state.

---

721 *Contra Costa Times*, December 16, 2005.

722 California Chamber of Commerce Statement Regarding the Appointment of Susan Kennedy as Governor Schwarzenegger's Chief of Staff, November 30, 2005 http://www.calchamber.com/PressReleases/2005/Pages/11302005PR.aspx

723 "PUC earmarks $300 million for solar energy subsidization," *Contra Costa Times*, December 16, 2005.

THE GLOBAL WARMING SOLUTIONS ACT AND CALIFORNIA AS THE WORLD'S "GREEN" POLICEMAN

A GOOD MOVIE IS built around the art of illusion. Actors pretend to be people they're not, speaking lines out of fictional plots and creating make-believe drama to entertain the audience. A setting that may appear to be on a mysterious foreign city's streets actually might be staged on a dusty Hollywood back lot. Illusion tricks the eye, and the audience. And, of course, special effects can present the appearance that heroes are in perilous danger, when more often than not, they're safe and sound behind a camera, and in front of what's called a "green screen." It makes sense, then, that a Hollywood superstar, a master of the *green* screen, would attempt to be the hero to usher in blockbuster *green* legislation to save the environment, with the flare and staging of a Hollywood movie premier.

In late September 2006 Governor Arnold Schwarzenegger signed into law Assembly Bill 32, a sweeping piece of legislation intended to reduce California's "carbon" footprint worldwide. Because the signing was timed just a few months before his re-election, Arnold and his handlers took advantage of AB 32's enactment as an elaborate press-generating show to lift the Governor's election prospects with California's "green" voters in both northern and southern California. Global dignitaries were tapped to speak at the event. "You are showing brilliant leadership that will inspire people around the world," said former British Prime Minister Tony Blair, who refuted the criticism that the global warming regulations would stifle job creation. "What we've actually found is, we've grown our economy . . . we have created hundreds of thousands of jobs in environmental technology."[724] Borrowing a few tricks of illusion from his tradecraft, at the signing at picturesque Pepperdine University in Malibu,[725] Arnold said, "[w]hen we sign this bill we will begin a bold new era of environmental protection here in California that will change the course of history." In truth, Schwarzenegger's signature on the bill would do little to "begin a bold new era of environmental protection" and that wasn't the only fib told by the governor. He was also doing some acting when putting his signature on the bill. In fact, the Governor had already signed the bill earlier in the day in San Francisco, at an event overlooking the city skyline and iconic Treasure Island.[726] "In a few minutes when I sign Assembly Bill 32 we will begin a bold new era of environmental protection here in the state of California that can change the course of history," he told the crowd at the morning event in the Bay Area, with the exact words he would mirror later in the day in Malibu.

Illusions and white lies are perfectly acceptable in action and adventure film scripts. But, in public policy decisions, when people's livelihoods are at risk, the truth matters a great deal. In many respects, Arnold's pretending to sign the bill a second time can be seen as a metaphor for the illusion and truth of AB 32, which has become one of the biggest job-killing pieces of legislation in California history. California officials cannot plead ignorance; rather, they were repeatedly warned in advance of AB 32's consequences.

---

724 http://gov.ca.gov/news.php?id=5176

725 Governor Schwarzenegger Signs Historic Legislation at Pepperdine, http://www.pepperdine.edu/pr/releases/2006/september/governor.htm

726 "State's war on warming," *San Francisco Chronicle*, September 28, 2006, http://www.sfgate.com/green/article/State-s-war-on-warming-Governor-signs-measure-2487887.php

Jack Stewart, the president of the California Manufacturers and Technology Association, cautioned that legislature's good intentions would devastate California's economy. "The economic graveyards of California are littered with the jobs that are the unintended consequences of good intentions by legislators and governors," he said.[727] "It could also have the unintended consequence of reducing emissions here but increasing global emissions—a lose-lose situation."[728] Stewart's worst case scenario was echoed by none other than the governor's own Climate Action Team. "If the state implements the program without other western states, there will be an incentive for activities that emit GHGs [greenhouse gases] to shift to neighboring states to avoid the emission cap," the committee of supportive aides wrote in March 2006. "If this occurs, emissions may decline in the state, only to increase in neighboring states."[729]

Democrat legislators dismissed these concerns as political rhetoric. "Those criticisms are more about political rhetoric than about what's really happening in our economy," one Democrat state Senator from San Diego said. "California is gaining jobs. And we're gaining good jobs, professional jobs, high-tech jobs, clean jobs."[730] Democrat legislators received some backup from the liberal editorial boards throughout California. The *Los Angeles Times*, in a classic case of political sophistry, twisted the argument— claiming that AB 32 created jobs. "California—and California business—needs AB 32," the paper editorialized in August 2006, prior to the legislature's vote

727 http//www.washingtonpost.com/wp-dyn/content/article/2006/08/31/ AR2006083100146.html

728 Jack M. Stewart, "California needs to get it right on climate change policies," August 29, 2006, http://www.sfgate.com/opinion/openforum/article/California-needs to-get-it-right-on-climate-2554057.php

729 Climate Action Team, March 27, 2006, Cap and Trade Program; Design Options Report of the Cap and Trade Subgroup of the Climate Action Team.

730 http://www.utsandiego.com/news/2006/sep/17/ governor-local-gop-disagree-on-global-warming/all/?print

on the bill. "In fact, AB 32 could help create jobs."[731] With the job argument muddled, far left environmentalists went on the offensive. In the fall of 2006 a Northern California Democrat Assemblywoman claimed at a community event, "I think the California Global Warming Solutions Act of 2006—in the long run—will be essential to our very survival."[732]

She obviously wasn't talking about the very survival of California's businesses. The numbers speak for themselves. In July 2006 when the legislature was hotly debating AB 32, California's unemployment rate was just 4.9 percent. Within three years, California's jobless rate reached a 70-year high of 12.2 percent. To find a comparable unemployment rate you have to go back to the Great Depression, according to a spokesman for the California Employment Development Department.[733] To be fair, the global economic crisis is largely to blame for rising unemployment rates throughout the United States, including California. But, it doesn't explain the extent of the problem facing California nor does the economic crisis account for the entire problem.

In the years prior to 2006, the unemployment rates of California and Texas largely mirrored each other, occasionally shifting by a few tenths of a percent. For example, in July 2006, the unemployment rate in Texas was 5 percent. That was a statistically insignificant tenth of a percent worse than California's rate of 4.9 percent. But by 2010, after the initial period of implementation of California's Global Warming Solutions Act, California's unemployment rate had more than doubled to 12.4 percent, while Texas' rate was much lower at 8.1 percent. Those comparative numbers do have statistical significance. According to an economic analysis conducted by Sanjay

731 "Be a cool leader," *LA Times* Editorial, August 13, 2006, http://articles.latimes.com/2006/aug/13/opinion/ed-global13

732 Assemblywoman Patty Berg, Climate Protection Campaign, Speech on September 16, 2006, http://www.skymetrics.us/news/news50.php

733 Jennifer Steinhauer, "California Joblessness Reaches 70-Year High," *New York Times*, September 18, 2009, http://www.nytimes.com/2009/09/19/us/19calif.html

Varshney, Dean of the business school at California State University-Sacramento, the economic impacts of AB 32 are dire. "In summary, the implementation costs of AB 32 could easily exceed $100 billion upfront," the academic found.[734] Those economic impacts could have played a role in the remarkable increase in unemployment in California in comparison to Texas.

The media largely ignored reporting the differences in unemployment losses between Texas and California and their potential relationship to California's implementation of AB 32. However, the *Sacramento Bee* picked up on the data and noted that AB 32 could "cost the average household $3,857 a year, kill more than 1.1 million jobs, and cut the state's economic output by nearly 10 percent."[735]

What is AB 32 and what does it attempt to accomplish?

In order to reduce California-based carbon pollution emissions, AB 32 established the California Air Resources Control Board (CARB) as "the sole state agency responsible for monitoring and regulating sources" of greenhouse gas emissions in the state.[736] By 2020, CARB is tasked with reducing the state's greenhouse gas emission limit by 25%.[737] CARB now has the authority to monitor, regulate, and mandate greenhouse gas emission levels for businesses operating in California. The appointed board has the authority "to impose administrative, civil, and/or criminal penalties." AB 32 also lays

734 CCost of AB 32 on California Small Businesses – Summary Report of Findings, Varshney & Associates, June 2009, http://www.killcarb.org/602-AB32costanalysis.pdf

735 "California State dean predicts major fiscal impact from climate law," Sacramento Bee, October 19, 2009, http://www.mcclatchydc.com/2009/10/19/v-print/77369/california-state-dean-predicts.html

736 LAO Report, Analysis of the 2007-08 Budget Bill: Resources, http://www.lao.ca.gov/analysis_2007/resources/res_04_anl07.aspx

737 California State Assembly Bill Analysis AB 32, http://leginfo.ca.gov/pub/05-06/bill/asm/ab_0001-0050/ab_32_cfa_20060905_120408_asm_floor.html

the framework for CARB to establish controversial "cap and trade auctions," whereby a distribution system for pollution allowances is established.[738] Under the program, companies labeled large-scale "polluters," such as a vegetable processing facility, are assigned an annual cap on the amount of carbon they can lawfully emit, declining slightly each year. Companies exceeding their limit are either forced to reduce their business activities or purchase additional emissions credits from the state or other companies to keep doing business as usual. Some businesses feel their limits are too tight and that they get little in return for paying for carbon credits. A spokesman for Woodland-based Morning Star Co., which processes tomatoes, says there wasn't a viable trading market last fall when the company was forced to go and bid at auctions by AB 32. He said that carbon credits, even when gained, are "not an asset of substantial value."[739] The state auctions a small amount of credits on its own every three months through CARB.[740] Under the regulations established by CARB, the cap and trade program affects any business that emits more than 25,000 metric tons of carbon dioxide per year, a standard that is estimated to cover more than 600 facilities operated by 360 businesses in the state. [741] In 2015 CARB will expand to include more regulations "to account for the emissions from all the vehicles in the state."[742]

So, what can the transportation industry expect when CARB begins to regulate the emissions of all vehicles in the state? Sadly, diesel truck drivers know all too well the cost of CARB's regulations. In December

---

738 *Washington Post*, September 1, 2006, http://www.washingtonpost.com/wp-dyn/content/article/2006/08/31/AR2006083100146.html

739 http://www.sacbee.com/2013/08/29/5690290/sacramento-judge-tentatively-says.html

740 http://www.sacbee.com/2013/08/29/5690290/sacramento-judge-tentatively-says.html

741 http://www.mercurynews.com/ci_21972739/californias-landmark-global-warming-law-becomes-real-this

742 Id.

2008 the agency approved new regulations of buses and trucks in an effort to reduce "particulate matter." Nearly a million vehicles are subject to the new restrictions, which, in turn, affect approximately 170,000 businesses in nearly every sector of the state's economy.[743] Construction-based businesses, which rely on heavy equipment to operate, have been forced to retro-fit or replace equipment in order to avoid CARB's punitive fines. One construction company, MCM Construction, spent nearly $3 million on CARB compliance costs. Yet, the company's general counsel says that there's no guarantee that those expenditures will be enough to satisfy CARB. "Our concern is we're shooting at a moving target," Ed Puchi of MCM Construction, one of the biggest bridge builders in California, told a CBS affiliate. "We've spent this kind of money and we don't know whether that's going to put us in compliance or not."[744] The company doesn't know because the scientific basis of CARB's diesel regulations were found to be flawed. A 2010 investigation by the *San Francisco Chronicle* found that "California grossly miscalculated pollution levels in a scientific analysis used to toughen the state's clean-air standards."[745] The newspaper, in the bastion of California liberalism, reported that the diesel regulation was 340 percent higher than it should have been. Oops! Skip Brown, the president of Delta Construction in Sacramento, whose CARB compliance costs were pegged at $5 million, aptly stated, "It's called trust me science."[746] This "trust me science" is costly, too, for workers. Brown laid off 15 of his workers as he struggled with CARB's new regulations. Other business leaders have echoed this refrain. "From what I can tell, joblessness is far more unhealthy than

---

743 CARB Fact Sheet, Truck and Bus Regulation Reducing Emissions from Existing Diesel Vehicles, REVISED July 20, 2012, http://www.arb.ca.gov/msprog/onrdiesel/documents/fsoverview.pdf

744 http://sacramento.cbslocal.com/2010/11/04/on-the-money-air-pollution-fight-gets-dirty/

745 http://www.sfgate.com/green/article/Overestimate-fueled-state-s-landmark-diesel-law-3250576.php

746 http://sacramento.cbslocal.com/2010/11/04/on-the-money-air-pollution-fight-gets-dirty/

the air we breathe anywhere in this state today," Rob McClernon, a small business owner and president of the California Dump Truck Owners Association, told *Better Roads Magazine*. "Food on the table, a roof over your head, and healthcare for your family are just as important if not more than nominally cleaner air."[747] Of course, lay-offs, unemployment, and low wages are exacerbated by rising energy rates. As one utilities expert bluntly put it, "When power shortages occur and rates go up, the people who are hurt the most are the ones least able to afford it."[748]

CARB regulators, who receive very good government paychecks and generous pensions, don't have to worry about joblessness or poverty. In 2007 the first year that AB 32 became law, the state budget included a $35.8 million increase for various state agencies to fund the program and begin implementation of the new regulations. The new budget outlay created 151 new government positions. CARB would receive the lion's share of the new funds, or more than $24 million.[749] The independent Legislative Analyst's Office then warned that the state was relying on unsustainable budget sources to fund AB 32. Not to worry, CARB has developed a cottage industry of complementary businesses that work to justify new taxes, fees, and fines.[750] There is now a financial incentive for liberal academic institutions to publish studies on air quality that are not thoroughly vetted, or that twist and turn the data until they have a publishable finding. "That's how it works," Lois Henry, a columnist with the *Bakersfield Californian* explains. "A study says we're all gonna die and CARB rides in to slay whatever dragon a handful of scientists claim to

---

747 http://www.betterroads.com/ca-dump-truck-owners-association-sues-carb/

748 *Washington Post*, September 1, 2006, http://www.washingtonpost.com/wp-dyn/content/article/2006/08/31/AR2006083100146.html

749 LAO Report, Analysis of the 2007-08 Budget Bill: Resources, http://www.lao.ca.gov/analysis_2007/resources/res_04_anl07.aspx

750 Id.

see."[751] Such was the case with the original diesel regulations that missed the mark by 340 percent, but even the revised regulations used contrived science. Using eight models, the authors of the new study could not find evidence that premature death was linked to "particulate matter." So they created a new model called "conurbation," which merged past studies together. These findings were, after all, from *accredited* scientists— not all of CARB's scientific authorities have valid credentials. One CARB employee falsified his resume by claiming to have a PhD from the University of California-Davis. Hien Tran had, in fact, through the mail purchased a useless piece of paper for $1,000 from a diploma mill. The agency conducted an investigation only after significant criticism from a CARB board member. CARB board member John Telles believes that the issue tainted the regulatory process. "Failure to reveal this information to the board prior to the vote not only casts doubt on the legitimacy of the truck rule, but also upon the legitimacy of CARB itself," he said.[752] The regulations, however, remained in place just like the phony scientist, whose only punishment was a 60-day suspension. The journalist, who first reported on the story, lamented the agency's response, "The liar not only didn't get fired, he continues to write state regulations."[753]

The same cannot be said for a brave scientist that questioned CARB's authority and scientific credibility. James Enstrom, an epidemiologist and physicist at the UCLA Jonsson Comprehensive Cancer Center, was one of the few academics to publicly criticize CARB. "If you were strapped for cash and lived in North Dakota, would you spend money on hurricane insurance?" Enstrom and Henry Miller, a physician and molecular biologist at Stanford University,

751 http://www.bakersfieldcalifornian.com/health/x560461816/
New-study-doesnt-hit-the-mark-for-air-pollution-deaths

752 http://www.ocregister.com/articles/tran-222324-board-carb.html

753 Chris Reed, CalWatchdog.com, November 5, 2012 http://calwatchdog.
com/2012/11/05/carb-scandal-also-shames-california-media/

wrote in a *Forbes* column. "That would be no dumber than the regulations of the California Air Resources Board, designed to reduce the form of 'air pollution' known as diesel particulate matter."[754] CARB didn't take kindly to a professor questioning their authority. Within a month, UCLA informed Enstrom that his contract would not be renewed. The university's excuse: his "research is not aligned with the academic mission of the Department."[755] The professor has filed a lawsuit for wrongful termination that, as of August 2013, was still being litigated.[756] CARB's intimidation tactics didn't stop Enstrom's truth-telling. He pointed out to Fox News some of the flaws with CARB's diesel regulations. "The Scientific Review Panel of Toxic Air Contaminates in 1998 declared diesel exhaust a toxic substance based on studying truckers and railroaders from back in the '50s, '60s and '70s, when emissions were much higher," he said. "They never factored in, for example, that a very high percentage of truckers are also smokers when evaluating heath issues they may have had, yet they were using this research to declare that all diesel exhaust is a toxic substance."[757] Academic institutions have a vested interest in keeping CARB happy because some fine revenue goes back to colleges. In the second quarter of 2011 one Bay Area college district received $52,000 from the fines against 37 businesses who had failed "to properly conduct and pass self-inspections aimed at measuring vehicle smoke emissions to ensure state requirements are met."[758] At

---

754 http://www.forbes.com/2010/06/08/california-diesel-regulation-pollution-opinions-columnists-henry-i-miller-james-e-enstrom.html

755 Nature.com, Dissident air pollution researcher sues university over firing, June 16, 2012, http://blogs.nature.com/news/2012/06/dissident-air-pollution-researcher-sues-university-over-firing.html

756 "Will House Science Panel Need an Ethical Review?" Science Magazine, August 12, 2013, http://news.sciencemag.org/climate/2013/08/will-house-science-panel-need-ethical-review

757 http://www.foxnews.com/us/2010/08/31/pc-professors-firing-fueling-exhaustive-debate/

758 CARB Press Release, Businesses fined for air quality violations, Release #:11-42 September 23, 2011, http://www.arb.ca.gov/newsrel/newsrelease.php?id=243

an individual level, some scientists fear losing funding for studies or prestigious invitations to speak before the agency as a part of its "Air Resources Board Chairman's Lecture Series."[759] Seemingly petty, the speeches are important for academic careers and achieving tenure.

Is It Leading When No One Follows?

Back in 2006, environmental leaders and politicians rushed to make grand pronouncements about AB 32 leading the global warming regulatory effort. "The success of our system will be an example for other states and nations to follow as the fight against climate change continues," Schwarzenegger vowed. "AB 32 strengthens our economy, cleans our environment, and once again establishes California as the leader in environmental protection."[760] At the elaborate signing ceremony, British Prime Minister Tony Blair explained "that if we can get the leadership, not just from countries that have traditionally been very strong on this issue, but from states within the United States of America as well, and hopefully in time from the whole of America, if we can get that leadership, then this has enormous possibilities."[761] The liberal establishment rushed to reinforce this message and cement it as conventional wisdom. "Where California goes, others will follow," promised a spokesman for the San Francisco-based environmental group Natural Resources Defense Council.[762] The then-Speaker of the California Assembly and co-author of AB 32, Fabian Nuñcz, said, "For us, this is not just about

---

759 ARB Press Release, Release #:13-44, August 12, 2013, MEDIA ADVISORY: UCLA professor/author to speak on Climate Change: Its Impact on California's Cities and Economy, http://www.arb.ca.gov/newsrel/newsrelease.php?id=477

760 http://abcnews.go.com/US/GlobalWarming/story?id=2374968

761 Governor Schwarzenegger Signs Low Carbon Fuels Standard Executive Order.

762 http://www.utsandiego.com/news/2006/sep/17/ governor-local-gop-disagree-on-global-warming/all/?print

California. This is about making a push from the bottom up to get the Congress to take action."[763] Even the *New York Times* acknowledged that the left-wing push came to a stop in 2010, when federal cap-and-trade legislation died in Congress.[764] But, the Environmental Defense Fund takes the cake for over-the-top rhetoric. EDF's James D. Marston, said, "We'll look back in 10 years and say this was the final breakthrough and the final political consensus that we have to do something meaningful on global warming."[765]

Seven years into that ten year assessment, the environmental platitudes and political promises have proven faulty. California hasn't led anyone to follow its substantial boondoggle. It's exactly as the Cato Institute's Senior Fellows Jerry Taylor and Peter Van Doren warned: AB 32 had devastating effects on California's economic climate without any meaningful impact on the environment. "Were we environmentalists, we'd be annoyed that politicians were being let off the global warming policy hook so easily," the pair wrote in 2006. "But we're not, so let's just say that it's the political cynicism—not the economic consequences—that bothers us the most."[766] Other states have feared that adopting California's draconian limits on emissions would further undermine their fragile economies. [767] It's no wonder that no other state has followed California down the path of global warming regulations, or as one Republican state senator dubbed AB 32, "the road to economic ruin for California." [768] Even the *New York Times* has acknowledged that California "is making a huge bet:

763 *Washington Post*, September 1, 2006, http://www.washingtonpost.com/wp-dyn/content/article/2006/08/31/AR2006083100146.html

764 http://www.nytimes.com/2012/11/14/business/energy-environment/california-to-hold-auction-of-greenhouse-gas-emissions.html

765 http://www.nytimes.com/2006/09/15/us/15energy.html?pagewanted=all

766 http://www.cato.org/publications/commentary/californias-global-warming-dodge

767 National Geographic News, November 16, 2012, http://news.nationalgeographic.com/news/energy/2012/11/121116-california-cap-and-trade/

768 NBC News, August 31, 2006, http://www.nbcnews.com/id/14590345/ns/us_news-environment/t/calif-moves-cap-greenhouse-gas-emissions/#.UhjcTpKTTMs

that it can reduce emissions without wrecking its economy, and therefore inspire other states—and countries—to follow its example on slowing climate change."[769]

The road to economic ruin for California led businesses to setup shop elsewhere. A big problem with AB 32 is that the regulations put California businesses at a disadvantage in facing competition from out-of-state companies that aren't being forced to reduce their emission at the same robust levels. Out-of-state oil refiners, for example, don't have the need to offset their carbon emissions with California-based refiners, who are subject to limits and must either reduce operations or pay for credits for additional emissions from the government or at auction. In this manner AB 32 makes it much more expensive for California businesses to operate, and during a recession and a period of high unemployment, the law becomes yet another self-imposed obstacle to the economic well-being of the state.

Air regulations are so devastating that they've even managed to undermine some of California's traditional powerhouse industries. If you've seen the old television advertising campaign, you know that once "happy cows come from California." Not anymore. The number of dairy farms operating in the Golden State has consistently declined during the last decade. In 2003 California was home to more than 2,100 dairies. However, it has plummeted to just 1,563 in 2012.[770] Dairy farmers are moving out of the state because of high feed prices, low milk prices, and government regulations. Cows, which consume large amounts of water and emit plenty of methane, are major "polluters." A 2006 United Nations report labeled cattle as "the greatest threat to the climate, forests, and wildlife."[771] "The large share of dairy and beef cattle in California agriculture has important implications for greenhouse gas emissions," concluded one UC study on

769 http://www.nytimes.com/2006/09/15/us/15energy.html?pagewanted=all

770 http://articles.latimes.com/2013/mar/30/business/la-fi-california-dairies-20130330

771 http://www.independent.co.uk/environment/climate-change/cow-emissions-more-damaging-to-planet-than-co2-from-cars-427843.html

the agricultural effects of AB 32.[772] California's regulatory climate isn't lost on dairy farmers. One dairy family sold their farm in Corona and moved to Colorado, where they were constructing a $250 million facility. "We searched for a place that had better long-term prospects," the dairy farmer, Mark Vander Dussen told the *Los Angeles Times*. The state's $8 billion dairy industry is quickly losing market share to other states. Wisconsin and Idaho, which do not have their own versions of California's "Global Warming Solutions Act", and which produced a combined 39.4 billion pounds of milk in 2011, are on pace to top California. "Ten years ago, California was the low-cost producer," an agriculture economist at UC-Davis who specializes in the dairy industry said. "It's become more difficult to dairy here."[773]

While California also appears in retreat as a leader in manufacturing, entertainment, education, job creation, and energy production, there is one area where California is being recognized as an international leader, and that is its implementation of what is described as the "first economy-wide cap-and-trade program" to reduce worldwide carbon-dioxide emissions.[774] Almost immediately after California hosted America's very first state-level cap-and-trade auction in November 2012, the problems with CARB's regulations became apparent. "California carbon market launches, permits priced below expectations" read the headline for the Reuters news agency.[775] Nevertheless, Mary Nichols, chairwoman of the air resources board, described the auction results as a success. "The auction was a success and an important milestone for California as a

---

772 Daniel A. Sumner and John Thomas Rosen-Molina, "Impacts of AB 32 on Agriculture," Giannini Foundation of Agricultural Economics, University of California, Vol.14 no. 1, Sep/Oct 2010,

773 http://articles.latimes.com/2013/mar/30/business/la-fi-california-dairies-20130330

774 http://blogs.edf.org/californiadream/2013/06/04/california-a-national-leader-in-an-international-trend/

775 http://www.reuters.com/article/2012/11/19/us-california-carbonmarket-idUSBRE8AI13X20121119

leader in the global clean tech market," she said in a prepared statement released on CARB's website. "By putting a price on carbon, we can break our unhealthy dependence on fossil fuels and move at full speed toward a clean energy future. That means new jobs, cleaner water and air—and a working model for other states, and the nation, to use as we gear up to fight climate change and make our economy more competitive and resilient."[776] Yet no such jobs have materialized that are attributable to AB 32, as California faces historic unemployment levels. Only a few jobs for government regulators have been the result.

State regulators were simply unprepared or unqualified to oversee the market. The state received just $300 million from the first auction. One month after the first auction, a Bloomberg analysis found that the state had to disqualify 66 percent of companies' offers for the carbon credits. "After the disqualifications, the state had 1.06 legitimate bids per permit for the 23.1 million permits put up for sale on Nov. 14," the Bloomberg report found. [777] "The auction barely squeaked by." The number was a surprise because state regulators had happily sold to the press a number triple that amount. In advance of the auction, when the state's regulators were trying to propagandize its importance, the state claimed to have 3.1 bids for every permit available.[778]

California's carbon auction, the world's second largest auction system, only surpassed by the European Union, doesn't just have problems with the numbers. It also can't keep the public informed of its proceedings. Prior to the auction, CARB Chairwoman Mary Nichols said, "We've erred on the side of making this program

776 CARB Press Release #12-55, Date 11/19/2012, Statement by Air Resources Board Chairman Mary D. Nichols on California's first cap-and-trade auction, http://www.arb.ca.gov/newsrel/newsrelease.php?id=367

777 http://www.bloomberg.com/news/2012-12-06/california-carbon-permits-bids-averaged-15-60-last-month.html

778 Id.

transparent and enforceable."[779] Despite repeated promises of open-
ness and transparency, CARB has kept the bidding process hidden
from public view. CARB chief Nichols predicted revenue of "$500
million to $1 billion in the first year." Yet the auction netted the
state's new Air Pollution Control Fund just $55 million.[780]

California's cap-and-trade auctions, conducted by CARB, have
been challenged in court and after seven years only recently been
upheld by a Superior Court Judge.[781] The California Chamber of
Commerce sees the carbon auctions, which have the potential of
raising billions in state revenues, as an illegal form of taxation not
properly enacted. Governor Jerry Brown has reportedly said he is
weighing use of cap-and-trade revenue to help balance the state
budget,[782] which suggests the state's elected officials may be treating
the pollution income as something like a tax. But whether through
a withering California economy as a result of businesses leaving
the state, or success in carbon reduction efforts, California's carbon
emissions are now reportedly projected to be lower than expected
through 2019.[783] Brown won't have much government funding by
way of selling carbon emission permits in the future; neither will he
see any improvement in unemployment rates in the meantime while
job-killing legislation like AB 32 remains on the books.

779 http://calwatchdog.com/2012/12/09/
ready-evidence-keeps-building-of-flaws-in-states-carbon-auction/

780 Id.

781 http://www.sacbee.com/2013/08/29/5690290/sacramento-judge-tentatively-says.
html

782 http://cleantechnica.com/2013/08/27/
california-cap-and-trade-comes-to-a-crossroads-as-carbon-prices-fall/

783 http://www.environmentalleader.com/2013/09/11/
california-carbon-price-forecast-plunges/

SILICON VALLEY ENTREPRENEURS: "A GAME CHANGER?"

LIBERAL TAX-AND-SPEND THINKING AND liberal Democratic dominance in California could be turned back if just a handful of the creative, independent, self-made and self-reliant entrepreneurs of the Silicon Valley make a decision to focus their values and immense high-tech organizing skills on solving California's economic problems. Indeed, such a shift from their current disengagement could be a game changer that could lift California out of its stagnant and toxic one-party control and get the economy rocking again. It's not just a game changer because of the potential for wealthy Silicon Valley political donors to enter into the political stream in support of candidates and causes backing reform. Rather, if they are up to the challenge, a new generation of successful Californians in the Valley could make a huge difference by direct engagement. We've seen their brilliant minds transform our lives with technology. Now, we need Silicon Valley applying its way of thinking to government and politics.

It is indeed curious that the bright young problem solvers in the high technology community have had so little influence, or even interest, in helping to solve California's problems. Politics of course, is a different science from electrical engineering. One clue may be that Silicon Valley's insular and isolated nature has led its innovators to distance themselves from the rest of the state. First, they prefer to develop gated work communities that are much less affected by daily travails of California life. Second, too many of those who have actually delved into public policy have seemed to waste time and resources on perpetuating the current liberalism that isn't working for California, or fringe Libertarianism such as Ron Paul's losing presidential campaign, without achieving any tangible results. Opportunities to engage and work on real problems and practical solutions to California's busted economy get ignored. Finally, and perhaps worst of all, to the extent they have engaged in the political process rather than follow the example of their own innovations and thought, tech entrepreneurs have tended to rely on high-priced political consultants, who are usually deeply compromised by California's out-of-balance power structure, and who employ the same tired, traditional, and status-quo oriented strategies to their political engagement.

Insular, Isolated and Disengaged

In May 2013 the *New Yorker* delivered an in-depth look inside public policy advocacy emanating from Silicon Valley. It revealed the pervasive alienation from general society that is very much a part of the withdrawn and disengaged Silicon Valley culture. For starters, most technology companies have situated themselves to be physically removed from the rest of us. Google, Facebook, Apple and many more technology companies have built campuses "to be fully functioning communities, not just places for working."[784] The perks available on these campuses to keep workers close to home include on-site dentists, dry-cleaning, free gourmet meals, daycares, gyms, massages, and almost every other conceivable human need

---

784 George Packer, "CHANGE THE WORLD: Silicon Valley transfers its slogans—and its money—to the realm of politics," *New Yorker*, MAY 27, 2013.

and desire. All of the well-publicized perks at these companies have the collective effect of largely removing the brilliant cadre of people working for the technology firms from interaction with the general populace, where they might experience firsthand some of the failings of government itself. As the *New Yorker* described it, "These inward-looking places keep tech workers from having even accidental contact with the surrounding community."[785]

One of the most fundamental exposures to real life for employees of any companies, let alone tech companies, is on the daily commute to work. Yet most Silicon Valley employees don't have to deal with public transportation, traffic jams, or one-hour commutes from home to work. They can leave the frustrations of driving to someone else. Google has its unmarked "Google Bus" to pick up their employees from home and drop them off at the company's headquarters. As one San Francisco resident aptly described this occurrence in the *London Review of Books*, "Sometimes the Google Bus just seems like one face of Janus-headed capitalism; it contains the people too valuable even to use public transport or drive themselves."[786] Silicon Valley is so successful their culture can carve themselves out from the rest of the residents of the state, including having to deal with agencies like the Department of Motor Vehicles, perhaps one of government's worst examples of efficiency. Perhaps because these individuals do not need to fully experience the direct consequences of liberalism that the rest of us in California are left to deal with, they have been able to succeed in spite of California's overall decline.

Yet, no matter how hard technology entrepreneurs try to isolate themselves, inevitably their businesses and innovations will be obstructed by government. One such example of a successful Valley business running head-on into government regulations is Lyft. The

---

785 Id.

786 Rebecca Solnit, Vol. 35 No. 3, February 7, 2013, pages 34-35, London Review of Books, http://www.lrb.co.uk/v35/n03/rebecca-solnit/diary

new and appropriately named service is designed to add necessary competition in the taxi market. California might be known for its car culture, but it still has a healthy supply of taxis, which are tightly controlled by government regulations. In San Francisco, whenever a cab driver tries to sell their medallion—the license to operate a taxi cab—the city collects a cool $100,000 commission on the transaction.[787] Los Angeles is no better with its own regulations on the cab business. The city of Angeles' draconian restrictions on taxi drivers have kept taxi drivers in poverty. According to a UCLA study, "Taxi drivers work an average 72 hours per week, sometimes putting in 18-20 hours per day driving in Los Angeles traffic." All of these long days result in a median hourly salary of just $8.39 per hour. That's less than the city's "living wage" ordinance. Researchers found that "the City regulates the lives of drivers in minute detail, specifying what they can charge and even what they can wear." Nearly half of all citations during an eight-month period in 2006 were for "dress code" violations, according to the UCLA study.[788]

Lyft has created a cheap, useful taxi service that is free of government interference and market control. The work of a start-up company, Zimride, the Lyft smartphone app allows people to log on and find a driver willing to give them a ride. Drivers' criminal and driving records are reviewed to ensure passengers' safety.[789] Vehicles are also regularly inspected, and passengers are encouraged to rate their drivers in order to weed out anyone who is unsafe.[790] And the fares, well technically, they're optional. That's in order to escape the government regulations and avoid being considered a taxi service.

Governments aren't about to let Lyft disrupt their monopoly

---

787 http://blog.priceonomics.com/post/47636506327/
the-tyranny-of-the-taxi-medallions

788 http://www.taxi-library.org/driving-poor.pdf

789 http://business.time.com/2012/09/04/
need-a-lyft-ride-sharing-startup-zimride-hits-the-gas-pedal/

790 http://business.time.com/2012/09/04/
need-a-lyft-ride-sharing-startup-zimride-hits-the-gas-pedal/

without a fight. Predictably, the company has run into problems in Los Angeles because of government regulations. As the *Daily Caller* reports, "The Los Angeles transportation department ordered the companies to immediately halt operations within the city limits, handing local taxi drivers a major victory over their chief competitors."[791] That might leave the future of Lyft in doubt. Regulators are even fighting amongst themselves over who should regulate these innovative businesses. Recently the California Public Utilities Commission (PUC) stepped in and created an entirely new category of businesses that are now subject to its regulations. The California PUC will impose insurance requirements, driver background checks, and drug tests.[792] Of course, it's worth noting that Lyft was already meeting these requirements without the government's intervention.

Lyft's biggest problems are political. Yet, the company isn't actively working to change the political landscape of California. Even if the company can persuade Los Angeles to give it a pass, there will be more cities and more businesses facing the same problem. Lyft offers something new, and it runs against the tired-old thinking of big government liberalism. But the thinkers at Lyft are not invested in changing the system that holds them back. Lyft's absence of political activism may simply be a reflection of the Valley's Libertarian impulses. In the last few decades, many of Silicon Valley's executives have displayed a libertarian instinct to stay as far from politics and government as possible. Reid Hoffman described the attitude this way: "Look what I can do as an individual myself—everyone else should be able to do that, too. I can make a multibillion-dollar company with a little bit of investment. Why can't the whole world do that?"[793] Hoffman's view erroneously assumes that all the other residents of California share his genius and investment portfolio.

---

791 http://dailycaller.com/2013/06/26/uber-lyft-defiant-in-face-of-los-angeles-ban/

792 "http://www.npr.org/blogs/alltechconsidered/2013/08/08/209885782/californias-new-rules-could-change-the-rideshare-game

793 http://www.newyorker.com/reporting/2013/05/27/130527fa_fact_packer.

Public policy outcomes can only be as good as those who reach out to shape and mold public opinion.

Other Valley leaders that have become engaged have had little effect on outcomes. For example, Jim Gilmore, one of the co-founders of the Electronic Frontier Foundation, has donated thousands to a website: http://www.toad.com/gnu/ that publishes out-of-the-mainstream 9/11 conspiracy information as well as some other fringe information. Peter Thiel, who is arguably the single biggest Silicon Valley political donor, spent $4.7 million in campaign donations primarily to support Ron Paul, who lost his quixotic campaign for President by playing the role of a spoiler. Such funding, if directed instead to oppose Governor Brown's Proposition 30 tax increase, probably would have changed the election outcome and guaranteed that initiative's defeat. In the long run, Prop. 30's defeat would have best aided Thiel's professed pro-free enterprise philosophy and helped save California jobs and avoid the exit of more businesses and high income residents. Instead, Thiel's millions to Ron Paul resulted in nothing tangible and long lasting.

Silicon Valley's right of center leaders need to think more deeply about not only their own political interest, but also the best interests of the state that has allowed them a place to make their billions. They should embrace the GOP and mainstream politics, instead of dabbling with the political fringes. Skeptical attitudes about government are useful to reform-minded thinking in California. These attitudes are inherent in many of the Valley's skilled workers, millionaires and billionaires, and those attitudes are definitely not in-line with the economic results of liberal Democratic political dominance in the state. If this army, currently in political stasis, were to become politically engaged, it could revolutionize the state.

Yet, not all Silicon Valley entrepreneurs are fringe libertarians. Much of the Valley's political engagement is going directly to the liberal politicians responsible for bankrupting the state. Of 684 donors in the Valley who gave $13,000 or more during the 2012 presidential election, only 31 percent of the contributions were given exclusively to Republicans.[794] Democrats received 55% of the Valley's big-donor money given exclusively to Democratic candidates. According to one study, such giving patterns "essentially flip" giving patterns in the rest of the nation, where Republicans generally have the edge with large donors who provide funds to exclusively one-party candidates.[795] Silicon Valley remains captive of the Democratic party, regardless of the fact that liberal Democratic policies are so contrary to the principles of entrepreneurship that have fueled success there. Some Silicon Valley mega-millionaires surely are committed liberal Democrats. Chris Hughes, a co-founder of Facebook, is reportedly a member of the Democracy Alliance, an invitation-only organization that includes billionaire George Soros in its ranks.[796] Democracy Alliance makes funding recommendations to its members, who pay annual dues of $30,000 and are required to contribute at least $200,000 to favored liberal causes, such as backing President Obama's political agenda.[797] The group has reportedly contributed $500 million since 2005 to liberal causes.[798] At a recent retreat in charming Laguna Beach in Orange County, members heard from Governor Jerry Brown, Lt. Governor and former San Francisco Mayor Gavin Newson, and liberal economist and former Clinton-era Labor Secretary Robert Reich, along with leaders of the SEIU.[799]

But perhaps the greatest problem with the Silicon Valley's political activism applies to both right and left. For all its innovative new thinking in business, the Valley is remarkably traditional in its political strategies, and that is best demonstrated by the region's biggest political player, the Silicon Valley Leadership Group. Started by

---

794 http://www.bizjournals.com/sanjose/news/2013/07/09/the-10-biggest-republican-super-donors.html?ana=RSS&page=all

795 Id.

796 http://articles.latimes.com/2013/may/04/nation/la-na-donor-network-20130504

797 Id.

798 Id.

799 Id.

David Packard, one of the co-founders of technology giant Hewlett-Packard, it was originally intended to be an outlet for pro-business political action. Packard was a "regular guy," attending Stanford in the 1930s and lettering in basketball, football, and track.[800] He became an electrical engineer, worked at General Electric, and eventually started his company with William Hewlett, producing innovative products including the first handheld calculator and inkjet printer. While Hewlett focused on design, Packard was the successful manager of the business. He became a generous donor to the conservative Hoover Institution located on Stanford's campus and served on the board of the American Enterprise Institute. With a keen interest in international affairs, in 1969 he was appointed Deputy Secretary of Defense in the Nixon Administration, and Packard continued to be a life-long Republican. In 1977, Packard pushed Silicon Valley to engage in the political process by forming the Silicon Valley Leadership Group. "Our job as CEOs is not to sit on the sidelines and cheer or jeer," Packard said at the time. "Our job is to get in the game and move the ball forward."

But over time, despite Packard's pro-business leadership, political action emanating from Silicon Valley either seemed directionless or leaned Democratic. In 1992 Hewlett-Packard's Chief Executive Officer John Young endorsed Democrat Bill Clinton for President, even though Packard remained Chairman of the Board of Directors. At the time, Packard wrote a letter to the editor of the *San Jose Mercury* saying, "my friends have overlooked the fact that the Democratic Party has been the party of socialism."[801]

Today, the Silicon Valley Leadership Group has embraced political activism without any clear political ideology. In 2010 Daniel Weintraub, a longtime political columnist on California state government, wrote that "the group stands out as a small island of

---

800 http://capitalresearch.org/2013/01/a-reaganite-entrepreneurs-flawed-philanthropy/

801 http://capitalresearch.org/2013/01/a-reaganite-entrepreneurs-flawed-philanthropy/

ideological diversity in a sea of partisan polarization."[802] It is both for and against tax increases. In some cases, it backs new regulations, while other times, it opposes them. Writing in the *New York Times*, Weintraub observed that "when it comes to politics, the group is decidedly retro." One of the group's biggest political activities is an annual report on the state of business in California. While the report contains valuable statistical information, it is a reaction to state policy rather than a driving force of new public policy. Rather than using its member's brilliance and innovations to shape politics, it is allowing traditional approaches not calculated to reform the state to shape its actions.

The Silicon Valley Leadership Group isn't alone in this regard. In 2011 venture capitalist John Doerr hosted a political dinner for tech bigwigs with President Obama. Facebook founder Mark Zuckerberg describes that dinner as the impetus for his effort to change politics with Fwd.us.[803] From the start, the group promised to approach politics differently. In March 2013 the *Los Angeles Times* quoted one political operative involved in the project, "This is different. This is about political work, which is new. This is the next generation of political groups."[804] Just a few months old, the group has already resorted to politics as usual. As the *New Yorker* described it, "Rather than bringing fresh ideas to the project of organizing Americans and their elected leaders behind immigration reform, the group has hired veteran Washington operatives from both parties, who, following their standard practice, are spending Silicon Valley money on harsh and cynical political ads."[805] In late April 2013 the group began running ads defending South Carolina Senator Lindsey Graham that attacked President Obama's healthcare law.[806] The group isn't con-

802 http://www.nytimes.com/2010/01/03/us/politics/03slpolitics.html?_r=0

803 http://www.newyorker.com/reporting/2013/05/27/130527fa_fact_packer

804 http://articles.latimes.com/2013/mar/29/business/la-fi-silicon-valley-politics-20130329

805 http://www.newyorker.com/reporting/2013/05/27/130527fa_fact_packer

806 http://www.calbuzz.com/2013/06/zuckerberg-fwd-us-and-cynical-civic-psychobabble/

cerned with healthcare, but wanted to bolster Graham because of his support for comprehensive immigration reform. That seems best described as Machiavellian politics, and appears especially craven in that the group largely supports President Obama and ObamaCare. It even used a shell organization called Americans for a Conservative Direction to mask its involvement. CalBuzz, a prominent left-wing political blog, said of the move, "The notion that Zuckerberg's organization represents a new maturity in Silicon Valley's approach to politics ignores years of history."[807]

For all the traditional political strategies and largely rudderless political ideology by major advocacy groups, there remains much hope for Silicon Valley's political activism. And that optimism doesn't spring from any group or association, but the common viewpoints of individual leaders. Despite the Silicon Valley Leadership Group's varied positions at an organizational level, most of their members have conservative, reform-minded views. According to the Silicon Valley Leadership Group's own survey, half of their members believe that Governor Brown's pension reform doesn't go far enough.[808] Overall, 53 percent believe that California is on the wrong track.[809] About 45 percent of members that believe business regulations are a problem specifically cited the California Environmental Quality Act (CEQA) as a key challenge to their businesses.

Silicon Valley is posed to lead. But such leadership should not be confused with simply running for office. eBay's self-made billionaire Meg Whitman flung herself into the political arena in her 2010 race for governor, advocating change. Her message was indeed accepted by California Republicans in a contested primary she won, against another Silicon Valley millionaire, then Insurance Commissioner Steve Poizner. Just a few months before the general election

---

807 Id.

808 Silicon Valley CEO Business Survey 2013, http://svlg.org/wp-content/uploads/2013/03/CEO_Survey_2013.pdf

809 Id.

polls even showed her winning the race against Jerry Brown. In the end, liberal Democrats and the public employee unions exploited tangential weaknesses and defeated her. Whitman showed courage; but her experience should not discourage. The real challenge for Silicon Valley is not about finding an ideal self-funded candidate every election cycle. Rather, it is about the possibility of Silicon Valley stretching its wings and accepting responsibility for rational problem solving for government in California.

Some younger, enterprising engineers are already starting to accept the challenge of public policy problem solving, and right in the center of liberal San Francisco. Leap Transport, is a privately owned bus company started by Kyle Kirchhoff. Its buses compete with the slow and dangerous public system, called the "Muni." While the fare to ride down crowded Market Street is $6 on Leap rather than the Muni's $2, Leap is a faster, safer, cleaner service with added comforts like leather seats and Wi-Fi.[810] Progress on the route can be monitored with an iPhone application. As Kirchhoff and his young colleagues in Silicon Valley examine other such urban problems to tackle, this author believes that their solutions offered will be vastly different and far more rational than those advocated by California's public employee unions. Silicon Valley needs to apply its genius to build the type of sustainable movement David Packard envisioned; one that is smart, focused, and "moves the ball forward" to achieve rational policy solutions to California's problems. Rather than reacting, Silicon Valley needs to put the liberal Democrats in control on the defensive by offering compelling alternative solutions and support for candidates and measures that represent reform and economic expansion for everyone.

---

810 http://www.newyorker.com/reporting/2013/10/14/131014fa_fact_heller?currentPage=8

CALIFORNIA'S LONG SHOT TO REBOUND

CALIFORNIA IS CLEARLY BROKEN and urgently needs to be fixed. This view is not unique to this book. The very idea of "fixing" the state is shared by a broad range of people and groups concerned with how far the state has fallen and the need for new solutions. For example, the *San Diego Union-Tribune* has established a regular Sunday column dedicated entirely to the issue of "Fixing California" and what it terms its "broken system of governance" that includes lively commentary and debate on the state's economic and policy woes. The Pacific Research Institute, a right-leaning San Francisco-based think tank, has published *Eureka! How to Fix California* by Art Laffer that includes a number of recommendations, including adoption of a "revenue-neutral single low-rate flat tax." Former *Los Angeles Times* reporter Joe Matthews and Mark Paul have written *California Crack Up, How Reform Broke the Golden State and How We Can Fix It*. And the Manhattan Institute has published a book entitled *The Beholden State: California's Lost Promise*. All these works include important content about the problems the state of California faces and how they can be addressed.

Clearly, as a senior analyst at the think tank California Forward has observed, it will not be easy to "bring institutional change to an organizational structure that has been built over a 40-to 50-year period."[811] The fact is that California's current political structure, dominated as it is by liberal Democrats who have created the rotting institutional structure in the first place, won't allow for the changes California needs, and in that sense California is very unhealthy, and lacking of the cyclical ebb-and-flow that provides the necessary balance for reforms to arise. Restoring some political balance is the most obvious initial step California can take on the road to fixing its economic woes. Bluntly, that means the special interests need to lose some control, and state politics needs to become more competitive with more Republicans winning more seats to the state legislature.

In the longer term, California needs a fundamental realignment of its political system to get "healthy" again. The liberal historian Arthur Schlesinger, Jr., has observed that under the "political realignment theory," changes occur when "exigent new problems emerge."[812] When new, serious political problems arise:

> "[i]ssues that once galvanized the electorate fade into irrelevance. The new issues cut across party lines, split each party internally, and confront the established system with questions it struggles to dodge or ignore. Frustration produces voter restiveness, awakens new constituencies, and leads to ideological division, third parties, and high-intensity politics. The process culminates when a crucial event produces a fundamental shift in the pattern of voting and in the direction of national policy."[813]

Schlesinger has his doubts about wholesale party-based political realignment in an electronic age, believing political parties have become more-and-more irrelevant as a means to initiate change.

---

811 http://www.newjerseynewsroom.com/nation/
after-six-years-did-arnold-schwarzenegger-succeed-in-blowing-up-california-government

812 Arthur M. Schlesinger Jr., *The Cycles of American History*, (City: Mariner Books, 1999), 34.

813 Id.

Nevertheless, change doesn't have to be initiated from the bowels of a political party—Proposition 13 in 1978, an environmentalist movement, and the advent of the Tea Party prove that point. Conditions now exist that would seem to put California at the cusp of a "crucial event" politically. Its taxes are far too high and they are contributing to sustained high joblessness. The public employee pension system is gravely underfunded and seems out of control. State and local governments are spending too much. Cities are filing for bankruptcy. Strikers have even been shouted down by riders upset with BART's high fares and generous wages.[814] Special interests have too much control. "Rome is burning" and those in control don't have the political will to put out the fire. The combination of California's growing economic maladies and intractable liberal Democratic control, from a perspective inspired by Schlesinger's cyclical theory of history, suggest an unwelcome "big bang" may be waiting to occur in the not too distant future that will force the issue of political realignment, and push the political pendulum hard in the other direction regardless of the liberal Democrats and their special interest allies' current control.

Or maybe not. Some observers might conclude that California is "beyond fixing" because of the intractable control of the levers of power by the public employee unions and their opposition to meaningful reforms. Other ailing states like Wisconsin and Indiana have revitalized their economies in part by reforming pensions, reducing taxes and spending, but also by enacting controversial laws that have been seen as undermining public employee union power in those states. However, Indiana and Wisconsin are states that, though they have had serious financial problems, remained in general political balance between Republican and Democrats in elected offices.

---

814 A poll in August 2013 found 70% of Bay Area residents oppose a strike by BART transportation workers and 92% think a strike will have a significant impact on the economy. A majority in the poll said that BART workers are already fairly compensated. http://www.bayareacouncil.org/news/2013/08/02/bay-area-council-poll-shows-resounding-opposition-to-bart-strike/

California has no such balance in its politics, and attempts at the ballot box through the initiative process to eliminate mandatory union dues and thereby equalize the public employee unions' lock on power have lost miserably each time they have been voted on.

It is sadly unlikely that changes will happen anytime soon without a massive shift in political thinking. Yet modalities for "fixing" California are rather obvious and include that *public employee pensions must be dramatically reformed.* Changes in programs from overly-generous set benefits to self-directed retirement accounts, with employees contributing a greater share to their own retirement programs, as currently advanced in cities such as San Jose and San Diego, must be implemented by local governments across the state.

Taxes must be lowered. California cannot expect to regain its position of leadership in manufacturing, defense, and entertainment, or hold on to its positions of leadership in high technology and agriculture, if businesses and high-income residents continue to move out of state. Capital flight out of California means job losses. Unemployment in California at the unacceptable level of 1,700,000 unemployed, twice the level of just five years ago, is both unhealthy for the state and unacceptable in the long term. California needs to cut its taxes, not raise them, to spur the business investment necessary to reach full employment. There has never been a more appropriate time to cut taxes than now, when California's total tax burden is at the highest levels in the nation.

Spending must be brought under control. Even California's smaller cities and governing bodies can find many ways to reduce government spending without dramatically cutting government services, if they just try. The city of Corona in Riverside County recently cut $225,000 a year from its budget by eliminating a department and consolidating functions into another department, combining its Library services with its Parks and Recreation services. The motivation for the reorganization was unusual—the city couldn't find anyone to accept the job as permanent director of its Parks and Community Services Department. Rather than just fill the position because it was authorized, the city instead eliminated the job, with little affect on public services.[815] In San Luis Obispo County, the Board of Supervisors similarly combined the offices of auditor-controller and treasurer tax-collector into one department, saving the county $250,000 per year.[816] A spokesman said the taxpayer savings would "be much higher over time" as the county works to use more technology and automation to reduce costs.[817] Chipping away at even the smallest redundant and duplicative bureaucracies and finding efficiencies in all the inexpensive new technologies available can make a difference. That is good decision-making, and if replicated by the state and in localities across the state could save millions of dollars in public employee salaries and pension liability for localities over time.

Implement major provisions of Schwarzenegger's shelved "California Performance Review." California state government already has a blueprint to fix itself. Drafted nearly a decade ago, the California Performance Review has many ideas that could immediately begin to turn California around. When she was running for governor, Meg Whitman was quoted as saying of the report, "I've read the Performance Review cover to cover, twice, and I can tell you that most of the recommendations are no-brainers."[818] The major cost-saving recommendations of the Performance Review are not partisan political proposals; rather they are rational, fully vetted steps that the state can take to start fixing itself. Billions of dollars can be saved if the California Performance Review is fully implemented. All that is required is the political will to do the right thing by the state; and if Democrats won't do it, they ought to take the blame for the dire consequences of their inaction and be called out of office.

---

815 http://capoliticalnews.com/2013/07/24/
city-of-corona-combining-departments-saves-more-efficient-fewer-administrators/

816 http://www.sanluisobispo.com/2013/07/25/2600311/auditor-controller-treasurer-tax.html

817 Id.

818 http://www.newjerseynewsroom.com/nation/
after-six-years-did-arnold-schwarzenegger-succeed-in-blowing-up-california-government

Perhaps one reason why the California Performance Review has failed to shape the conversation about reform in California is the overwhelming nature of the report. It runs more than 2,500 pages. For politicians that think in 30-second sound bites and a public that limits its attention span to 140 characters or less, this document presents a challenge to digest. In an effort to correct that, the report should be abbreviated to focus on three key areas: government consolidation, using technology to modernize state services, and disposing of unnecessary government assets and functions.

First, California should follow the California Performance Review's advice to combine and consolidate duplicative functions of government. Immediately, many liberals will respond that this is an effort by Republicans to cut programs that affect the poor, minorities, and children. However, consolidation is about eliminating the bureaucratic layers that actively block those in need from receiving assistance. There's no better example of this than the duplicative bureaucracy in the area of education. The state could save millions with the consolidation of its multi-layered education agencies. The elimination of county superintendent of education offices and county boards of education, which largely duplicate statewide programs, would make it easier to get more dollars directly into the classroom. This story repeats itself throughout California government. Per the California Performance Review's recommendation, 11 state agencies and 79 departments could be consolidated into a more efficient system of just 11 overall departments. This consolidation would make it easier for consumers and businesses to interact with government. Twenty-five state entities could be merged into one California Infrastructure Department. Another 20 state entities could be combined into one new Department of Education and Work Force Preparation.

Secondly, California must use technology to make government more convenient and efficient. In this area, tech entrepreneurs need to step up and identify ways to fix a broken government bureaucracy. The California Performance Review's technological recommendations included some basic ideas, such as allowing more payment of state bills online, reducing lines at the Department of Motor Vehicles by letting Californians renew driver's licenses online, and allowing vehicles to be registered every other year. These recommendations were suggested back when most Californians were on a dial-up connection and Mark Zuckerberg was still in high school. Imagine, with the ubiquity of smartphones and the power of apps how much more California could do with technology to revive and reform government. Even some Democrats have moved in favor of this issue. California's Lt. Governor Gavin Newsom has championed government use of technology in his book, *Citizenville: How to Take the Town Square Digital and Reinvent Government*. Newsom has suggested coding contests to address social problems, use smartphone apps to highlight potholes, and start rating government services like Yelp. "We can begin to rate our DMV services compared with your DMV services in your neighborhood, or rate the interaction at the parks department," he told *Fortune Magazine*. [819] Shockingly, Newsom is even willing to let these innovations reduce the government workforce. He told the *New Yorker* that sometimes "government can do best by simply getting out of the way." [820]

Finally, based on the California Performance Review's recommendations, California needs to divest itself of unnecessary and wasteful government functions. The state should sell more surplus state property and do so using online tools such as eBay. The state could easily eliminate 118 of 339 boards and commissions in the Executive Branch, transfer more state highways to local governments, and cut the growth in state jobs. Here are just a few of the state agencies that could be eliminated: Integrated Waste Management Board, Fair Employment and Housing Commission, Industrial Welfare Commission, Air Resources Board, Board of Forestry and Fire Protection,

819 http://money.cnn.com/2013/03/21/technology/gavin-newsome-citizenville.pr.fortune/

820 http://www.newyorker.com/reporting/2013/05/27/130527fa_fact_packer

California Transportation Commission, High Speed Rail Authority, Board of Prison Terms, and the California Energy Commission.

Democratic officeholders must embrace more moderate solutions, especially in education reform. Hyper-local control in small school districts should be addressed through consolidations. Consideration of student academic performance in evaluating their teachers should not be a partisan controversial issue—it simply makes sense. Yet the CTA and the liberals they have elected to most school district board of trustees strongly resist the reform. In their view, teacher performance is a confidential matter between the district and the teachers. But no less liberal institution than the *Los Angeles Times* has sued to make non-personal data of student achievement test results and related teacher evaluations public, because of the significant public interest in the state's educational problems and the need to fix them.[821] Test results of California's student population are lacking, less than they should be, and pose a threat to the economic health of the state in the future. Tying teacher pay and placement to student performance is a reform that makes sense. Some Democratic politicians, such as former Los Angeles Mayor Antonio Villaraigosa, have had the courage to support use of student performance data in teacher evaluations. More Democrats should join that bandwagon if California is ever to see any improvement in teacher accountability and student test results.

In her book on education, author Amanda Ripley cites with some disdain the fact that there are more than 50 local Superintendents of Public Instruction in Oklahoma, each with their own deputies and aides, and that this bureaucracy weighs down and presents obstacles to gains in children's education because of the complex administrative overhead. Yet in California, the Legislative Analyst's Office

---

821 http://latimesblogs.latimes.com/lanow/2012/10/times-sues-la-unified-for-teacher-ratings.html

has estimated that there are 950 school districts statewide.[822] For every school board, there is a highly paid Superintendent, an array of highly-paid deputies, at least five members of the elected school board, and ample contracts with law firms representing the district.

Currently, about 40 percent of public school districts in California are "small" (serving fewer than 1,000 students), and about 10 percent of all districts are "very small" (serving fewer than 100 students). Under state law, minimum district size is very low—average daily attendance of six for an elementary district and 11 for a high school or unified district. [823] California also leaves the decision over whether to consolidate school districts up to local communities, with local stakeholders required to initiate the consolidation process and ultimately a majority of the local electorate required to approve any merger.[824]

Compared to larger districts, very small districts tend to dedicate a significantly bigger share of their budgets to covering overhead costs and a smaller share to instructional staff and leaders. Moreover, very small districts are more difficult to hold accountable for student outcomes because their small enrollments do not yield statistically significant results.[825]

Despite challenges that would push in the direction of consolidation, small districts still tend not to pursue it, according to the Legislative Analyst's Office. The system may seem to present fiscal incentives for districts to remain small and certain disincentives for districts to consolidate. Specifically, the state encourages districts to remain small by providing them substantial funding advantages. These benefits are especially evident in very small school districts, which on average receive more than twice as much funding per pupil

822 "Update on School District Finance in California," LAO, May 2012, http://lao.ca.gov/reports/2012/edu/year-three-survey/year-three-survey-050212.pdf

823 http://www.lao.ca.gov/laoapp/pubdetails.aspx?id=2472

824 Id.

825 Id.

compared to midsize and large districts. Additionally, certain state laws, including those related to environmental reviews and district staffing, coupled with community preferences for small districts, serve as disincentives for districts to consolidate.[826] Yet student performance appears slightly better in midsize districts.[827]

California could save millions of dollars and improve children's educations by consolidating its hundreds of school districts, both large and small, into fewer, better managed units. "Hyper-local control" is not working, as the test scores indicate, and the redundancies inherent in more than 900 local school districts statewide ought to be recognized and addressed through mergers and consolidations.

Republicans must become competitive by real outreach and empowerment of Hispanics. If California is to be restored to political health and balance, Republicans need to start winning more elections, and to do that they need to win more votes from Latinos. Unlike Texas, which has elected a number of Hispanic officeholders including Tea Party-backed U.S. Senator Ted Cruz, California has no notable Latino officeholder. Former State Senator Abel Maldonado was appointed by Governor Schwarzenegger to fill a vacancy in the office of Lt. Governor, but lost his run to retain that office in 2010 and was defeated in a run for Congress in 2012. Maldonado has launched a campaign to challenge Jerry Brown for re-election as Governor in 2014,[828] but many conservatives in the GOP have not forgiven him for his support for tax increases in 2009.[829]

It has been said before that typical Latino families and the Republican Party share core family values. The GOP needs to seize on that

---

826 Id.

827 Id.

828 http://www.sacbee.com/2013/05/03/5393533/maldonados-long-shot-bid-for-california.html#mi_rss=Latest%20News?utm_source=feedly

829 Id.

point more effectively. GROW Elect is an effort by Latinos to help elect Latinos who are Republicans at the local level and build a leadership team within the GOP. The effort seems to be gaining widespread support among Republican activists in the state, but one of its leaders has told *The Economist* magazine that the task is enormous and could be a 20-year effort.[830] In twenty years, California's Latino population will be the most dominant demographic in the state. The California Republican Party's future depends not only on winning some elections right now, if it is to have a future, but also to turn over the keys to its headquarters to Latino Republicans.

California must open its shores to new oil and natural gas drilling and allow fracking to quickly transform the state economy. The most important single step that California can take to improve its economy is to change its energy policy to allow more oil and natural gas extraction. Fracking in the Monterey Shale formation itself could be a transforming event, but adding highly regulated offshore oil drilling could completely eliminate California's budget deficit for years to come, reduce residents' energy bills and stabilize energy sources, and inject so much new capital into the economy that unemployment could finally drop below national averages.

Silicon Valley entrepreneurs must be encouraged to take leadership in public policy—and turn their drive for success and natural distrust of government into a real "game-changer" for California's future.

The likelihood, at least in the short-term, is that California will not reform itself, and that its economics will continue to crumble as political control remains in the hands of the chief special interest

---

830 http://www.economist.com/blogs/democracyinamerica/2013/05/republicans-and-latinos-california

power in the state, the CTA. Yet the reality is that a teacher who is paid $67,000 a year to ineffectively instruct the state's students has more political power, through his or her public employee union, than the Silicon Valley entrepreneur who makes $6.7 billion a year. As we have seen, CTA's pervasive influence is proving itself unhealthy for California. In the long term, California will only be able to reform itself when that fact comes to general realization. In 1974, not too long after the Santa Barbara oil spill, Democrat Assemblyman Ken Cory was elected State Controller, winning the election with the slogan "the man the oil companies fear most."[831] When Michael Barone of the American Enterprise Institute later asked Cory what the job of State Controller had to do with oil companies, "he laughed and said 'Nothing.'"[832] Cory's success nevertheless had everything to do with the electorate's perceptions that the oil companies had too much special interest power, and that they had harmed the state's environment. Cory retired after serving four consecutive terms as State Controller.

California will be on the road to real reform when its citizens can come to a similar conclusion about the out-of-balance power and control of its current biggest special interest, and when a person running for statewide office can connect with the public by saying he or she is "the candidate the California Teachers Association fears most."

831 http://articles.latimes.com/1998/nov/14/news/mn-42652

832 http://www.aei.org/article/politics-and-public-opinion/legislative/gangster-government-attack-on-oil-companies/

ACKNOWLEDGMENTS

I could not have written *Taxifornia* without the support and real interest of my law partner, business colleague, wife, and best friend, Janice Lacy, who surely is the foremost of those I wish to acknowledge and thank.

After the Proposition 30 tax hike passed and the Democrats completed their demolition of the Republican Party in the state legislature and California Congressional districts in the 2012 elections, I decided that it was time to focus debate on their failed liberal economic policies and the special interests behind them. I felt it was time to force the liberal Democrats and their public employee union allies to start taking ownership of the economic train wreck they have created in California. I settled on writing a book about the subject in March 2013 after attending the national Conservative Political Action Conference in Washington, D.C., on whose board of directors I serve, and which inspired me to take action.

It took me about six months of daily work, research, and writing to complete the book. About half-way through the manuscript, I engaged John Hrabe, a promising young journalist with a fresh outlook and a couple of Master's Degrees, as my research assistant, and he not only ably executed himself, he had a major hand in the development and writing of the chapters on Arnold Schwarzenegger's failure as governor, the Global Warming Solutions Act, and Silicon Valley. He also helped me make some sense of the material on energy policy, particularly fracking, and helped me organize the manuscript.

My friend Brian Calle, Opinion Page editor of the *Orange County Register*, introduced me to Owen Brennan, a gifted videographer, who introduced me to my literary agent Jennifer Cohen in New York City. Jennifer believed in my book project from the very first moment and I am so grateful for her work in placing such a "California-centric" book with a new national imprint, Post Hill Press, and in Post Hill's decision to publish it. I am thankful to you all.

My primary daily research for *Taxifornia* started with a visit to each of five news aggregation and political opinion websites: www.flashreport.com, a leading site published by my friend and California political operative Jon Fleischman, who also offered encouragement for my authorship of the book and some helpful comments; www.capoliticalreview.com, a news and opinion website in which I am co-owner and publisher; www.rtumble.com, a nonpartisan California news aggregation site; www.foxandhoundsdaily.com, an excellent business-oriented opinion site published by Joel Fox; and www.capoliticalnews.com, owned by long-time California Republican Party official and operative Steve Frank. Steve and I also met to discuss the book, he read the manuscript before I sent it off to the publisher and he offered some very helpful comments. My favorite feature on Steve's website is his compilation of articles from various local business journals throughout the state, usually entitled "What Recovery?" which offers excellent and otherwise overlooked grassroots information about local businesses and their challenges.

My daily reading would usually take me to further research of various newspaper and government archives on the internet. Part of my research included many discussions with elected officials at all levels, their aides, and government officials whom I have come to know over time, including a couple of city managers. You know who you are, and thanks to you all.

I also read a number of books, including Professor Gerston's text on California mentioned in the Introduction; *The King of California* by Mark Arax and Rick Wartzman, (though I did not use much of the material, it is a great book); *Eureka! How to Fix California* by Art Laffer with Wayne Wunegarten; *The Cycles of American History* by Arthur M. Schlesinger; and *Governor Reagan* by Lou Cannon. I was frankly surprised by the rather inaccurate personal characterization of iconic and long-time California taxpayer advocate Lew Uhler, a product of Yale University, and a contemporary of William F. Buckley and author M. Stanton Evans, in Cannon's otherwise impressive book.

I relied on Joe Mathews' *People's Machine* for its insightful information on Schwarzenegger's political rise. As I was writing *Taxifornia*, Joe was kind enough to solicit and publish on Zocalo Public Square, (www.zocalopublicsquare.org) an original piece I wrote about Howard Jarvis on the 35th anniversary of the passage of the Proposition 13 tax-cut, which was picked up by the opinion pages of the *San Francisco Chronicle*, *Los Angeles Daily News*, *Bakersfield Californian* and *San Gabriel Valley Tribune*. The small success of that piece gave me encouragement to keep writing.

Alex Tomescu, a lawyer in Janice's and my law firm, Wewer & Lacy, LLP, was very helpful in compiling public record information, especially the detailed information reflected in the campaign finance chart in the book.

Fellow Los Angeles Kings hockey club fan and business associate Tim Carey, business partner and friend Floyd Brown, and a long-time friend who is a Superior Court Judge in California, provided invaluable personal advice and support and I thank them.

My friend and client Joel Fox, the President of the Small Business Action Committee, and a successful author himself, very kindly offered me some original insights into his policy work on the Schwarzenegger campaign and as a state commissioner who participated in the development of the California Performance Review. I also enjoyed re-reading Joel's *The Legend of Proposition 13*.

I met with John Suttie, an executive and board member of the Howard Jarvis Taxpayers Association (HJTA), to discuss the book, and both John and his colleague Kris Vosburgh, the Executive Director of HJTA, read a copy of the manuscript and offered valuable information and insights that helped me polish parts of the book. Though we did not counsel together specifically on *Taxifornia*, I am grateful for the hard and determined work of Jon Coupal, the Sacramento-based President of HJTA, who in my opinion is just about always right on California politics.

Congressman Darrell Issa has played an enormous role in the fight to reform California, not only as an elected official but also as a supporter of other candidates and causes. The successful recall of Governor Gray Davis would not have happened without his personal intervention and financial support. Congressman Issa has a keen knowledge of the failings of government tax and regulatory systems. He has accomplished much for taxpayers and government transparency in Washington, D.C. I am so grateful to have the honor of working for him as a lawyer, and humbled by his willingness to write the Forward to *Taxifornia*. I also appreciate the valued insights and support for *Taxifornia* of Congressman Issa's able and long-time Chief of Staff, Dale Nugebauer.

My mom and dad passed away about twenty years ago. My mom, Romalda Stetsky, came to the United States as an immigrant from a foreign land and moved to a welcoming San Francisco, where she met my dad, James C. Lacy, Jr., a second generation San Franciscan whose Irish-American mother, Mary Agnes Morrissey Lacy, had survived the famous earthquake and fire of 1906. My parents loved California. They would have been pleased that I wrote a book about the state. They sacrificed to be sure I had an education to write it, and I remember them for that.

I am pleased to take sole responsibility for *Taxifornia* and remain so very thankful to have in my life my wife, Janice Lacy, a veteran of Washington, D.C., where we met, and a brilliant political observer. She touches my heart every day, challenges me, and makes me a better man, and I love her very much.